CRITICAL INSIGHTS

Family

CRITICAL INSIGHTS

Family

Editor
John V. Knapp
Northern Illinois University

SALEM PRESS
A Division of EBSCO Publishing
Ipswich, Massachusetts

Cover Photo: © Ben Welsh/Corbis

© 2013 by EBSCO Publishing
Editor's text © 2013 by John V. Knapp

∞ The paper used in these volumes conforms to the American National Standard for Permanence of Paper for Printed Library Materials, Z39.48-1992 (R1997).

Library of Congress Cataloging-in-Publication Data
Family / editor, John V. Knapp.
   p. cm. -- (Critical insights)
 Includes bibliographical references and index.
 ISBN 978-1-4298-3734-7 (hardcover)
 1. Families in literature. 2. Literature--History and criticism--Theory, etc. I. Knapp, John V., 1940-
 PN56.F3F36 2012
 809'.93355--dc23

                  2012010662

Contents _____

Critical Contexts

Critical Readings

Resources

About This Volume

John V. Knapp

Part I

Almost all of us have lived in families—whether growing up or in families we ourselves have created—and can all appreciate the stories, poems, and dramas that have emphasized family life. Following this introduction that briefly describes the essays in this volume, I will detail the critical reception to major works on families in literature. As I will remind us ahead, families, in literature and in life, emerge from being a mere aggregate of individuals to becoming dynamic entities in their own right. Readers will note the newer psychologies employed in several essays in this volume: family systems, evolutionary psychology, cognitive science, and other more eclectic models. I will suggest the reader consider moving his or her expectations away from traditional psychoanalysis—as a critical model of one-at-a-time character consideration—to thinking about characters as also explainable by embedding them inside their families, as inhabiting systems of people, all of whom are subject to their evolutionary inheritances.

The first example of such systems thinking is my essay on the British novelist D. H. Lawrence and *Sons and Lovers* (1913), his famous early novel of a young man growing up in the coal-mining region of Northern England. A good example of a bildungsroman (a novel of a young character growing up), *Sons and Lovers* was revised in 1992 (Penguin edition) by a team of scholars at Cambridge University in England; the revision restored almost seventy-five pages of missing text, edited out by Lawrence's first editor who missed the central fact of a plural in the title: the other son, William Morel, and his experiences with his parents, Gertrude and Walter. Although the character dies early in the work, William illustrates some central truths in family life: to truly understand any one member of the family, the observer must embed that individual (literary character or living being) into the very fabric of family life generally. The greater textual detail of William's character in the new edition of the novel, describing his love and affection for both parents, gives readers a whole new understanding of the issues in the family life of the Morels and the main character, Paul.

The next essay, by Steven Mintz, a historian from Columbia University, takes us through a brief survey of how selected historians have viewed families over the years. As Mintz explains so well, a "defining feature of modern times" is a "nostalgia for a world that never was." By that, Mintz argues that we often tend to "romanticize the past and confuse historical fantasy and reality" when it comes to understanding how earlier families were constituted and behaved. Such terrors as divorce, domestic violence, and single parenthood are not recent phenomena, nor were families always constructed along the lines of a breadwinner father, a stay-at-home mother, and a haven for elderly grandparents and infirm relatives. Mintz suggests that these problems and myths need corrective analysis to better understand who we are and where we fit in the historical record.

Finally, we end the opening section of this volume with an essay by Catherine Leen, who explores two Hispanic American novels that illustrate comparatively some issues on families as dramatized in Tomás Rivera's novel . . . *And the Earth Did Not Devour Him* (1971) and Sandra Cisneros's *Caramelo* (2002). Each is reflective of its differing historical periods, and the first novel's "almost exclusive concentration on male characters" indicates fiction as written via the initial wave of Chicano nationalist writers who emphasized community and solidarity (Leen, in this volume). Cisneros, by contrast, turns her attention to "a young woman who longs to fashion her own identity," but questions whether any individual can ever truly represent a whole family. Leen suggests that Chicana writers like Cisneros use the family motif both to reflect on women's home lives and even to rewrite the history of the Chicano movement by "talking back" to Chicano nationalist language and the very patriarchy itself. The two novels offer contrastive perspectives on the Chicano and Chicana family, perspectives profoundly shaped by the generational and gender differences between their authors.

Part II

The next section of essays emphasizes dramatic pieces of literature, beginning with the English-speaking world's foremost dramatist, William Shakespeare. The opening essay, by Joseph Carroll, is an evolutionary psychological reading of *King Lear*, one of William Shakespeare's most profound tragedies. Carroll suggests that his emphasis on an evolutionary perspective will offer first a "metaphysical vision that corresponds with that of the play"; second, a set of ideas concordant with human motives and values found in the play; and third, an integrated awareness of those universal aspects of human nature with recognition of the play's historically specific features. Carroll is the godfather of evolutionary psychology as a literary critical tool and his explanation about the tribulations of old age is among the most stimulating of the collection.

The next essay, by Tom McCann, is also on Shakespeare, but this one is about the romance *The Tempest*. In direct contrast to the family torn apart in *King Lear*, *The Tempest* represents, according to McCann, Shakespeare's "image of a stable family," an appropriate model for ruling and functioning in a civilized society. Although some have criticized the Bard for seeming to condone European imperialism, McCann thinks Shakespeare was aware of the abuses of colonizers, but was more interested in supporting the home family's status quo: the Elizabethan era concept of a patriarchal structure within the family based on the great chain of being.

The third essay in this section moves us from sixteenth-century England to Chicago, Illinois, where Susan Callahan closely examines a mid-twentieth-century family in Lorraine Hansbury's *A Raisin in the Sun* (1959). Using narrative theorist Alan Palmer's ideas of "doubly embedded narratives," Callahan explains how the play's various characters have created stories that are "versions of themselves. . .

and versions of other characters" and that these stories "can show the whole of a character's various perceptual and conceptual viewpoints, ideological world views, and plans for the future." Walter, the father in the play, can only tell his son about "stories about how rich white people live" given his own lack of a compelling personal narrative, while Mama holds up her tale about her husband (and Walter's father) as the dream story to which the children should all aspire.

The last play discussed in this section is on Henrik Ibsen's *A Doll's House* (1879), in an essay by Beth McFarland-Wilson and John V. Knapp. A play about a marriage built on unexamined cultural expectations about spousal roles and proper wifely behaviour, *A Doll's House* ends with what has been called the most famous slamming door in theater history. Nora, the "little songbird" in the mind of her husband, Torvald, discovers to his dismay that his "little squirrel" is actually a competent woman who was forced to borrow money, deceptively, in order to save her own husband's life—in spite of his express wishes against taking any sort of loan. In a moment of truth-telling, Nora realizes that her own father, Torvald, and her close friend, Dr. Renk, have all treated her more like a precious child rather than a mature and capable woman and, worse, she is perpetuating these attitudes toward her own children. McFarland-Wilson explains through family systems the dynamics of the various triangles into which members of the Helmer family are embedded and from which Nora must extract herself, if need be by wrenching herself away violently via a slammed door.

Part III

The essays in the next part of the collection are devoted to poetry. The first essay, by James Postema, selects two poems by Robert Frost: "Home Burial" (1962) and "Death of a Hired Man" (1905). Postema explains that, as a child, Frost was himself abused physically and emotionally by an alcoholic father, and became a neurotic during adulthood. His pain allowed him to explore "the implications of his own lost childhood indirectly, after the fact and from the points of view of parental figures." According to Postema, although there are no children in Frost's poetry, Frost uses poetry to "explore what his own childhood presence or absence might have meant to his parents," and in doing so, recoups some of what was valuable about himself in his parents' eyes—and thus in his own.

The second essay, by Nicla Riverso, is about Dante's *Inferno* from *The Divine Comedy* (written between 1308 and 1321). This essay may be among the first to explore from a specifically familial perspective how the fourteenth-century Italian poet Dante described "the attitudes of his age with respect to family dynamics," emphasizing "conjugal love, affection for children, and relationships to ancestors." Because each story represents the particularity of domestic life "in a very specific social and political environment," Riverso thinks the *Comedy* offers many insights concerning marital unions and those circumstances bringing them "to either respect and love, or despise and detest their spouses."

The last poetry essay, by Brian Edwards and John V. Knapp, shifts from fourteenth-century Italy to twentieth-century England and selected poetry by Philip Larkin, Seamus Heaney, Eavan Boland, and Stevie Smith. Edwards discusses the large cultural changes wrought upon Great Britain during the aftermath of two world wars and their expression in the poetry of the time. As Great Britain contracted and England evolved, the traditional families and Victorian values that undergirded the separate spheres in which men and women circulated lost value in the shortages after World War II, and were challenged by emerging female voices who continue to unmask a legacy that would "bandage up the history" and "make a rhythm of the crime."

Part IV

The final series of essays is devoted to fiction. In the first essay in this section, Brett Cooke, a professor of Russian literature and language, explores Leo Tolstoy's nineteenth-century Russian masterpiece *Anna Karenina* (1873 to 1877). The famous opening line of the novel—"All happy families are alike; every unhappy family is unhappy in its own way"—sets the stage for the discussion of several families and the rise and fall of five married couples from the perspective of evolutionary psychology. Cooke analyzes how and why Russian families in the 1870s were often reluctant to divorce, no matter how miserable they might be, also describing the issues surrounding the custody of children in a conservative patriarchal society. Cooke also details some of the intricate Russian naming practices within nineteenth-century extended Russian families.

The next essay, by Massimiliano Morini, takes us back another several decades to Jane Austen's early nineteenth-century novel *Pride and Prejudice* (1813). Morini tells us that few novelists have explored family life with the thoroughness and consistency of Jane Austen, and that *Pride and Prejudice* is perhaps the universally most popular of all of her works. The Bennet family's five daughters—Jane, Elizabeth, Mary, Kitty, and Lydia—all must be married since the family home has been entailed only to male relatives; one or more of the daughters and their mother could be homeless if their father dies while any is still single. Hence, marriage is constantly and obsessively on the minds of Mrs. Bennet and her daughters.

The next essay, by Tim Ryan, looks at selected fictions by African American writer Zora Neale Hurston, in particular *Jonah's Gourd Vine* (2008) and *Dust Tracks on a Road* (2010). Ryan argues persuasively that so much of Hurston's fiction is drawn on personal experience, but, like so many writers dissatisfied with merely recounting ordinary (but truthful) life experience, Hurston's accounts of her life are almost as fictional as her fiction itself. However, for readers so interested, having available "two distinct versions of the same basic story is incredibly helpful as far as interpretive analysis is concerned." Distinctions between her autobiography and her fiction "reveal a great deal about Hurston's use of the family as a symbol in her works" and also "helps to illuminate the meanings" of her protagonist's "triumphs, ordeals and failures in *Jonah's Gourd Vine*."

The fourth essay, by Gillian Lachanski and John V. Knapp, analyzes the marriage of two minor but important characters, Pauline and Cholly Breedlove, in Toni Morrison's *The Bluest Eye* (1970). Morrison informs readers immediately about the single most important event of the novel: the rape of the young girl, Pecola, by her own father, Cholly Breedlove. Although readers and the other characters are horrified by this despicable act of incest, Morrison begins the novel by indicating that she can explain the *how* of the act but not the *why*. Lachanski insists on understanding the *why* as well, and the importance of looking at the whole Breedlove family dynamic leading up to the acts of rape. Lachanski suggests that, while Cholly is the actual agent of the attack, an explanation of the emotional tensions and dependencies between the family architects, Cholly and Pauline, can offer possible answers as to the *why*.

The last essay of the fiction section, and of the whole volume, is by Sang-wook Kim, who analyzes a very different marriage—that of Gabriel and Gretta Conroy in "The Dead," James Joyce's most widely anthologized short story from *Dubliners* (1914). Kim notes Gabriel's changed perception of his wife Gretta—the crux of his epiphany—through a cognitive science explanation of their family process. Kim says that psychologist Jean Piaget and subsequent neo-Piagetians explain how people may change their cognitive structures to adapt to new experience, and that this sort of intellectual leap is pushed by emotions and anxiety. Gabriel is shown, imagistically and narratively, to display a brooding anxiety about ordinary experiences at the Christmas party he and Gretta attend. Once learning about a boy from her past who died for love of her, his initial shock and jealousy give way to a new ironic reality—of her existence separate from him and hitherto emotionally and cognitively incomprehensible. Freed from self-delusive constraints, Gabriel objectively evaluates himself and, in turn, accepts his wife's individuality as a being of free will.

On Family
John V. Knapp

The volume that follows explores the dynamics of some of the most well-known literary families in the Western world. What may be of particular interest to many readers is that much of what is discussed reflects the real-life experiences of many in relation to their own family experiences and their own personal development. Many developmental psychologists claim that the primary developmental task for those in their late teens or early twenties is to leave their families-of-origin, strike out on their own, and eventually create their own families. This volume explores that developmental task—its success, failure, and progression in several works of fiction, drama, and poetry that span from the fourteenth to the twenty-first century.

At the same time that many young adults are establishing material independence, they are often trying to establish physical and psychological independence from their families. The people and ideas that seem so attractive during early childhood and adolescence change and evolve as we grow older, and we may choose to follow paths that differ from those of our parents. In Jane Austen's *Pride and Prejudice*, for instance, the five sisters each take a different path toward independence, even as they come to understand and—to a degree—also reject the values and expectations of their parents. Yet, as is shown in this volume's essay on Sandra Cisneros's novel *Caramelo*, breaking away from the ideas espoused by those we have always loved can be terribly difficult. Parents and older siblings may take the rejection of their ideas and values as something akin to a rejection of themselves. In these cases, a young person may not only break away from the family, but also need to spend decades reconsidering and renegotiating his or her family, trying to balance independence against the need to retain emotional bonds with and loyalties to family members.

Lifespan developmental psychologists maintain now that people evolve over the whole courses of their lives, not just during their

On Family **1**

childhood and young adult years. Gabriel in "The Dead"—who, after years of marriage, finally begins to see his wife as she is, not as he wants to see her—is a positive example of personal evolution, but literature is full of negative ones, too. An example of an increasingly negative development is found in Toni Morrison's *The Bluest Eye,* in which the two spouses, Cholly and Pauline, are in constant conflict and their actions have tragic consequences for their children, even causing their daughter to go mad. The married characters in D. H. Lawrence's *Sons and Lovers,* Walter and Gertrude, suffer a similar fate, struggling for control and becoming so engaged in their war that, as Lawrence's narrator says, "end[s] with the death of one." Even William Shakespeare's King Lear, in spite of his raging against old age and the very elements of nature, changes during the final days of his life, recognizing what a "fond foolish old man" he had been as he reconciles with his estranged daughter, Cordelia. Other times, change may come from an outside force, like the death of a member, as we see in Robert Frost's poem "Home Burial," where the pain each parent feels over the loss of their child disrupts their spousal relationship.

Yet though they are made up of individuals, families are also greater than just the sum of their members and may be said to have a life of their own. Like individuals, families go through their own life cycles: from the courtship and later marriage or cohabitation, forming two-person dyads, to the birth of their first child, which forms a triad. The life events that follow—the births of subsequent children, their maturation and marriages, and the parents' deaths—are all developmental tasks that the family members must perform together. Though literary scholars often treat characters singularly rather than as part of a familial unit, psychologists recognize that it is often more revealing to consider an individual as part of a "family system." They see that even though members may grow up, move away, or otherwise change, the family itself still remains. It reconstitutes itself in its daily life and even re-forms when members return for holidays or weddings, for instance.

However, despite the separations and difficulties a family may encounter, as can be seen in this volume's essay on Lorraine Hansberry's *Raisin in the Sun*, it is often the stories families tell about themselves that can keep them together through hardship. The stories the Youngers tell about their success gives them pride, and they still remain closely connected through stories of failure.

One family therapist describes families as having collective emotional reflexes: any change in any one part of the family has reverberations throughout the whole family. For instance, Nora's slammed door in Henrik Ibsen's *A Doll's House* not only signals a change within her, but also shakes up her whole family. In the best cases, families learn to become more tolerant of one another and more forgiving of each other's idiosyncrasies, mistakes, and difficulties. In some families, however, as we will see in this volume's essays on Dante's *The Divine Comedy* and on Leo Tolstoy's *Anna Karenina*, forgiveness is difficult if not impossible. Both of these outcomes can be found in Shakespeare's comedies and his tragedies. *The Tempest*, like most of his comedies, ends with a marriage and a reconciliation, while *King Lear* shows the death, betrayal, and destruction that can come from unforgiving, torn apart families.

Where in times past it was rare to find families that were legally divorced from one another, today such families are relatively common. As Steven Mintz reminds us in his survey of the history of the family, almost half of the marriages in North America end in divorce and some four of every ten children are born into families with only one legally sanctioned parent. Relations may become all the more complicated in these families as they often grow to include stepparents and stepsiblings. Add to that most children's early allegiance to one or more biological parents, siblings, or extended families, and we see that growing up in the world of the twenty-first century can require significant adjustment and negotiation. What psychologists and literary authors have known for a very long time is that children's mental and emotional health benefit enormously from having an adult, in or out of the family, who can be an emotional caregiver. Zora Neal Hurston, for example, has enormous praise for her "godfather," who, in her childhood, acted as her first teacher and emotional confidant because her own biological father was quite literally "out of town" when she was born and seemed distant generally to her during her growing years.

It is often said that even in intact families, each child is raised in a slightly different home by slightly different parents. This truism merely reflects the sense that families evolve even as we do.

CRITICAL
CONTEXTS

Critical Reception of the Family in Literature _____

John V. Knapp

Many teachers of literature through the twentieth and into the twenty-first century have tended to think of characters in a singular fashion, rather than in terms of a collective, social, or familial dynamic. In this book, the focus will remain on characters within the family—as both individual entities but also as members of a family that exhibits what some psychologists call "emergent properties."[1] The family (in life and fiction) as a unit exhibits qualities that both imitate and differ from those exhibited by any single member or even subset of them. References to fictional families in this essay will be based on their being representations of real or living persons and the families they inhabit.

Hence, families emerge from being a mere aggregate of individuals to become dynamic entities in their own right. Conversely, individual literary characters also inhabit systems of people; this essay will discuss both individuals and families employing what is called family (or living) systems theory (FST). As noted in another critical essay in this volume, Leo Tolstoy opens his novel *Anna Karenina* with the famous line: "All happy families are alike; every unhappy family is unhappy in its own way." Yes, but while all families—unhappy or otherwise—are different in some respects, they often behave in ways that would be obvious and predictable to a critic of family theory. Each family constitutes a dynamic entity that emerges from the very individuals who belong to it.

Whether discussing characters individually or in families, many English teachers and professors often ask students to consider character representations through some rather stereotypical and critical patterns. Students are often asked to make a chart of traits where characters' dominant personalities or functional characteristics are categorized and labeled with terms like *adaptability* or *independence*. Some teachers suggest that "a character's physical description can tell us something about him or her" (Smith and Wilhelm 44, 192). While true in an obvious way, character reduction to a single static label cannot help readers to understand a dynamic textual figure for very long. Still other teachers discuss characters and characteristics in a highly generalized fashion that makes their model useful for middle school students, but less helpful for young adults.

Narrative scholar James Phelan has created a very useful tripartite scheme for discussing literary characters. He calls the three functions mimetic (like real-life people), thematic ("an idea with legs," in Phelan's quaint phrase), or synthetic (a character as plot device) (*Reading* 12). Phelan rightly says that most characters share all three functions in some ratio, depending on "a dynamics of character and event and a dynamics of audience response" (*Living* 161). Instead of putting characters into trait boxes, Phelan's schema stresses the importance of dynamism in both character behavior and the sequence of the narrative, as well as the change that "typically proceeds through the introduction, complication, and resolution (in whole or in part) of unstable situations within, between, or among the characters" (161). This volume will emphasize the examination of situations between and among characters as much as it will investigate what goes on within each.

There have been several literary scholars who have examined studies of family life in literature,[2] some thematically, with critic Tom Scanlan suggesting that "two ideal models of the family have emerged" in, for example, American drama (27). Each of these "two models has been accompanied by what we might call an ethos which animates, justifies, and perpetuates it" (27). The first model is that of a

> stable, ordered family life lost (or being lost) to the past; the other model is of a spontaneous, natural family life to be gained in the future. The first is animated by nostalgia and pessimism; the second by apocalypse and hope. . . . In a curious way these two models depend on each other even as they clash and are antagonistic. (27)

Other scholars have looked less to literary models for inspiration and instead looked to reality itself. Focusing not only on individuals within a family structure, but on the family collective as a whole and its emergent properties, they note multiple interactions inside that familial organization. Although literary readers have been interested in examining individual characters in families for years (cf. Joseph Carroll's discussion of *King Lear* in this volume), thinking about and observing characters embedded in their family's social system is relatively recent; indeed, a newer element of literary study is the consideration of families and familial systems as composed of characters representing dynamic components. By contrast, real persons needing psychological counseling have been seeking help through family systems therapy, a type of clinical practice that is among the most popular in North America, Europe, and other parts of the world (Piercy, xi). This clinical model is widely employed to better understand challenged family dynamics. Although a relative latecomer to therapeutic intervention techniques, it owes its beginnings to a group of theoreticians, most of whom were psychoanalysts, that formed in the 1950s in Palo Alto, California.

Their history is outside the scope of this chapter, but their intellectual legacy is still practiced in countless psychotherapeutic clinics all over the world. The intellectual origins of family therapy were originally derived from cybernetic systems research and theory, from communication and cybernetics research, from sociologists, and from those early therapists. These therapists, frustrated with the limitations of individual analytic outcomes (especially in psychoanalysis), converted the elements of the previously mentioned research programs into a paradigm that assumed the individuals' embedding in his social fabric—particularly the most intimate fabric of all: the family. More recently, theoreticians of family dynamics have moved away from the older, more mechanical cybernetic model and have referred to their work, after psychiatrist Murray Bowen, as "living systems analysis" or "living systems therapy."[3]

An interesting complement to the FST model in literary study is the collection of ideas of independent scholar Alan Palmer. Whereas family systems therapy was developed to deal with real people and real-life issues, Palmer is among the first major narrative critics who emphasized literary characters embedded primarily in their social milieu, drawing the attention of several other talented narratologists who now play such an important role in literary study (cf. Phelan); indeed, linguist James Paul Gee maintains that generally "thinking and reasoning are inherently *social*," noting that "they are also *distributed*" and that the "power of distribution—of storing knowledge in other people, texts, tools, and technologies" created the network of knowledge (196–97). In his "fictional minds toolkit" Palmer has also explained that "our hitherto privileging of *inner speech* obscures the fact that only *some* of our thought, though not all of it, occurs as inner speech" (*Style* 2011 217–19; emphasis added). Second, he thinks we must focus on representations of "*embodied consciousness*," including kinesthesia, awareness of physical sensations generally, and a character's perceptions of the physical storyworld. Third, Palmer speaks of aspectuality wherein characters can only experience their storyworlds from one perspective at a time; these storyworlds will therefore be unique to each unique character and come from that character's particular background and experience (*Style* 2011 212).

Fourth, Palmer speaks of intermental thought, since as in real life, "much of the mental functioning that occurs in novels is done by large organizations, small groups, work colleagues, friends, families, couples, and other intermental units" (*Intermental* 427). A large amount of the subject matter of novels is the formation, development, maintenance, modification, and breakdown of these intermental systems. Finally, this essay will also briefly mention the ways in which other critical models have dealt with literary characters in order to shed further light on some of the differences between characters thought of as individuals versus those embedded in their families.

It would be worth briefly exploring why literary characters have not been seen until recently as part of a living system so much as they have been considered primarily as individuals—and why then it seems obvious that readers should consider characters only individually, and not also as embedded in their social milieu. While formal literary study in schools and universities is only a little more than one hundred years old, human beings have been enthralled with storytelling and the characters who inhabit popular stories for thousands of years. But during this last century or so of a more formal analysis of tales and fictional people in them (cf. Graff), the primary psychology available to scholars and teachers of novels, poetry, and drama has been only psychoanalysis. By the mid-1990s, the usefulness of Freudian psychology waned for literary people and was largely replaced by other psychological domains, including evolutionary psychology; forms of cognition; and, for counselors, family or living systems therapy.

One interesting theorist in literary cognition is Jonathan Culpeper, whose *Language and Characterization* (2001) asks questions about the role of prior reader knowledge in the understanding of characterization, how readers make inferences about characteristics in a novel, and how textual cues are used in characterization in fiction. Culpeper says of the subject of character in drama that "dialogue of plays is the primary focus of this book." He also discusses surveys of earlier literary character studies including issues on character in the journals *Poetics Today* (1986) and *Style* (1990), but regrets that in both issues, "only one article addressed the issue of character in drama" (1). I agree that most postmodern theorizing seems troubled when transforming largely textual analyses into studies of dramatic collaboration. Collaboration is the nature of the drama (Knapp, *Introduction* 2), and it is the gap between the solitary author's contribution and the drama company's contribution wherein Culpeper makes a fascinating contribution—albeit by focusing primarily on written verbal elements. The greater interest is that drama consists primarily of overt character interaction and what Palmer would specify as intermental thought.

Culpeper's major interest is in the process of character formation—"how we form impressions of characters in our minds—not just characters themselves or their personalities." He employs ideas of "character impression" borrowed from "research on impression formation in social psychology," insisting that "the mind is not a passive recipient of information, but an active manipulator of that information" (2–3). Culpeper surveys "previous approaches to characterization developed in literary studies" (cf. Hochman 11–30; Margolin 105–20; Sacks 19–21) and compares them with the linguistic analyses of a real person's conversational discussions. Culpeper argues that such "knowledge of real people" can be a superb source of knowledge "used in understanding characters" in literature, although clearly "knowledge of real people is not the only knowledge used in understanding" figures in drama or other literature (87). It is ultimately an "empirical question" finding distinctions among alternative types of knowing (88).

Culpeper examines cognitive psychology's view of "real people" through discussion of "attribution theories" that are "designed to explain how aspects of personality are inferred in real life situations" (113–14). Citing major theorists who have investigated attributional studies,[4] Culpeper speaks of two issues important to literary readers: the first is the "theory of correspondence" (the degree of correspondence between a person's behavior and his or her disposition or temperament) and concludes that this model tends to think about characters "in an idealized way with single behaviors in a vacuum" (121). The second issue connects characters and environment; readers want to contextualize the situations in which characters act, and are as fascinated with environmental inferential validity as they are with merely "person-based sources of inference" (126–27). The two are complementary within certain limitations, and Culpeper asserts that foregrounding theories emphasizing either characters' personalities or their environments (in FST, for example) are "analogous to attribution theory" (129) where attribution models "are different sides of the same coin"—both have "concentrated on non-linguistic behavior," although "foregrounding theorists have focused on linguistic behavior" and speech. Agreeing with Palmer, Culpeper thinks there "seems no reason why there should be a division" when trying to understand the person and his or her environment even though "foregrounding theory does not contain explicit mechanisms with which to distinguish different types" of causes (134–35).

Culpeper distinguishes between the kinds of evidence, saying we "cannot assume that the characteristics of real people are inferred in exactly the same way as those of literary characters" (144–45). First, "we have access to that character's whole life—complete and finite" unlike real persons for whom we never see the complete trajectory of a life. Second, "character behaviors have greater relevance and significance" since interactions reveal that "any character behavior is part of an act of communication between playwright and the audience/reader" (145).[5] Culpeper says that "by looking through a character's eyes (including their mind's eye) a reader gets to view the fictional world as if they were that character" (147), as in Palmer's aspectual focus, and so "attribution theory can act as an explanatory framework for a reader's character inferences" (153).

In sum, there is always a tension between situation and person speaking. Culpeper reiterates (from social psychology) that most human beings "tend to underestimate the impact of contextual factors when inferring characteristics of people"—"the fundamental attribution error" (171). Although we are "predisposed to accept at face value what characters say about other characters" (172), at least initially, the act of reading becomes one of verifying, modifying, or even rejecting those initial views, depending on the text and on authorial intent.

III

As a type of therapy, family systems counseling (and in literary study, family systems theory) is really a clinical form of social psychology, and therefore requires psychoanalytic critics to look more in social rather than intrapsychic (internal psychology) directions, trying thus to avoid the fundamental attributional error. Those using family systems in the act of criticism are asked questions about terminological variants: is FST really just using different names taken from critical practices employing psychoanalytic theory? Is Freud's *family romance* in this regard merely the same basic idea as the *family dance*? If so, then is FST just a variation of what psychoanalytic critics have been using during most of the twentieth century? To answer all such questions requires a single word: no.

Responding to such questions requires contextualizing the problems many see in Freudian criticism. Specifically, I will point to literary critics employing the works of Sigmund Freud as psychological and critical anatomies. By contrast, most practicing psychoanalytically-oriented therapists see themselves mostly as eclectic practitioners, grounded in neopsychoanalysis, yes, but stealing, begging, or borrowing from whatever clinical practice or theory is useful. Since the early 1990s, however, literary theoreticians and critics of a psychoanalytic nature have mostly died or retired, and those remaining sometimes go off in very unusual directions. One good example of odd trajectories is feminist critic Marianne Hirsch's *The Mother-Daughter Plot* (1989), and although Hirsch "question[s] the flexibility of psychoanalytic frameworks," she asserts their "compelling usefulness for feminist analyses of femininity as culturally constructed and internalized by individual female subjects." Generally ignoring the male of the species, Hirsch wants to repeat "the triangular structure of the nuclear family, with narrative occupying the place of the paternal" (11). Of course, if the reader happens to be male—or happens not to think of male-female identities as socially constructed, but as having a biological component, and happens to think of families as quite often containing fathers—then Hirsch's psychoanalytic family model exhibits some noticeable limitations.

She is, unfortunately, not alone in self-prescribed limitations of family definition. A 2008 study by Mary Jean Corbett goes a bit further in idiosyncratic definitions of families. Although Corbett appears almost apologetic in speaking of family life but "concentrating only on prose works by women writers" (viii), she insists that the "fictions of biology as just one among other grounds for defining the family unit." For her, "the practice of adoption establishes paradigms for family and marital relationships in which affinity . . . takes precedence over consanguinity in determining kinship" (89). Although some of Corbett's argument appears unexceptional, one wonders if male-authored literary works would suggest similar values.

Freud's theories are now over one hundred years old and, like the human science generally, psychology and especially biologically-oriented psychology have evolved well beyond such anachronistic theorizing about mentalistic categories as *the unconscious*. The Freudian unitary mind he called the unconscious, a cornerstone of Freud's understanding of human motivation, evolved in his thinking out of Eduard von Hartman's *Philosophy of the Unconscious* (1870). In the twenty-first century, Freud's unitary unconscious is considered just an early primitive mentalistic concept; contemporary psychologists have known for decades that many activities of the brain are unavailable to conscious introspection, or available only in moderate degrees (Carr 26). Hence, Paul Ehrlich repeats what many others have noted about the unconscious and about Freudian thinking generally: there "are few data to support most of his original ideas which have little influence in the scientific community today and must be categorized as 'interesting even if not true'" (367; cf. Grunbaum). Some critics have, unfortunately, dismissed such factual connections to reality. One literary critic says that the "argument that Freudian notions are inapplicable fails to convince, for the very ideas which we have detected in the works of Freud . . . also surface in some of the most influential writings of the Augustan age" (Nelson 43–44).

The Oedipus complex is yet another concept hitherto important to literary critics but bearing almost no weight in contemporary science. In his monumental study of families, sibling relationships, and parents, Frank Sulloway says that it would be tantamount to committing evolutionary suicide for a young child to kill a parent; it would also be an evolutionary time waster even to wish to kill a parent, even if one never acts on this wish—although obviously, raw emotion is hardly rational (122–23). That has not stopped some contemporary psychoanalytic scholars from still evoking *oedipal revolt* to explain twentieth-century drama as composed of many *prodigal sons* who rebel against family life and "its stasis, its strictures, its economic responsibilities." Men do not want to "be married to an angel with little angel children" but prefer "a life much more fluid and sensual" (Proehl 81–82).

Still a different critic of this type of Freudian thinking is Jeffrey Masson, who speaks of Freud's "abandonment of the seduction theory" as the origin of the Oedipus complex (189–91). Sigmund Freud was shocked into disbelief when hearing of sexual assaults on children by their parents. Indeed, for the bourgeoisie of late nineteenth-century Vienna society, Freud needed to stoutly deny their existence. Once Freud had "decided that these seductions had never occurred, that the parents had never done anything to their children in reality, then [the child's] aggressive impulses [toward sexually abusive parents] replaced seduction in Freud's theories" (113). Masson also notes: "By shifting the emphasis from an actual world of sadness, misery, and cruelty to an internal stage on which actors performed invented dramas for an invisible audience, Freud began a trend away from the real world" (144).[6]

Though Freud's views have become dated over the course of a century, many apologists—including Paul Ricoeur—now emphasize that Freud and Freudian concepts are not so much scientific truths, but are rather useful tools for hermeneutic (theories of interpretation) understandings. But that defense also has some difficulties. Given the lack of verifiable premises in its scientific grounding, psychoanalysis remains immune to empirical investigation. Nonetheless, some like Ricoeur would maintain that Freudian themes are so intimately woven into our cultural fabric that Freud remains for many one of the big three thinkers—alongside Karl Marx and Charles Darwin—who helped create the modern world as it is understood in the twenty-first century. By contrast, Adolph Grunbaum would have readers remember two issues. The first suggests our remaining alert to Freudian-based thematic connections, yet wary of their beguiling causalities. Second, Grunbaum insists that criticism promoting explanations of Freudian thematic dogmas remain "explanatorily sterile or bankrupt. At best, they have *literary* and reportorial value"; at worst, they are mere just-so stories that "foster *ideological hostility* to scientific thought" (139). Granted Freud himself could not know of the evolution of the biological sciences and the unmasking of the human genome but those who have tried to follow him do.

IV

As Jaak Panksepp has pointed out: "modern brain imaging has demonstrated, time and again, that psychotherapy has demonstrable and beneficial effects on the brain. This is creating a sea-change in our conception of who were are and what we are seeking to accomplish in therapeutic interventions" (184). In family systems thinking and its theoretical underpinnings the biggest change is recognizing that—for the self inside family systems psychotherapy—the family system as a whole becomes the ultimate source of identity, rather than the individual character.[7] Hence, the origin and cause of a given conflict in maturation (and into adulthood) may be traced not so much to a specific person or a single event, but more toward an emotional process linking people and events (Minuchin and Nichols 112). The term used here (and discussed above) is that the whole is greater than the sum of its parts—a phenomenon called *emergence*.

By contrast, one must also remember that in FST the family is made up also of independent, but simultaneously interdependent, literary characters or human selves and that requires the reader to reduce his or her attention at times to one or more of those individuals (Vancouver 166). Thus, FST readers (and therapists) move their attention up and down the abstract scales between emergence and reduction as the need arises. The concept of reduction—in therapy, literary criticism, and psychological research—is, therefore, a necessary complement to emergence. To understand a single member of a given family, the reader needs to understand the family system—whether it is a biological family or stepfamily (Minuchin, Lee, and Simon 63; Visher and Visher 34–39). In both FST-oriented literary criticism and in therapeutic practice, the observer is always aware of an irresolvable and fluctuating tension between the hard reality (or its representation) of the biological self, according to Jerome Kagan, and the living system into which that self is embedded: the family network. The latter comprises a softer or cultural reality. It seems to be a truism among family therapists that, inside a single family, each child is raised by different parents: "every child experiences the very same family in sharply idiosyncratic ways" (Goleman 155). Similarly, in literature readers must always consider this irresolvable perceptual tug-of-war between the individual character and the social, familial, and biological context in which that character is embedded.

According to Gregory Bateson and C. West Churchman, a second corollary following from the first is that families represent a coevolutionary ecosystem. That is, inside the family's system, each person (or character) determines to a significant degree the living conditions for the other family members' development. As a unit, families are also formed inside a surrounding sociocultural system as they interact to form the coevolutionary ecosystem. These include the individual, the family, and the social environment of work, school, churches, social clubs, and even online social networks such as Facebook and Twitter. All of these represent an interwoven three-tiered feedback system of varying hierarchical orders. Marion O'Brien, who analyzes biological families, speaks even more generally: she notes that there are two guiding frameworks for individual and family development, and so the processes of change "operate at multiple levels, from the cellular to the cultural," where both principles are "transactional and reciprocal" (881).

As Robert Kegan and Murray Bowen have discussed, a very important task for any family is providing support for the whole family's integration into a solid unit and, where age-appropriate, helping the children to differentiate into relatively independent selves, thus learning to act, think, and feel as individuals. These twin polarities form a lifelong tension, as members of the family-of-origin create a new family through marriage, or as they join another system of close-knit intimates where much depends on mutual caring, trust, and loyalty. This rhythm between separateness and closeness is somewhat different developmentally for male and female (Haley 40). In well-functioning families, every member develops a solid self—able to act, think, and feel so that the inside and outside of the self are usually congruent. Bowen has also noted that, in what are known as dysfunctional families, anxiety and fear usually force individual members to create a pseudo-self—separating inner feelings and outer behavior so they are not said to be *congruent.*

The notion of a T-bond is another part of family systems. At the top of the family hierarchy are its twin architects: the parents who form the horizontal bar at the top of the T. Below the middle of the T are the children, beginning with the first-born child and the others following in birth order. In more abstract language, all families are said to have subsystems: parent-parent (at the top of the hierarchy), parent-child, and sibling-sibling (Simon et al. 183–85). Parents are assumed to maintain boundaries between both themselves and their children, as well as between individual children. Various subsystems may range from rigid to diffuse and the boundary between parent and children is clearly separated by financial responsibility, sexuality, and authority (Minuchin, Lee, and Simon 226–27).

The two parents, the original pair-bond, form a dyad. Most of these dyads are considered inherently unstable during the early years of a relationship because each of the pair-bonded must create a new self who is now part of a larger entity. During the inevitable tugs and adjustments necessary to establish a balance between this initial intimacy and former independence, most pair-bonds do become periodically unstable and it is typical for one or both to call in a third entity (a parent, a friend, a child, or even their career) in order to reduce the tension and reach an equilibrium. When the third entity is one of the family's children, as Mara Selvini Palazzoli has theorized, therapy "implies relationally redefining the symptoms in terms of a protective-sacrificial conduct the patient is said to be enacting for the benefit of someone else in the family" (7).

If the third entity, a child in this example, is inducted into the pair-bond, he or she then becomes part of a triangle, and the original relationship is thus said to be triangulated (Imber-Black, *Families* 64–66). One spouse or the other may be enmeshed (or overly involved) with the child while the other spouse is, through complementarity, disengaged or uninvolved (Palazzoli et al. 143–48). Parentification may be said to occur when parents assign the child a task or a role that properly belongs to one of the parents, either the primary emotional bond or even a major breadwinner task (Framo 143–212). Typically, inducting this third element does indeed reduce tension, but it also reduces intimacy even if either one of the original pair-bond really wants the other spouse to change so that they may both revert to their former state. Of course, this reversion must always be on one partner's own terms, and, absent a resolution satisfactory to both, the triangle remains, even if it often creates secrets.

The effects of secretiveness on the whole family is often devastating because it introduces distortion at the fact-gathering level (Imber-Black, *Secrets*). For example: if a father tells his son something about his wife (the boy's mother), it will affect the child's feelings and behaviors toward her; this change is based on one-channel information obtained about his mother. If the child is asked to keep it a secret by his father, the child cannot independently verify the information. Secrets help maintain illusions and prevent evidence contrary to fixed perceptions. Thus the child cannot easily, if ever, change the relationship with his mother based on new information.

In the vocabulary of early cybernetic theory, families are said to maintain homeostatic balance through constancy loops. By contrast, families change through what are called variety loops. Homeostatic balance is a term used to denote equilibrium in the system. Equilibrium is not always a good thing, especially if the homeostatic balance is maintained by creating a scapegoat of one family member. One of the first activities many therapists recommend to a family in some interpersonal pain is to break up and change the balance. While family life can be considered a generally open system, there are limitations to its openness (Simon et al. 81–82).

For suffering families in psychic trouble, morphogenesis, or change, is required—a deviation from the usual set of interactions among the difficult relationships in the system. Morphogenesis is the risk all dysfunctional families must take: change or die (divorce, or death of the family) because homeostasis is far stronger in families than morphogenesis. Once such a pattern (a triangle, for example) is set in motion, Salvador Minuchin thinks it might last the lifetime of the members involved (cf. Bowen). Divorces may be thought of as the act of last resort for troubled families (Reiss et al. 23–31).

As do individuals, families also undergo a life cycle: a typical life cycle in a family goes from the courtship of the dyad, to marriage or cohabitation, to the birth of first child—making the family a threesome. This cycle continues with subsequent children, career changes, moves, illness, the parents' empty nest and aging, the renewed life cycles of children and grandchildren, and finally the death of a partner or sibling. Kegan has also noted that, in healthy families, both parents and children must cope with developmental tasks appropriate to a given stage in the life cycle. With the birth of the first child, the pair-bond (parent-parent) must become a triad; the two parents must now each relate to the child both separately and as a pair-bond, and must adjust to meet their own needs as well as the needs of their infant. In brief, things become different from what they were before the first child and, without major attempts at redefining roles and expectations, marital tensions often arise.

For literary people, the use of language rates among the most important concepts of FST. Borrowing the terminology of linguistics, one could say that all family interaction is governed by transactional rules: if one spouse does something, then the other will counter it with another action or behavior. Each subsequent action or behavior will elicit a measured response. Thus family behavior is an adjustive process where cues are given and individual members respond to those stimuli. These rules are largely unspoken, circular, and—oftentimes, until spouses learn alternative argumentative strategies—an endless set of claims and counterclaims. Hence, viewing events in a family conversation is best understood by a cyclical model of causality. Looking for an origin to the argument is termed punctuation. It is an attempt by individuals to separate or divide cyclic processes into origins, middles, or ends, as every parent knows who has tried to referee squabbling children.

The context of any communicative act sees cues for action—as small as a nod or closing of the eyes as exemplified through metacommunication. Metacommunication is communication and information about the very act of communication itself. It may take almost any communicative form: eye-rolling, shrugs, tonal qualities, and facial gestures. Outsiders may be puzzled by a family member who becomes outraged at another family member by nothing more than a smile or furrowed brow that passes between them; both know intimately how to translate such cues into precise meanings.

Families are also influenced by themes, transmitted via narratives, family stories of correct behavior from one generation to the next. These themes are illustrated by myths and cycles of family behavior—often relating to perseverance, morals, and communication—that take the form of maxims or adages. William Randall suggests that what holds families together is, in part, a "collection of stories—however differently compiled and told by different family members—through which each of us sees ourselves, interprets others, and makes sense of our world." He notes that existence becomes experience through this kind of storytelling (196).

Related to such themes are family myths that may be loosely categorized into myths of harmony, or charming pictures of a family's past problems overcome. Some are myths of agency—or of forgiveness and atonement—where, for example, a single family member may be made solely responsible for the family's problems. Alternatively, this family member may be assigned agency for what are called rescue myths, a subset of the above, where either a family member, or perhaps even an individual outside the family, is attributed magical powers and is regarded as the savior and benefactor. Occasionally, there will be someone in the family who all other members heap expectations on, often setting lofty, and sometimes unattainable, goals.

FST is not without its critics and, for humanists, one charge seemed to need a particularly strong response. Early critics of FST complained that, by focusing on the present, some FST practitioners have tended to minimize family history and individual responsibility from the past (Palazzoli et al. 159–60). More recently, many FST clinicians have addressed such charges and have tried to integrate knowledge of previous actions within the family (example: an alcoholic's inability to manage both the addiction and the history of violence when under the influence) and plans for solving contemporary familial issues. It should also be pointed out that FST is but one of several emerging psychologies for literary studies (that is, emerging into the consciousness of people in the humanities) that is considered a useful tool for reading literature.

Notes

1. The phenomenon of *emergence* includes the properties, functions, and behaviors of living systems, and many of their constituent subsystems. Emergent phenomena manifest themselves as inexplicably unpredicted novel properties, behaviors, or functions—ones not observed in their subsystems or components. These are not explainable or predictable from even a complete understanding of the components' properties, functions, and behaviors considered in isolation from the system that embeds them. Families as living systems have such novel properties and a given family's behavior cannot necessarily be predicted from even detailed knowledge of any one or several of its members (cf. Vancouver).

2. See an early example on Lawrence by Jerome Bump from his article "D. H. Lawrence and Family Systems Theory" in the fall of 1991 issue of *Renascence*. In 1997 and in 2010, special summer issues of *Style* featured FST in literature; both issues were edited by John V. Knapp and Kenneth Womack. In 1999 Bernard Paris discussed the work of the neo-Freudian psychoanalyst Karen Horney regarding mother-child relationships, but Horney's work tends to neglect the role of the father in her analysis of early parental bonding.

3. Early works include, for example, Jay Haley's *Problem Solving Therapy* (1976); Virginia Satir's *Conjoint Family Therapy* (1967); Charles P. Barnard and Ramon G. Corrales's *The Theory and Technique of Family Therapy* (1979); Paul Watzlawick's *Change: Principles of Problem Formation and Problem Resolution* (1974); Milton Erickson's *Healing in Hypnosis* (1983) and *My Voice Will Go with You: Teaching Tales of Milton Erickson* (1982); and Salvador Minuchin and John P. Nichols, *Family Healing* (1993). The best single work aimed at a general audience is Augustus Napier and Carl Whitaker's *The Family Crucible* (1988).

4. Including E. E. Jones's *Interpersonal Perception* (1990) and H. H. Kelley's "Attribution in Social Psychology" from the *Nebraska Symposium on Motivation* (1967).

5. This is despite the limitations of what Gerrig and Allbritton (1990) refer to as the "fundamental attributional error." That is, ascribing behavior to a character's or person's personality rather than the situation.

6. Family therapist Jay Haley says that what "Freud was offering in 1896 was a family theory of neurosis. He found that in 13 out of 13 cases there had been sexual abuse in childhood. Had Freud continued with this view, he would have established family therapy. He would have had to adapt the focus of family therapists today, who must take into account not only abusers but mothers who failed to protect their children. His thinking would have become triadic and would have involved not an oedipal fantasy, but real-life family behavior. . . . However, Freud changed his mind a short time later. He decided that the sexual abuse of these patients did not actually occur but was a false memory, a fantasy they constructed of their world. By taking that position, Freud brought the therapy world back inside the mind of the client and away from what actually happens in the social context of the family" (93).

7. In more abstract and mathematical terms, Ludwig von Bertalanffy says that a system may be defined as "a set of differential equations with the property that information about the state of the system influence(s) the system's rate of change." Concerned with human applications of von Bertalanffy's ideas, Jeffery Vancouver has discussed what he calls Living Systems Theory (LST). LST is a paradigm in organizational science that, first, "provides a framework for describing the micro (i.e., human), macro (social organizations), and meso (interaction between the two) levels of the field without relying on reductionism or reification. The more parsimoniously it can do this, the better"; second, "provide(s) a model of the major processes of dynamic interaction among individuals, situa-

tions, and behavior, addressing major phenomenon like behavior, cognition, and affect"; and third, "provide(s) [interesting] research ideas" (165).

Works Cited

Ariel, Shlomo. *Culturally Competent Family Therapy*. Westport: Prager, 1999.

Bateson, Gregory. *Steps Toward an Ecology of Mind*. New York: Balantine, 1972.

Beach, Richard, Deborah Appleman, Susan Hynds, and Jeffrey Wilhelm. *Teaching Literature to Adolescents*. New York: Routledge, 2006.

Bertalanffy, Ludwig von. *Robots, Men, and Minds*. New York: Braziller, 1967.

_____. *General Systems Theory: Foundations, Development, and Application*. New York: Braziller, 1968.

Bowen, Murray. *Family Therapy in Clinical Practice*. Northvale: Aronson, 1978.

Carr, Nicholas. *The Shallows: What the Internet Is Doing to Our Brain*. New York: Norton, 2010.

Churchman, C. West. *The Systems Approach*. New York: Delta, 1968.

Cooper, Sara, ed. *The Ties That Bind: Questioning Family Dynamics and Family Discourse in Hispanic Literature*. Lanham: UP of America, 2004.

Corbett, Mary Jean. *Family Likeness: Sex, Marriage, and Incest from Jane Austen to Virginia Woolf*. Ithaca: Cornell UP, 2008.

Culpeper, Jonathan. *Language and Characterization: People in Plays and Other Texts*. Essex: Pearson, 2001.

Davis, Todd, and Kenneth Womack. "'O My Brothers': Reading the Anti-Ethics of the Pseudo Family in Burgess's *A Clockwork Orange*." *College Literature*. 29.2 (2002): 19–36.

Erlich, Paul R. *Human Natures: Genes, Cultures, and the Human Prospect*. New York: Penguin, 2000.

Flint, Christopher. *Family Fictions: Narrative and Domestic Relations in Britain, 1688–1798*. Stanford: Stanford UP, 1998.

Framo, James L. "Rationale and Techniques of Intensive Family Therapy." *Family Therapy: Theoretical and Practical Aspects*. Ed. Ivan Boszormenyi-Nagy and James L. Framo. New York: Brunner, 1965.

Gee, James Paul. *What Video Games Have to Teach Us About Learning and Literacy*. New York: Palgrave, 2007.

Gerrig, Richard J., and David W. Allbritton. "The Construction of Literary Character: A View from Cognitive Psychology." *Style* 24.3 (1990): 380–91.

Goleman, Daniel. *Social Intelligence: The Revolutionary New Science of Human Relationships*. New York: Bantam, 2006.

Gottman, John, and Nan Silver. *The Seven Principles for Making Marriage Work: A Practical Guide*. New York: Three Rivers Press, 2000.

Graff, Gerald. *Professing Literature: An Institutional History*. Chicago: U of Chicago P, 1987.

Grunbaum, Adolph. *The Foundations of Psychoanalysis: A Philosophic Critique*. Berkeley: U of California P, 1984.

Haley, Jay. *Learning and Teaching Therapy*. New York: Guilford, 1996.

Hirsch, Marianne. *The Mother-Daughter Plot: Narrative, Psychoanalysis, Feminism*. Bloomington: Indiana UP, 1989.

Hochman, Banich. *The Test of Character: From the Victorian Novel to the Modern*. East Brunswick: Associated UP, 1983.

Hoffman, Lynn. *Foundations of Family Therapy: A Conceptual Framework for Systems Change*. New York: Basic, 1981.

Imber-Black, Evan. *Families and Larger Systems: A Family Therapist's Guide through the Labyrinth*. New York: Guildford, 1988.

_____. *Secrets in Family and Family Therapy*. New York: Norton, 1993.

Jones, E. E. *Interpersonal Perception*. New York: Freeman, 1990.

Kagan, Jerome. *Galen's Prophecy: Temperament in Human Nature*. New York: Harper, 1994.

Kanthak, John F. "Legacy of Dysfunction: Family Systems in Zora Neale Hurston's *Jonahs Gourd Vine*." *Journal of Modern Literature* 28.2 (2005): 113–29.

Kegan, Robert. *The Evolving Self: Problem and Process in Human Development*. Cambridge: Harvard UP, 1982.

_____. *In Over Our Heads: The Mental Demands of Modern Life*. Cambridge: Harvard UP, 1994.

Kelley, Harold H. "Attribution in Social Psychology." *Nebraska Symposium on Motivation*. Ed. D. Levine. Lincoln: U of Nebraska P, 1967: 192–238.

Knapp, John V. "Introduction: Family Systems Psychotherapy and Literature/Literary Criticism." Ed. J. V. Knapp and Kenneth Womack. *Style* 31.2 (1997): 223–54.

_____. "Introduction: New Psychologies and Modern Assessments." Style 44.1–2 (2010): 1–59.

_____. "Introduction: Self-Preservation and Self-Transformation: Interdisciplinary Approaches to Literary Character." *Style* 24.3 (1990): 349–64. Rpt. UP of America, 1993: 1–16.

_____. *Reading the Family Dance: Family Systems Therapy and Literary Study*. Newark: U of Delaware P, 2003.

_____. *Striking at the Joints: Contemporary Psychology and Literary Criticism*. Lanham: UP of America, 1996.

Loewenstein, George F., Elke U. Weber, Christopher K. Hsee, and Ned F. Welch. "Risk as Feelings." *Psychological Bulletin* 127.2 (2001): 267–86.

Margolin, Uri. "The What, the When, and the How of Being a Character in Literary Narrative." *Literary Character*. Ed. John V. Knapp. Lanham: UP of America, 1993.

Masson, Jeffrey M. *The Assault on Truth: Freud's Suppression of the Seduction Theory*. New York: Farrar, 1984.

Meutsch, Dietrich. "Mental Models in Literary Discourse: Towards the Integration of Linguistic and Psychological Levels of Description." *Poetics* 15 (1986): 307–31.

Minuchin, Salvador. *Families and Family Therapy*. Cambridge: Harvard UP, 1974.

Minuchin, Salvador, Wai-yung Lee, and George M. Simon. *Mastering Family Therapy: Journeys of Growth and Transformation*. Hoboken: Wiley, 2006.

Minuchin, Salvador, and Michael P. Nichols. *Family Healing: Strategies for Hope and Understanding.* New York: Touchstone, 1993.

Nelson, T. G. A. *Children, Parents, and the Rise of the Novel.* Newark: U of Delaware P, 1995.

O'Brien, Marion. "Studying Individual and Family Development: Linking Theory and Research." *Journal of Marriage and Family* 61.4 (2005): 800–90.

Osment, Steven. *Ancestors: The Loving Family in Old Europe.* Cambridge: Harvard UP, 2001.

Palazzoli, Mara Selvini, Luigi Boscolo, Gianfranco Cecchin, and Giuliana Prata. *Paradox and Counterpardox: A New Model in the Therapy of the Family in Schizophrenic Transaction.* New York: Aronson, 1978.

Palazzoli, Mara Selvini, Stefano Cirillo, Matteo Selvini, and Anna Maria Sorrentino. *Family Games: General Models of Psychotic Processes in the Family.* New York: Norton, 1989.

Palmer, Alan. *Fictional Minds.* Lincoln: U of Nebraska P, 2004.

_____, ed. "Social Minds in Fiction and Criticism." *Style,* 45.2 (2011).

_____. *Social Minds in the Novel.* Columbus: Ohio State UP, 2010.

Panksepp, Jaak. "Affective Neuroscience and the Ancestral Sources of Human Feelings." *Consciousness and Cognition: Fragments of Mind and Brain.* Ed. Henri Cohen and Brigitte Stemmer. Burling: Academic P, 2007: 173–88.

Paris, Bernard. *A Psychological Approach to Fiction.* Bloomington: U of Indiana P, 1974.

_____. *The Therapeutic Process: Essays and Lectures.* New Haven: Yale UP, 1999.

Phelan, James. *Living to Tell About It: A Rhetoric and Ethics of Character Narration.* Ithaca: Cornell UP, 2005.

_____. *Reading People, Reading Plots: Character, Progression, and the Interpretation of Narrative.* Chicago: U of Chicago P, 1989.

Piercy, Fred P., Douglas Sprinkle, and Joseph L. Wetchler, eds. *Family Therapy Sourcebook.* 2nd ed. New York: Guilford, 1996.

Proehl, Geoffrey S. *Coming Home Again: American Family Drama and the Figure of the Prodigal.* Cranbury: Associated UP, 1997.

Randall, William Lowell. *The Stories We Are: An Essay on Self-Creation.* Toronto: U of Toronto P, 1995.

Reiss, David, Jenae M. Neiderhiser, E. Mavis Hetherington, and Robert Plomin. *The Relationship Code: Deciphering Genetic and Social Influences on Adolescent Development.* Cambridge: Harvard UP, 2000.

Ricoeur, Paul. *Freud and Philosophy: An Essay on Interpretation.* Trans. Denis Savage. New Haven: Yale UP, 1970.

Sacks, Sheldon. *Fiction and the Shape of Belief.* Berkeley: U of California P, 1964.

Scanlon, Tom. *Family Drama and American Dreams.* Westport: Greenwood P, 1978.

Short, Mick. "Discourse Analysis and the Analysis of Drama." *Language, Discourse, and Literature.* Ed. R. Carter and P. Simpson. London: Hyman, 1989: 139–68.

_____. "From Dramatic Text to Dramatic Performance." *Studying Drama: From Text to Context.* Ed. Jonathan Culpeper et al. London: Routledge, 1998: 6–18.

Semino, Elena. *Language and World Creation in Poems and Other Texts*. London: Longman, 1997.

Simon, Fritz B., Helm Stierlin, and Lyman C. Wynne. *The Language of Family Therapy: A Systemic Vocabulary and Sourcebook*. New York: Family Process, 1985.

Smith, Michael W., and Jeffrey D. Wilhelm. *Fresh Takes on Teaching Literary Elements*. Urbana: NCTE, 2010.

Thornton, E. M. *The Freudian Fallacy: An Alternative View of Freudian Theory*. New York: Dial, 1984.

Tulving, E. "Episodic and Semantic Memory." *Organization of Memory*. Ed. E. Tulving and W. Donaldson. New York: Academic, 1972: 382–403.

Vancouver, Jeffrey B. "Living Systems Theory as a Paradigm for Organizational Behavior: Understanding Humans, Organizations, and Social Processes." *Behavioral Sciences* 41 (1996): 165–204.

Visher, Emily, and John S. Visher. *Therapy with Stepfamilies*. New York: Brunner, 1996.

Wade, Nicholas. *Before the Dawn: Recovering the Lost History of Our Ancestors*. New York: Penguin, 2006.

Whitaker, Carl A., and William M. Bumberry. *Dancing with the Family: A Symbolic-Experiential Approach*. New York: Brunner, 1988.

Womack, Kenneth. "Passage to Italy: Narrating the Family in Crisis in Forster's *Where Angels Fear to Tread*." *Mosaic* 33.3 (2000): 129–44.

Literary Characters and Family Systems: D. H. Lawrence's *Sons and Lovers*_____

John V. Knapp

As discussed in the Critical Reception essay, this essay will employ the tools of family systems theory (FST) and Alan Palmer's concepts of aspectuality and situated identity to discuss *Sons and Lovers* (1913), a bildungsroman by D. H. Lawrence. Set in northern England during the turn of the twentieth century, Lawrence's novel is a family story concerned with the life trajectory of a married couple, Walter and Gertrude Morel, their four children—William, Paul, Annie, and Arthur—and the influence family dynamics has on the children growing up and into their young adulthood. The novel opens, after some brief discussion of the parents' life before marriage, with the Morels' ongoing marital issues, their discovery of one another's personality characteristics after their wedding, the births of their children, their growing estrangement, and, eventually, Gertrude's inevitable turn to her sons (first William, then Paul) as emotional replacements for her husband. Various scenes dramatize Walter's bitterness at being pushed out of the mother-child triangle, also demonstrating how this triangularization affects William and Paul in their relationships with the women in their lives. After the early death of William, the emotional bond between Gertrude and her son Paul becomes the dominating focus in the novel; the second half of the narrative details Paul's romances with two women—Miriam and Clara—who both love him, but also realize that he cannot commit because of his intense tie to his mother. Gertrude's eventual death leaves Paul adrift; Lawrence ends the novel as Paul's moving finally "towards the faintly humming, glowing town, quickly" (464).

Previous commentary on Lawrence's masterpiece has emphasized the mother-son relationship and diminished the other characters' importance to background for the so-called Freudian Oedipus conflict of

Gertrude and Paul. This critical bias has allowed the reader to take sides in a family fight, with many readers either dismissing the father as relatively unimportant while blaming Paul's mother, Gertrude, as the one who has kept him from emotionally maturing. A different group of critics has blamed the father's brutality for the mother's emotional attachment to her sons, and none seems to have discussed the dynamics motivating both spouses' misunderstanding about life with the opposite gender.

One of the reasons for the critical diminution of Walter's character in *Sons and Lovers* is textual: between 1913 and 1992, the version of the novel available to readers was a variation of the first edition that had been severely edited by Edward Garnett. Garnett cut the the length of the novel by ten percent and, in doing so, reduced the role of Paul's brother, William—and, therefore, William's relationship with Walter (Lawrence xvi). The missing text was eventually reinstated by editors Helen Baron and Carl Baron in the 1992 Cambridge edition (used in this essay), and William's place in the novel was restored, enhancing his role in the story and his interactions with Walter. The second reason for the critical response to *Sons and Lovers* was the domination of psychoanalysis as the primary psychological tool in literary criticism for understanding the Morel family dynamic. Given the psychoanalytic penchant for comprehending characters (and people) one at a time, many critics were seduced by the narrative bias that had chosen sides in the family fight. A third reason suggests that the familial social fabric, out of which mimetic characters emerge, has been relatively under-discussed. Characters addressed in three recent models of mind analysis (psychoanalytical, cognitive, and adaptationist or evolutionary psychology) have all tended to emphasize representations of biological or social characters, primarily one-at-a-time and individually, rather than, more importantly, as characters that are part of a larger coevolutionary ecosystem called the family.[1]

By noting what could be called the primacy in human families— what critic George Butte refers to as a "field of mutual consciousness"—the emphasis is placed on longitudinally integrated social systems displaying emotional intensity. The most obvious example being that of the family, but one might argue for analogies that include small groups of men (and woman) in extended combat situations. Especially in families, but also in long-term intimate social units, the "system and its environment are a unity and must co-evolve" (Rosenblatt 13). Hitherto, most discussions of fictional family dynamics through an individual character's development had seen the emergent family relegated largely to settings where individual minds could play out their monodramas. Now, the focus on the whole family may find readers reconstituting their attitudes toward several of the critical difficulties repeated in earlier criticism of Lawrence, with the major difficulty still unresolved: that of assigning singular blame or responsibility for the marital discord and for the subsequent damage to Paul's emotional development.

The usefulness of the vocabulary and the conceptual apparatus of FST for literary study—a clinical mind-set that allows readers to reappraise attitudes both toward Lawrence's novel and toward the whole sense of family power struggles—may be amenable to assignments of blame and singular psychological responsibility. For family therapists such as Jay Haley, assigning blame only continues the endless unresolved sets of claims and counterclaims typical of family feuds (157–61). This critical lens focuses less on the notion of fault, but asks about the dynamics of the conflict, emphasizing not guilt, but the graduated levels of responsibility in an area where a character may conveniently look over his shoulder at his parents, they at their parents, and so on, with each generation blaming the last for its current malaise, and all with some justification. Even a lengthy examination of acquired behaviors and predispositions may not reveal their origins or explain their underlying causes. Although very few family members are ever totally innocent inside the family dance, the final weight of immediate responsibility falls to the mother and father as the architects of the family.

For many readers who do attempt to account for the rest of the family, the views of Lawrence and his protagonists and narrators are often taken at face value as a set of unbiased facts, instead of opinions (cf. Schapiro 356). Even before the Cambridge edition of *Sons and Lovers* was published, however, most readers had agreed that the narrator in the novel was highly biased, particularly regarding the characters Miriam and Clara (Martz 84–91; Pittock 236). Some readers think similarly about the narrator's assessment of Walter (Sklenicka 54). Wayne Booth has argued that this narrative "inconsistency" can be reframed to demonstrate one of Lawrence's strengths, not necessarily a weakness:

> In his practice, all rules about point of view are abrogated: the borderlines between author's voice and character's voice are deliberately blurred, and *only criticism of the whole tale will offer any sort of clarity* to the reader seeking to sort out opinions. . . .
>
> . . . Again and again Lawrence simply surrenders the telling of the story to another mind, a mind neither clearly approved nor clearly repudiated yet presented in a tone that demands judgment. I don't know of any novelist, not even Dostoyevsky, who takes free indirect style further in the direction of a sustained surrender to a passionate mimicry that gives us two or more voices at once: the author's and the independent character's. (16–17; emphasis added).

Booth's thinking points to inconsistencies between what readers are told and what they are shown concerning Walter and his oldest son, William. The most serious obstacle remains the narrator's (and therefore the reader's) mixed feelings about Walter Morel and, subsequently, the understanding of the dynamics of the whole Morel family as mediated by the Paul-Gertrude dyad. Hence, the narrative voice and the original editing of Lawrence's text have come together in a perfect storm of criticism, overlooking the intermental unit of father and son in Walter and William. When Lawrence's pre-1992 version of *Sons and*

Lovers downplayed the importance of this unit, it treated Walter and William as synthetic surrogates for the heart of the novel: the mimetic bond and conflicted attachment of Paul and Gertrude. The 1992 edition makes the importance of this relationship apparent, in both what Lawrence's narrator does not say about them, or merely alludes to, and in what is made explicit.

By paying closer attention to both Walter and William in the more general family dynamic, and by employing the theoretical constructs from FST, I intend to persuade the reader toward a more balanced final response to the novel and the Morel family, arguing that the problematic relationship of Paul and Gertrude is only one part of a much larger dysfunction in the whole family. Finally, I will suggest that previous psychoanalytic discussions of Paul's early emotional and sexual rumination via the Oedipus complex should be reconsidered by looking instead at typically occurring biological and psychological family dynamics. Sensitizing ourselves to William's role in the family, we will see by analogy that both parents have responsibility for his and Paul's development.

III

Further discussion of *Sons and Lovers* should begin with a brief overview of the Morels' origins as a family employing both FST and Palmer's new critical tools. Examining the families-of-origin for both Walter and Gertrude, one can see where they learned the emotional lessons that each brought to the marriage. Each was also taught, as was Paul, the proper behavior toward loved ones and members of the opposite sex, as well as expectations for their own treatment by others. In short, the child of either sex learns from his parents a sense of self in the context of familial reciprocity (Bowlby 9–11; Herring and Kaslow). Hence, many family therapists see family life as existentially problematic and marvel that, as a species, most people have survived their parents only to burden their children with many of the same difficulties they once faced (Haley 153). It is part of the human condition that many people spend the middle part of their lives overcoming and, ideally, forgiving the mistakes perpetrated on them by their parents—just as they had to do with their own parents. One of the founders of family therapy, Carl Whitaker, used to joke that he no longer believed in individuals; he believed, rather, in scapegoats, sent out by their families-of-origin to do battle with new spouses over whose family they would re-create (56).

In the Morel household, Walter and Gertrude brought with themselves, as scapegoats, some lessons learned from their parents. While readers know almost nothing about Walter's father (although his grandfather "was a French refugee who had married an English barmaid——if it had been a marriage" (Lawrence 17), his mother (perhaps abandoned by the father) asked or pushed Walter to work in the mining pits from a very young age (Rose 237–55). Thus, while apparently responsible for his family's financial survival, Walter was simultaneously taken care of by his mother in all other ways, and this traditional English working-class pattern remained an integral part of his emotional expectations going into his marriage. In the language of one personality theorist (Marcia 159), Walter's development was truncated, and his identity was foreclosed; he had virtually no time to develop beyond his childhood emotions and his role expectations. Growing up this way had psychological ramifications along class lines; a middle-class Gertrude was more emotionally developed simply by having more time to mature.

Thus, in a scene in which Gertrude discovers bills still unpaid after several months of marriage, she confronts a passive Walter. Unable to rouse him, she addresses what she learns is the real source of fiscal authority: Walter's mother. Walter and his mother had formed what Palmer calls an intermental bond, tacitly agreeing that in exchange for Walter's working childhood, she would continue to look over his finances, even after he married. Gertrude had not yet learned of this distributed cognition of the mother and son mental unit. Walter's mother was highly indignant that Gertrude would even question their common agreement: "'It is lucky to be you,' said the elder woman bitingly, 'to have a husband as takes all the worry of the money, and leave you a free hand'" (Lawrence 21). Contrastively, Gertrude had also formed an intermental unit with her father and his values, and so during the conversation, Gertrude remains "white and silent. She was her father now" (21) as Walter sits by, letting his wife discover the overpriced house rental.

While Walter finds his mother's control of his finances both familiar and comfortable, Gertrude's feelings evolve from fear, to anger, and finally to indignation. Taking on her psychologically dominant parent's values while rejecting her subservient mother's behavior, she now becomes the worrying spouse. After all, her "father was to her the type of all men," even though she "hated her father's overbearing manner towards her gentle, humourous, kindly-souled mother" (18, 15). Ironically, even though she became more like her father before Walter could become him to her, Gertrude was initially attracted to Walter precisely because he was "different: soft, non-intellectual, warm," a dancer who moved "as if it were natural and joyous in him to dance" (17). This choice of a marital partner who appears to be the opposite of the rejected parental personality is typical of the desire to re-create the family-of-origin dynamic, the only ones both spouses know intimately (Haley 15; Satir 112–34).

From Walter's perspective, Gertrude was fascinating because she was so different; she "was to the miner that thing of mystery and fascination: a lady," in part because her "southern pronunciation and purity of English . . . thrilled him to hear" (Lawrence 17). Indeed, therapist Salvador Minuchin said of his own experience: in "these first years of marriage, this trek of transformation from me to me-and-you" (what Palmer calls "we" narratives), "occurred like the formation of the self in childhood—a slow accretion of small moments"—albeit not always positive ones (55). For family therapists, this capacity—to marry one's opposite and then react with angry surprise when the spouse exhibits contrary behavior—is the stuff of the human condition. However fascinating he or she finds the the other's differences, each newlywed expects reflected emotions when the couple confronts life's initial joint crises. Since many young couples begin marriage without each having a well-defined sense of self, the urge to merge into a single identity as a couple is so powerful that when conflicts arise as to whose version of self will predominate, the battle is often intense. Minuchin says that often young married couples lack "both the capacity to see each other's perspective and the sympathy that allows tolerance of differences, so that every issue [becomes] a struggle for survival of the self" (73). It was, as the narrator says of the Morels' first years: "a fearful bloody battle that ended only with the death of one" (Lawrence 22). Recall Palmer saying, "characters in a story-world can only ever experience the story-world from a particular perceptual and cognitive aspect at any one time, and be experienced differently by, the various minds of the characters" (*Style*). Reading this novel for the first time, it is important to remain aware of the narrator's and characters' seductive voices, and not be mislead by any one of them.

Early on, Gertrude tried to connect to her husband and "open her heart seriously to him" in the way she knew best—verbally, telling him what she felt and expecting verbal, perhaps somewhat intellectual, responses back (Lawrence 17). In addition, as a "Puritan," Gertrude wanted Walter to be more like her father. She wanted "to make him undertake his own responsibilities, to make him fulfill his obligations. . . . She tried to force him to face things." He, on the other hand, had a nature that "was purely sensuous . . . [and] what he felt just at the minute, that was all to him." Often, he "did the right thing by instinct"; nevertheless, when she tried to verbalize herself to him, she "saw him listen deferentially, but without understanding. This killed her effort at finer understanding, and she had flashes of fear" (19). To get away from her disappointment in him, he drank and relaxed with more accepting friends in the neighborhood pub; the more he drank, the more "she scathed him with her satire," but, to Walter, her rage was incomprehensible and he "could not endure it—it drove him out of his mind." The "estrangement between them caused him, knowingly or unknowingly, grossly to offend her where he would not have done" (23).

Readers have generally agreed that Lawrence's narrator early in the novel is as balanced and as objective as it ever gets (Moore 70; Martz 74). From that initial objectivity, however, the narrator all too often takes on the emotional aspects of the mother, and draws many critics into their shared sympathy (Sklenicka 46, 50). But it was a sympathy that even Lawrence in his later years felt was overdrawn: "my mother was wrong and I thought she was absolutely right" (Frieda Lawrence 57). Of course, as readers oriented to family systems and social minds, we assume the problem is less one of right-wrong and more one of balanced understanding of each character's aspectual view. Judith Ruderman, in correcting her (and Lawrence's) over-identification with Paul's view, believes that "Lawrence outgrew his Oedipus complex and shifted his allegiance from his mother to his father" (8). I would argue that using a Freudian model to move "allegiance" from one part of the system to another does not change the system at all. Rather, the pattern of interaction remains crucial to understanding Lawrence, the artist, not any switch in readers' allegiances (cf. Haley 127)

Following the Morels' early married life, they give birth to children, first William, then later Paul, Annie, and Arthur—a pattern that conflates Lawrence's real family's birth order (Pittock 242). The arrival of their children added an element to their marriage that helped keep the couple together in spite of early stresses. Family systems theorists have found that, since conflict within dyads is too intense to bear for long, the most typical gambit for unhappy married couples is to introduce a third element (a parent, friend, lover, or child) and create a triad or triangle. Although that third element could be anything, for Gertrude, it was the children. William arrived "just when her own bitterness of disillusion was hardest to bear; when her faith in life was shaken, and her soul felt dreary and lonely. She made much of the child and the father was jealous" (Lawrence 22). The Morels' parental decisions concerning this new subsystem merely continue the battle already in progress, as we see early during Walter's clumsy hair-cutting attempt to assert some masculine control and influence his developing son (23–24).

Most critics have largely dismissed Walter's influence following the narrative voice: during their fearful life-long battle, Gertrude "in seeking to make him nobler than he could be, she destroyed him. She injured and hurt and scarred herself, but she lost none of her worth. She also had the children" (25; cf. Ruderman, 8, 180). Too ready here to dismiss both the selfhood of the father and his familial value, the narrative voice also magnifies the self-worth and the family role of the mother. By taking the narrative view too easily here, and so dismissing Lawrence's famous remark about trusting the (whole) tale and not the teller (Booth 18), one stumbles in approximately the same way author Anthony Burgess does when he exposes his mixed feelings about the father and his absolute assurance about the role of the mother:

> [Walter is] the disruptive force that crashes in, drunk, dirty, selfish, aggressive, at the end of each idyllic day, but he is not antipathetic. He breaks easily in a crisis, he is comically repentant, his dialect is more engaging than the cold English of rebuke that Mrs. Morel levels at him. [In his] careless vigor, he represents a principle about which Lawrence always maintained a strong nostalgia—a rough and beautiful masculinity that stands out against female domination. (54–55)

Burgess makes no mention here that Lawrence's supposed masculinity principle is in fact a well-known concept in family clinical study: that is, both parents can be highly influential in a child's development—even when one is physically absent a great deal, as was Walter—and in Anglo-American culture, each carries the weight of gender values, even if only by negative example (Waters 220; Epstein 83; Bowlby 128).

Contrary to the narrator's opinion, however, much evidence in the new edition indicates that Walter was not merely a negative example, destroyed by an all-powerful wife and mother. Even disengaged, Walter influenced members of his family, including young Paul, as they learned the knowledge necessary to become adults in the twentieth century. Paul's familial education and its context are important since children learn as much, if not more, from their families in direct experience rather than from precept. In terms of therapy with families outside fiction, Jay Haley notes that the wise therapist, like the wise reader of *Sons and Lovers*, "learns not to naively take sides with one spouse against the other and learns the value of seeing how people actually deal with each other rather than listening to their reports about how they do" (157).

Early in the novel, when Walter is told that Paul has won a book about birds in a child's newspaper competition, he cannot respond suitably enough for the Paul-focalized narrative voice who pontificates that "conversation was impossible between the father and *any other member of the family*. He was an outsider. He had denied the God in him" (Lawrence 88; emphasis added). After Paul's pronouncement, the narrator tells readers that Walter was particularly "lavish of endearments to his second son," that "the children feel secure when he is in bed," and that he was particularly "gentle if anyone were ill" (89–91). Given Paul's own inability to truly see his father, and the narrator's lack of consistency in this scene about the Paul-and-Walter dyad, perhaps a better source for information about the father's early influence could come from William.

IV

Here are two brief examples to suggest that William's character was the precursor to Paul and his problems with his family. In the 1992 edition, William's case makes plain that the problems of the boys' maturation, emotionally and sexually, is the result of a family dynamic where both parents share major responsibility for their children's adult adjustments. This new edition shows clearly the consequences of previously making William a synthetic (plot-driven) figure, and Paul a mimetic (real-life) one, even as we question the reliability of that information about Paul. Early in the novel, Gertrude enmeshes (or bonds too tightly with) William just as she will do with Paul after William's death. The older boy has a more complex response to William's mother than Paul will ever have: "So [William] went out, hampered with his sister, while his mother worked. He was angry with her, for foisting the burden on him, and yet he grieved for her, because he knew something was the matter. So, with his love for his mother vexing his young growth, he made the best of things" (30).

Paul admits to feelings of sibling rivalry for his more athletic older brother, and even complains to Gertrude about her passionate attachment to William: "And why wasn't I the oldest son?" he asks, adding "You should have had me for your eldest" (282; see Moore 42). It is a strange complaint, in one sense, because Paul wanted to replace someone who resembled his father psychologically. Although William exhibits his mother's ambition to rise up out of the working class, he is much more sensual and spontaneous—a dancer just like his father. Indeed, for an ineffectual father, Walter must have wielded some heavy influence over William, for Gertrude "was afraid of her son going the same way as his father" (Lawrence 76). Whenever largely male issues are at stake, William is as interested in pleasing his father as his mother: "When he was seventeen, he won a bicycle race at Ilkeston. Morel, in one of his bursts of bragging, had challenged his son against any champion there in the public house. William felt it his duty to fulfill his father's boasts. Mrs. Morel did not approve." (70)

In spite of the family history of tension between husband and wife, William by no means distanced himself from Walter the way Paul would later on. This is exhibited in a scene in which father and son tease each other about dancing generally, and Walter's purported ability to do the waltz:

[Walter:] "When I was a bit nimbler, I could turn on a threp'ny bit."
    "I bet you could," said William skeptically.
    "I could an' all," protested Morel, with pride.

> "Go on then—let's have a look at you."
>
> But Morel was afraid to dance before his children . . . .
>
> "You see I'm following in my father's footsteps," [William] said.
>
> "An' more fool thee," said his father, "if iver tha does that."
>
> "That's all right when you're too stiff to dance anymore," said William.
>
> "I've niver danced for twenty year," cried Morel hotly.
>
> "An' I'll bet you found it hard work to give it up."
>
> But William persisted. He was a great favourite with the ladies. (73)

This teasing conversation does not hide William's pride in his father's past accomplishments, his father's enjoyment of William's interest, and the sense of continuity from father to son—in dancing and in romance. Naturally, Gertrude could not enter into this type of conversation, a kind of dialogue apparently witnessed by Paul and repeated often enough for her to worry that William was becoming like his father, Walter. At times, given her high standards, "he lapsed and was purely like his father" (78). Only Gertrude would use the word *lapsed* regarding her son's enjoyment of dancing and flirting—a common enough practice for young single men.

William, of course, has been buffeted by both parents in their battle, but especially by his mother. From early in his childhood she encouraged him to be her protector, but in doing so she kept him from ratifying those personality characteristics taken from the father—spontaneous joy, dancing, an eye for the ladies—that would be for him an expression of a major part of his own development. Like so many children caught up in a parent's battles, William thinks that he can save her, or at least can lift her out of her misery. A child so caught in triangles with his parents, says Virginia Satir, gets used to an emotional life that oscillates from "omnipotence to helplessness, from grandiosity to self-abnegation," and unable to predict relationships "his needs remain unvalidated, he is distrustful of others, yet dependent to a crippling degree on what others think of him" (61).

When he leaves home, William brings along with him the emotional baggage he carried all of his life. By expressing those qualities of his father's he antagonizes his mother, who wants him to succeed above all else. Her need for William's success goes beyond a parent's concern; Gertrude dreams that the success of both Paul and William will fill her sense of inner emptiness: they would "work out what *she* wanted; they were derived from her, they were of her, and their works would also be hers" (Lawrence 127). On the other hand, William is different from her; like his father, he needs and enjoys friends, women, and dancing. Therefore, like a dutiful son still enmeshed in the original family triangle, William tries to please himself internally by pleasing both sides of the triangle, sides that have now long since become a part of himself: he tries to both study and dance, and in doing so risks exhaustion.

In choosing dancing, William knows that he risks becoming a ne'er-do-well in his mother's eyes. If he chooses to study Latin instead, he gives up expressing that part of himself that comes from his father. Caught in a dilemma, and unable to experiment with his identity for fear of risking his mother's hopes for him, William once again oscillates from grandiosity to helplessness, returning home for a visit with Gyp. Gyp is a young woman who superficially appears the opposite of William's mother, but who, in fact, displays some of Gertrude's least desirable qualities. Like the young Gertrude with the miners' wives (10), Gyp acts superior toward the Morel family and cannot "realize them as people" (144). Her helplessness at times barely disguises her manipulative behavior, even though William is emotionally used to being manipulated by both parents. Walter responds to Gyp in his best version of a London dialect (143) and treats her gallantly, just as he once courted and performed for Gertrude. Walter's male behavior and attitude signal to William that he has indeed made a conquest, but that victory, won in front of his jealous mother, is at best ambiguous, for William's "heart was rather sore and he did not know why" (145).

Experienced observers of family systems see a rich set of interactions through the replaying of the inner struggles William has faced all of his life. Although biographers like Jeffery Meyers take Lawrence at face value and agree with him that William is killed "by a split between sex and soul" (114), a family systems–oriented interpretation would suggest otherwise. William's turmoil is not an earlier version of Paul's (supposed) Oedipus conflict—a version where William loves his mother and hates his father, the male head of household whose place he wishes to usurp. Rather, William's conflict is the product of his divided love for both parents as expressed by those personality attributes of theirs he has internalized. His conflict is thus between valuable parts of himself that are apparently equally strong.

Here is where Palmer's foci on the aspectual nature of human interactions, embodied consciousness, intermental thought patterns, and FST all come together to describe the interactions among Walter, William, and Gertrude. Few activities could be more embodied in one's physical consciousness than in dancing, and Palmer argues that "fictional mental functioning should not be divorced from the social and physical context of the storyworld within which it occurs" (*Style* 204). As mentioned earlier, Gertrude fell in love with Walter because he was a dancer, and because dancing embodied in him and for him the playful childhood he had never experienced. From Walter's perspective, Gertrude fell in love with all of him, the whole being and not merely those parts and experiences of which she approved. Walter is therefore befuddled when Gertrude rejects his personality as a whole—not just the parts she does not like. Furthermore, William displays the same problem in reverse. In trying to create a satisfying intermental unit (called a marriage), William falls in love with only the physical part of Gyp and actively rejects, as his mother did his father, those areas of mind and behavior incompatible with what he expects from women generally. What Gyp feels, however, is William's rejection of her; in one instance, as William discusses a book Gyp has apparently not read, she remains "miserably on the sofa," listening to his criticism right in front of her, when he tells his mother how there "is not a thing you can talk to her about" (Lawrence 161). Any married couple—married beyond a certain duration—exhibits what Palmer calls intermental thought, where through experience and profound emotional connections, the couple appears to know each other's thoughts without any need for verbalization; each can intuit those areas of conflict without need for explicit internal apprehension. As Palmer argues, "social minds are possible because much of our thought is visible" (*Social Minds* 2). William and Gyp have no future because they have no shared mind, repeating the problem of Walter and Gertrude.

The consequences of Paul's upbringing in his family-of-origin are evident in his relationships with both Miriam and Clara; with each of these women Paul alternately acts like, or responds as if, he were his mother and his father—unable to coordinate empowerment and kindness in a healthy adult way. Merely exchanging Clara for Miriam does little for Paul in helping him understand these basic issues. Likewise, Paul's father is also, at times, caring, but unable to coordinate his protectiveness toward his children and wife with his negative feeling toward them. As Jay Haley, has said, "underlying most marital problems is a protectiveness that keeps the problem going" (157). Hence Paul is angry at both parents, an anger in which sexuality is only part of the difficulty.

In addition to Paul's problem of coordination with Miriam, he displays the same ongoing difficulty with Clara, reenacting the family dance with each woman. On their seaside holiday, as Clara and Paul discuss possible marriage plans, Clara remains reserved, feeling that she cannot commit herself to Paul fully without being reassured that he is willing to do the same. Clara tells Paul that her husband Baxter "belongs" to her, as does Paul; he later picks at her, telling her, "I consider you treated Baxter rottenly." For the reader, what is most interesting is that Paul "half-expected Clara to answer him, as his mother would" (404). When she does not, when she takes him "seriously," Paul loses his temper and takes his father's point of view on the nature of man-woman control balances:

You imagined him something he wasn't. That's just what a woman is. She thinks she knows what's good for a man, and she's going to see he gets it; and no matter if he's starving, he may sit and whistle for what he needs, while she's got him, and is giving him what's good for him. (404)

Despite Clara's efforts, her ties to Paul remained tenuous: "So there went on a battle between them. She knew she never fully had him" (405).

In effect, Paul sees every love relationship as a battle, a view learned by witnessing the Morels' inability to coordinate their very different emotional expectations. Napier and Whitaker refer to this process of polarization and escalation as maintaining an (unhealthy) homeostatic balance in the family (81–83). Jay Haley attests to the power of homeostasis when he notes that, in his clinical experience, "couples followed sequences of behavior that they could not seem to change [even] when they tried . . . [It was] as if they had interpersonal reflexes" (152).

The family dance, thus, perpetuates itself from generation to generation, an *inter*psychic struggle as much as an *intra*psychic one. Literary critics, unless they wish to choose sides in the family dance, must move away from assessing blame for Paul's developmentally problematic future—away from either mother-alone or father-alone—and place responsibility where it belongs: on the saddest part of the human condition, the oftentimes unresolvable battles for authority and control with those whom we feel the most intimate. Only through the gaining of great wisdom later in life (Orwoll and Permutter 163–64) or the help of a systems-wise therapist can anyone learn to cope in what can sometimes be that most dangerous of places, the family circle.

Notes

1. This same place, the family circle, also has the potential for enhancing individual existence. As Minuchin says: "Loyalty, responsibility, tolerance, enjoyment, and kindness—these are the positive features of family life through which we expand and enrich each other. Family ties do not reduce the self they expand it" (*Family Healing* 284).

Works Cited

Bloom, Harold, ed. *D. H. Lawrence: Modern Critical Views.* New York: Chelsea, 1987.

Booth, Wayne. "Confessions of a Luke-Warm Lawrentian." *The Challenge of D. H. Lawrence.* Ed. Michael Squires and Keith Cushman, 1990: 9–27.

Bowlby, John. *A Secure Base: Parent-Child Attachment and Healthy Human Development.* New York: Basic, 1988.

Brown, Judith M. "The Milan Principles of Hypothesizing, Circularity, and Neutrality in Dialogical Family Therapy: Extinction, Evolution, Eviction . . . or Emergence?" *Australian and New Zealand Journal of Family Therapy* 31 (2010): 248–65.

Burgess, Anthony. *Flame into Being.* London: Heineman, 1985.

Butte, George. *I Know That You Know that I Know: Narrating Subjects from Moll Flanders to Marnie.* Columbus: Ohio State UP, 2004.

Carroll, Joseph. "An Evolutionary Paradigm for Literary Study." *Style* 42.2–3 (2008): 103–35.

_____. *Literary Darwinism: Evolution, Human Nature, and Literature.* New York: Routledge, 2004.

_____. Rejoinder. *Style* 42.2–3 (2008): 308–411.

Chambliss, D. L., and Thomas H. Ollendick. "Empirically Supported Psychological Interventions: Controversies and Evidence." *Annual Review of Psychology* 52 (2001): 685–716.

Christensen, Andrew, Brian D. Doss, and David C. Atkins. "A Science of Couple Therapy: For What Should We Seek Empirical Support?" *Family Psychology: The Art of the Science.* Ed. William M. Pinsof and Jay L. Lebow. New York: Oxford UP, 2005: 43–63.

Cooper, Sara, ed. *The Ties That Bind: Questioning Family Dynamics and Family Discourse in Hispanic Literature.* Lanham: UP of America, 2004.

Gottman, John, and Kimberly Ryan. "The Mismeasure of Therapy: Treatment Outcomes in Marital Therapy Research." *Family Psychology: The Art of the Science.* Ed. William M. Pinsof and Jay L. Lebow. New York: Oxford UP, 2005: 65–89.

Haley, Jay. *Problem-Solving Therapy.* San Francisco: Jossey-Bass, 1976.

Herring, Melissa, and Nadine Kaslow, "Depression and Attachment in Families: A Child-Focused Perspective." *Family Process* 41 (2002): 494–518.

Hoffman, Lynn. *Foundations of Family Therapy: A Conceptual Framework for Systems Change.* New York: Basic, 1981.

Knapp, John V. "Family Systems Psychotherapy and Psycho-analytic Literary Criticism: A Comparative Analysis." *Mosaic* 37.1 (2004): 149–66.

_____. "Introduction: New Psychologies and Modern Assessments." *Style* 44.1–2 (2010): 1–59.

_____. *Striking at the Joints: Contemporary Psychology and Literary Criticism.* Lanham: UP of America, 1996.

Knapp, John V., and Kenneth Womack, eds. "New Psychologies and Modern Assessments." *Style* 44.1–2 (2010).

_____. *Reading the Family Dance: Family Systems Therapy and Literary Study.* Newark: U of Delaware P, 2003.

Lawrence, D. H., *Sons and Lovers*. Ed. Carl Baron and Helen Baron. London: Penguin, 1992.

Lawrence, Fredia. *Not I but the Wind*. Carbondale: Southern Illinois UP, 1974.

Marz, Louis T. "Portrait of Miriam." Bloom 73–91.

Meyers, Jeffrey. *D. H. Lawrence: A Biography*. New York: Knopf, 1990.

Minuchin, Salvador. *Family Healing: Strategies for Hope and Understanding*. New York: Touchstone, 1993.

_____. *Family Therapy Techniques*. Cambridge: Harvard UP, 1981.

Moore, Harry T. *The Priest of Love: A Life of D. H. Lawrence*. New York: Penguin, 1974.

Napier, Augustus, and Carl Whitaker. *The Family Crucible: The Intense Experience of Family Therapy*. New York: Harper, 1988.

Orwoll, Lucinda, and Marion Permutter. "The Study of Wise Persons: Integrating a Personality Perspective." *Wisdom: Its Nature, Origin, and Development*. Ed. Robert J. Sternberg. New York: Cambridge UP, 1990. 160–77.

Palazzoli, Mara Selvini, Stefano Cirillo, Matteo Selvini, and Anna Maria Sorrentino. *Family Games: General Models of Psychic Processes in the Family*. New York: Norton, 1989.

Palmer, Alan. *Fictional Minds*. Lincoln: U of Nebraska P, 2004.

_____. *Social Minds in Fiction*. Columbus: Ohio State UP, 2010.

_____. "Social Minds in Fiction and Criticism." *Style* 45.2 (2011): 183–420.

Phelan, James. *Experiencing Fiction: Judgments, Progressions, and the Rhetorical Theory of Narrative*. Columbus: Ohio State UP, 2007.

_____. *Reading People, Reading Plots*. U of Chicago P, 1989.

Pinsof, William M, and Jay L. Lebow, eds. *Family Psychology: The Art of the Science.* New York: Oxford UP, 2005.

Pittock, Malcolm. "*Sons and Lovers*: The Price of Betrayal." *Essays in Criticism* 13.4–5 (1986): 235–54.

Rabinowitz, Peter J. *Before Reading: Narrative Conventions and the Politics of Interpretation*. Ithaca: Cornell UP, 1987.

Reiss, David. "Genetic Influences on Family Systems: Implications for Development." *Journal of Marriage and Family.* 57.3 (1995): 453–60.

Rosenblatt, Paul C. *Shared Obliviousness in Family Systems*. Albany: SUNY P, 2009.

Ruderman, Judith. *D. H. Lawrence and the Devouring Mother*. Durham: Duke UP, 1984.

Sagar, Keith. *D. H. Lawrence: Life into Art*. Athens: U of Georgia P, 1985.

Satir, Virginia. *Conjoint Family Therapy*. Palo Alto: Science and Behavior, 1967.

Sawyer, R. Keith. *Group Genius: The Creative Power of Collaboration*. New York: Basic, 2007.

Schaprio, Barbara. "Maternal Bonds and the Boundaries of the Self: D.H. Lawrence and Virginia Woolf." *Soundings* 69 (1986): 347–65.

Sklenicka, Carol. *D. H. Lawrence and the Child*. Columbia: U of Missouri P, 1991.

Squires, Michael, and Keith Cushman. *The Challenge of D. H. Lawrence*. Madison: U of Wisconsin P, 1990.

Stephens, John, and Ruth Waterhouse. *Literature, Language, and Change: From Chaucer to the Present*. London: Routledge, 1990.

Tallis, Raymond. *In Defense of Realism*. London: Arnold, 1987.

Whitaker, Carl, and William M. Bumberry. *Dancing with the Family*: A *Symbolic-Experiential Approach*. New York: Brunner, 1988.

Wood, James. *How Fiction Works*. New York: Picador, 2008.

Recovering the History of the Family _____

Steven Mintz

Nostalgia for a world that never was is a defining feature of modern times. From television, movies, and novels, many people have come to imagine that earlier families were more stable, secure, and harmonious than those today. This view is profoundly misleading. Like their contemporary counterparts, families in the past were fragile and diverse.

Far from a static or unchanging entity, the family is a dynamic, evolving institution whose structure, size, roles, functions, and emotional dynamics have changed dramatically over time and varied widely across class and ethnic lines. Repeatedly, wars, economic depressions, and such large-scale developments as urbanization and the Industrial Revolution disrupted and decisively altered family life. Although many think of the family as an island of stability in a sea of disruptive social change, this is an illusion (Mintz and Kellogg xiv).

Few subjects are as enshrouded in myths and misconceptions as families in the past. Many people today assume that most families earlier in time consisted of a male breadwinner and a female homemaker. In fact, through much of history, families were collective economic units in which all members—including wives and children—were expected to contribute to the family's economic well-being. Indeed, it was not until the 1930s that a majority of families in the United States had a breadwinner father and a homemaker mother. Far from being a timeless arrangement, the male breadwinner family represented a relatively brief interlude in the family's long history (Mintz, "Does" 4).

Historical perspective reveals that families in the past faced many of the same problems as families today. Desertion, child abuse, spousal battering, and alcohol addiction always troubled significant numbers of families. Death rates, not surprisingly, were far higher. As recently as 1900, most parents could expect to lose one or more children, while most children would lose at least one parent before reaching the age of twenty-one (Mintz and Kellogg 104).

Although the family is the primary unit of social organization in all known societies, the family's functions have shifted profoundly over time. Before the Industrial Revolution, which began in the mid-eighteenth century, the family's roles were far broader than they are in the twenty-first century. In addition to serving as an emotional unit, the family was also a workplace, where parents and children engaged in a variety of productive tasks. Families also served various economic, educational, religious, insurance, and welfare functions. Parents taught their children basic literacy as well as craft skills. In addition, families were responsible for caring for the sick and the elderly and transferring property to the next generation (6–7).

Since the Industrial Revolution, many of the family's traditional responsibilities have been shed to public and private institutions such as schools, hospitals, insurance companies, and nursing homes. Today, the family specializes in two functions. It is responsible for caring for the young and for providing love and emotional support for its members (xv).

Families in the Ancient and Early Christian World

The ancient world had no word that precisely corresponds to the modern word for family. The explanation is straightforward: within ancient societies, households varied widely by social class in size and structure. Whereas the wealthiest households contained dozens of slaves and servants, poor people, including slaves, often had no opportunity to establish independent households (Herlihy 2).

Marriages in the ancient world were not a matter of romantic love and personal choice. Rather, marriages were arranged by the heads of families in order to advance family interests. Women were often contracted to marry at a young age; in classical Greece, a girl might be married as young as twelve to a husband who could be as much as a decade older. This substantial age gap contributed to families that were strongly patriarchal. In families in ancient Rome, the household head, known as the paterfamilias, was endowed with absolute authority. Under Roman law, he could sell his children, abandon them, or even put them to death.

Ancient societies permitted a variety of practices that the contemporary Christian church would strongly condemn. In classical Greece and Rome, newborn children might be exposed—a practice in which handicapped or sickly infants were left outdoors to die. A disproportionate number of exposed children were female, resulting in a highly skewed sex ratio.

Many ancient societies permitted marriages that the Christian church reviled as incestuous. For example, in ancient Egypt, a man might marry his sister, and in many ancient societies, a widow was compelled to marry her deceased husband's brother. Easy access to divorce—a practiced forbidden by the early Christian church—was widespread in the ancient world. In addition, many ancient societies practiced polygyny (allowing husbands to take more than one wife) and concubinage (permitting husbands to cohabitate with a woman who was not his legal wife). Polygyny and concubinage not only symbolized elite status, these customs allowed a wealthy or powerful man to sire a son if his first wife failed to produce an heir.

In the early Christian era, family patterns in Western Europe began to diverge sharply from those in the classical and non-Western worlds. The Christian church, for example, forbade marriages to close kin, including marriages to a deceased spouse's siblings, the spouses of deceased siblings, various degrees of cousins, and godchildren. It also placed greater emphasis on the spousal bond than on other kinship relationships (Goody 8).

Especially noteworthy are changes in women's experiences. As early as the fourth century, a growing number of women in Western Europe never married or bore children, and in some parts of Western Europe, over a fifth of adults remained unmarried. Women also delayed marriage until a relatively late age, usually in their late teens and twenties, producing greater equality in marital relationships (Goody 8).

Christianity played a critical role in the emergence of new family patterns. The church encouraged young men and women to remain celibate and enter religious orders. It also condemned the exposure of infants and opposed concubinage, polygyny, arranged marriages, marriages with close kin, and divorce. The church's insistence on the indissolubility of marriage helped make the nuclear family and the marital bond more important than in the past.

Families in Medieval and Early Modern Europe

The Middle Ages witnessed the emergence of the concept of family as a domestic unit in which members were bound together by emotional and kinship ties. Although medieval households, like those in the ancient world, varied widely in size and complexity—with noble households consisting of forty or more members—most medieval households were small, containing just four or five members. As slavery declined, there was a proliferation of peasant households bound together by shared labor. With husbands and wives closer in age than in the past, marital relationships grew closer and more intimate. However, because of the high death rate, remarriages were common as well. A quarter of all marriages involved partners who had been married before. Consequently, many medieval and early families contained stepparents, stepchildren, orphans, and half-orphans.

In medieval and early modern Europe, most houses were cramped and lacked privacy. Relatives often shared beds and the same rooms were used for working, entertaining, cooking, eating, storage, and sleeping; not until the late seventeenth and eighteenth centuries did separate bedrooms and dining rooms become common. Nor was there a sharp separation between the household and the workplace during the Middle Ages or the early modern era. Whether farms or small urban craft shops, most European households were productive units. Wives preserved food, made textiles and clothing, tended gardens, and brewed beer. In addition to farming, many husbands engaged in crafts such as carpentry, ironworking, and barrel-making.

During the Middle Ages, conflict arose between the Church and wealthy families who were eager to preserve their land holdings and form alliances with other powerful families. Many wealthy families opposed church rules that allowed children to marry without parental consent and that barred marriages between kin. To prevent the fragmentation of family estates, many wealthy families in England adopted a custom known as primogeniture, in which parents left their estate to their eldest son, leading many younger sons to join the Church or the military.

One of history's values is that it defamiliarizes the present, revealing that many of contemporary society's arrangements and assumptions are anything but natural or universal. Consider childhood, for example. Whereas contemporary American society tends to view early childhood as life's formative period when a child's personality and character is shaped, earlier plays, novels, memoirs, and biographies devoted surprisingly little attention to this stage of life. Nor was much attention paid to the drama of adolescence—the storm, stress, sullenness, and rebelliousness associated with puberty that absorbs so much attention today.

Few books in medieval or early modern Europe provided explicit childrearing advice. The few that existed focused largely on discipline or religious training rather than on children's care, nurture, or education. The lack of attention to childhood derived, in part, from the relative unimportance attached to age before age-graded school classrooms became common. In contrast to contemporary society—in which children's age determines such aspects of their lives as their grade in school, the shows they watch on television, and the toys and games they play with—age was far less important during the Middle Ages or the early modern era than size, strength, social class, and gender.

Unlike contemporary Americans, who tend to associate early childhood with innocence and playfulness, medieval and early modern Europeans and colonial Americans regarded early childhood as a state of deficiency. Children supposedly lacked the attributes of full humanity, including the ability to speak articulately, reason, or stand erect. Rather than being a stage of life that was intrinsically significant, childhood was devoid of the seriousness and wisdom that came with maturity. Some religious groups, including the more orthodox Calvinists, went further and viewed even newborn infants as innately sinful and regarded play as devilish. Children's supposedly animal-like nature encouraged adults to use harsh physical punishments to discipline the young—including caning and paddling (Mintz, *Huck's Raft* 16).

Whereas contemporary parents tend to believe that young children need lots of sensory stimulation, in Europe, prior to the eighteenth century, many children were swaddled, or bound tightly in a swaddling cloth, which slowed their heartbeat and suppressed crying, freeing their parents to work. In contrast to contemporary society, which holds that childhood should be devoted to play and schooling, there was a widespread view prior to the nineteenth century that even young children should be put to work.

Today, it is commonly believed that, for children to grow up psychologically well-adjusted, they must have a firm attachment to a single nurturing figure and a stable upbringing. In stark contrast, children in the Middle Ages and the era of the Renaissance, the Reformation, and Counter-Reformation had multiple nurturing figures and underwent frequent dislocations; the young frequently moved between homes. Immediately after birth, children, especially those in more affluent households, might be breast-fed by a wet nurse. Then, after returning to a mother's or older sister's care, children around the age of six, seven, or eight might enter another household and work for a time as a servant or page. During their early teens, boys might enter an apprenticeship or work as a farm laborer, while many girls served again as servants. Because of a high death rate, remarriage rates were high; if a parent remarried, or if the surviving parent was poor, the children might be forced to leave the parental home and find residence elsewhere, perhaps with a relative or else as a servant or laborer in another household.

In predominantly agricultural societies, where a child's future status depended on the size of a dowry or the inheritance of land, sibling rivalry could be very pronounced. Sibling rivalry did not simply involve a competition for a parent's attention, love, and affection, but a struggle over tangible assets. At the same time, these earlier societies lacked any formal mechanisms to care for the elderly. Should older women and men decide to transfer their assets to their children, the elderly were very careful to draft highly specific deeds that spelled out in precise detail how they were to be cared for. There was a widespread view that elderly people without property were likely to be mistreated by their children in the absence of written guarantees.

Colonial and Nineteenth-Century American Families

In the American colonies, as in Europe itself, the family was the fundamental economic, educational, religious, and welfare unit. It was not only the center of production, but the institution responsible for educating children and caring for the elderly and infirm. Three centuries ago, most families lived on farms that were largely self-sufficient. Although specialized craftsmen made shoes and iron implements, most families produced much of the food, furniture, cloth, and other goods that they needed. The colonial family was not merely an emotional entity; it was an interdependent unit of labor, in which all household members contributed to a collective family economy (Mintz and Kellogg 6–7).

The colonial family was a patriarchal institution. Childrearing books were addressed to fathers, not mothers, and fathers had the right to give or deny consent to their children's marriages. In cases of divorce, the father received custody of the children. A man's control over inheritance, in turn, kept his grown sons and daughters dependent upon him for years while they waited for his permission to marry and to establish a separate household (9).

Families in colonial America were anything but uniform. Family life in the southern colonies contrasted sharply from the more stable patterns found in Puritan New England or in the Middle Colonies.

During the seventeenth century, a majority of immigrants to the southern colonies were young, unmarried male indentured servants, with women in short supply. Defining characteristics of family life in these colonies included a short life expectancy; high rates of out-of-wedlock births; frequent remarriages; and substantial numbers of orphans, bereaved parents, widows and widowers, stepparents, and stepchildren. In seventeenth-century Virginia, half of all marriages ended as a result of death within seven years, while two-thirds of all children lost a parent by the time they were eighteen (25, 37).

By the late eighteenth century, household self-sufficiency declined as farms began to specialize in the production of cash crops and use the proceeds to purchase households goods produced outside the home. As the economy changed, relations between spouses and parents and children underwent a profound transformation. Marriages came to be based not on family interests, but on romantic love. Relations between husbands and wives grew more affectionate and intimate. Perhaps most notably, parents devoted increased attention to the care and nurture of their offspring (43–44).

During the early nineteenth century, a new kind of family emerged among the urban middle class, characterized by a sharp gender division of labor. As wage labor expanded, there came a growing separation of the home and the workplace. Family roles were reorganized around the principle of separate spheres for women and men. Urban middle-class men, who left home to go to work, defined themselves as the family breadwinner and provider, while a growing number of middle-class wives defined their identity as full-time homemaker and mother (50–51).

The urban middle-class family was much more child-centered than its predecessors. Instead of sending children to work as servants or apprentices, middle-class parents kept children at home and in school into their teens. Viewing children as investments, rather than as economic assets, middle-class parents sharply reduced their birthrate (which, in the United States, fell from about seven children per family in 1800 to five in 1850 and just three in 1900), allowing mothers and fathers to invest more time and resources in each child. A new emphasis on family life was apparent in the rise of the "white wedding," the formal ceremony in which a bride dressed in a white wedding gown, and the appearance of the birthday party, the Christmas tree, and the family vacation (51).

During the nineteenth century, urban middle-class family patterns were confined to a small minority of the population. For many immigrant and urban working-class families, low wages and a lack of year-round employment meant that all family members had to work. While middle-class families could rely on a single breadwinner, working-class families had a family economy in which all members, including children, contributed. While wives might take in boarders and lodgers or perform wage work, such as sewing, which could be done at home, children under the age of sixteen earned about 20 percent of the family income, toiling in factories or selling matches, hawking newspapers, or blacking boots on city streets (88).

No families were more vulnerable to breakup or subject to greater stress than those of enslaved African Americans. During the decades before the American Civil War, slaves in the South had no legal right to marry. Yet despite legal prohibitions on slave marriages, most enslaved African Americans married informally and lived with the same spouse until death, and most slave children grew up in households containing both a slave father and a slave mother. This was the case despite the fact that slave owners dissolved at least a fifth of marriages by sale (67).

Slavery inflicted severe hardships on family life. Many slave husbands and wives resided on separate plantations and, as a result, many fathers could only visit their families with their master's permission. Slave cabins were cramped and crowded, offering little family privacy. These cabins were often shared by two families.

In spite of the threat of sale and family breakup, African Americans managed to forge strong family ties. A majority of slaves grew up in families headed by a father and a mother, and nuclear family ties stretched outward to an involved network of extended kin. Through the strength and flexibility of their kin ties, enslaved African Americans resisted the psychologically debilitating effects of slavery.

Families in the Twentieth and Twenty-First Centuries

During the second half of the nineteenth century, many Europeans and Americans became highly anxious about the family's future. Critiques of marriage and the family proliferated. Feminists, like the pioneering women's rights advocate Elizabeth Cady Stanton, denounced the patriarchal family as a miniature slave plantation in which every woman was a slave and a slave breeder. Yet far less radical figures advocated legal divorce as a "safety-valve" to allow couples to exit unhappy marriages. Most Protestant countries made legal divorce increasingly accessible, and while the rate remained low by contemporary standards, it was noticeably increasing. The annual number of divorces in the United States reached 10,000 in 1867, a number that increased fifteenfold by 1920. Further contributing to a sense of crisis was a sharp decline in the birthrate and the number of unmarried women. Meanwhile, the world's first organizations to combat spousal and child abuse appeared (109–10).

In literature, portraits of loveless, abusive, conflict-driven, or simply unsatisfying marriages became increasingly common. In the highly realistic novels and plays of writers like George Eliot, Gustave Flaubert, Leo Tolstoy, or Henrik Ibsen, resentment, regret, boredom, unrequited love, and quarreling characterized many marriages. These unions were anything but genuine friendships and partnerships, let alone passionate unions of souls.

To address the apparent breakdown of the family, psychologists, legal scholars, educators, marriage counselors, social workers, and academic social scientists popularized a new familial ideal. Called the "companionate" family, this new ideal called on husbands and wives to be "friends and lovers," and parents and children to be "pals." A successful marriage, according to this new companionate ideal, demanded close communication and healthy sexuality among partners. It also required hard work (113).

During the Great Depression of the 1930s, unemployment, reduced pay, lowered living standards, and the demands of needy relatives subjected families to severe stress and fundamentally altered family relationships. High levels of joblessness forced many people to postpone marriage and childbearing and tolerate unhappy marriages for financial reasons. The divorce rate declined, but desertions soared; by 1930, over 1.5 million married women lived apart from their husbands. Within many families, men—demoralized by their inability to support their wives and children—distanced themselves emotionally, while wives strove to supplement family incomes and children took up various chores and part-time jobs. Depression-era hardships left a lasting impression on many young peoples' psyches, encouraging many to become intensely security conscious and family-oriented as adults (136).

World War II also left an indelible imprint on family life. During the war, a sixth of families in the United States suffered prolonged separation from sons, husbands, and fathers. Five million wives of servicemen had to raise children alone. Wartime migration also added to familial stress. The war spurred an unprecedented tide of migration, as more than fifteen million Americans searched for jobs in industrial areas or followed loved ones from one military base to another. Few wartime developments had as great an effect on family life as the rapid entry of married women into the labor force. Nearly half of all American women held a job at some point during the conflict, and many families faced a severe shortage of adequate day care facilities. There were tens of thousands of unsupervised "latchkey" children. The end of the war and the return of husbands and fathers required a readjustment for many families and contributed to a sharp rise in the divorce rate in the wake of the war (152).

Depression hardships and wartime dislocations provoked a sharp reaction during the late 1940s and 1950s, as couples married earlier than their parents had and women not only bore more children, but also had them at younger ages and spaced the births closer together. The average age of marriage fell sharply to just twenty for women and twenty-two for men, while the birthrate soared, climbing 50 percent between 1940 and 1957. Meanwhile, the divorce rate, which had risen steadily since the late nineteenth century, stabilized. Rising incomes permitted millions of middle-class Americans to buy their own homes in the rapidly expanding suburbs (178–79).

Yet even amid the postwar celebration of family togetherness, there were undercurrents of discontent. Popular magazines ran articles focusing on the growing sense of discontent among many American women, who had received the same education as men but who were cautioned against pursuing a career and encouraged to find fulfillment as wives and homemakers. Reports of abuse of alcohol, barbiturates, and tranquilizers by suburban housewives received widespread attention. At the same time, there were many stories involving "careerism" among men—a compulsive concentration on work that excluded many other aspects of life. Men who found their family lives unsatisfying or who were anxious about family finances compensated by "losing themselves" in their work. Meanwhile, in 1961, pediatric radiologist Dr. C. Henry Kempe and his associates brought the issue of child abuse to public attention (194–97).

A growing source of public concern was also the purported breakdown of the family among the African American poor. Within this population, the number of births outside marriage increased dramatically, as did the proportion of children living in female-headed households.

The plight of the black family came to public attention in 1965 when the federal government released a confidential report called *The Negro Family: The Case for National Action*. The Moynihan Report, as it was known, was written by assistant secretary of labor Daniel Patrick Moynihan and it argued that the chief obstacle to black advancement lay in the crumbling of the family. To support this thesis, Moynihan cited startling statistics. Nearly 25 percent of all black women were divorced, separated, or living apart from their husbands, compared to

8 percent of white women. Out of wedlock births among blacks had risen from 17 percent in 1940 to 24 percent in 1963, while the rate for whites had only climbed from 2 to 3 percent. The proportion of black families headed by women had climbed from 8 percent in 1950 to 21 percent in 1960, while the rate for white families had remained steady at 9 percent. Crumbling families, the report concluded, contributed to a sharp increase in welfare dependency, delinquency, joblessness, drug addiction, and failure in school (210).

The Moynihan Report unleashed a firestorm of public criticism. Critics rightly argued that the report exaggerated the problems of absent fathers, single parenthood, and out-of-wedlock births; underestimated the differences between black and white families; and downplayed the strengths of the black family, including the support that single mothers received from networks of extended relatives and friends and institutions such as the black church. Yet the report was prescient in pointing to changes that would affect the entire society and that could no longer be addressed solely in terms of race (211).

Family life in the twenty-first century is markedly different than it was half a century ago. As recently as the early 1960s, an overwhelming majority of Americans took it for granted that a family consisted of a married woman and man and their minor children living in a common residence. The father single-handedly earned the family income and, as head of his household, gave his surname to his wife and children. A wife's responsibilities were to be her husband's companion and helper, as well as the facilitator of her children's education and development. Families that failed to conform to these givens were stigmatized as troubled or problem families.

In the decades since the 1960s these givens were overturned. No longer does the term "family" attach exclusively to a married couple and their children. It is applied to almost any group of two or more people domiciled together, such as single-parent households and cohabitating couples, including same-sex couples. In the span of a decade—from the mid-1960s to the mid-1970s—the divorce rate in the United States doubled, the number of working mothers tripled, and the number of couples cohabitating outside of wedlock quadrupled. Today, 40 percent of children are born outside marriage.

The causes of this radical transformation in family life lie in a profound shift in cultural values. The women's movement dramatically altered women's attitudes toward family roles, marital relationships, and housework. A growing majority of women came to believe that both husband and wife should hold jobs, do housework, and take care of children. At the same time, humanistic psychologies that stressed growth and self-actualization triumphed over earlier theories that emphasized adjustment, compromise, and avoidance of confrontations as the solution to marital problems. According to psychologists such as Abraham Maslow, Carl Rogers, and Erich Fromm, maturation is not a process of settling down, but of achieving one's potential. As expectations for personal fulfillment rose, fewer adults were willing to put up with loveless, unsatisfying, or inequitable marriages (206).

Today's families face many difficult challenges. In today's time-stressed society, fewer families eat dinner together. In many dual earner households, spouses lead parallel lives and spend less time with one another than the previous generation. At the same time, many parents find it hard to find reliable and affordable day care and after-school care for their children. When faced with family emergencies, few parents receive paid leaves that will allow them to take time off work. Meanwhile, as life expectancies rise, many parents find themselves responsible not only for caring for children, but for aging parents as well.

History offers no simple solution to the problems facing today's families, but it does offer a bit of reassurance as we look forward. The history of the family suggests that we need not be disturbed by change in and of itself because change—and not stability—has been the norm. Doomsayers of every era have worried that families are endangered, but families have repeatedly had to change to adapt to novel circumstances and have done so successfully. Nor do we need to worry obsessively about the diversity of family arrangements, since diversity has always been a defining characteristic of family life. Instead of focusing on shifts in family structure and roles, we would do better to focus on how actual families function, and whether they satisfactorily meet their members' emotional and material needs.

Works Cited

Balch, David L. *Early Christian Families in Context*. Grand Rapids: Eerdmans, 2003.

Balch, David L., and Carolyn Osiek. *Families in the New Testament World*. Louisville: Westminster John Knox, 1997.

Bradley, Keith R. *Discovering the Roman Family: Studies in Roman Social History*. New York: Oxford UP, 1991.

Coontz, Stephanie, Maya Parson, and Gabrielle Raley, eds. *American Families: A Multicultural Reader*. New York: Routledge, 2008.

Dixon, Suzanne. *The Roman Family*. Baltimore: Johns Hopkins UP, 1992.

Gies, Frances, and Joseph Gies. *Marriage and the Family in the Middle Ages*. New York: Harper, 1987.

Goody, Jack. *The Development of the Family and Marriage in Europe*. Cambridge: Cambridge UP, 1985.

Gottlieb, Beatrice. *The Family in the Western World from the Black Death to the Industrial Age*. New York: Oxford UP, 1993.

Hanawalt, Barbara A. *The Ties That Bound: Peasant Families in Medieval England*. New York: Oxford UP, 1986.

Herlihy, David. *Medieval Households*. Cambridge: Harvard UP, 1985.

Jabour, Anya, ed. *Major Problems in the History of American Families and Children*. Belmont: Wadsworth, 2004.

Mintz, Steven. "Does the American Family Have a History? Family Images and Realities." *OAH Magazine of History* 15.4 (2001): 4–10.

Mintz, Steven. *Huck's Raft: A History of American Childhood*. Cambridge: Belknap, 2004.

Mintz, Steven, and Susan Kellogg. *Domestic Revolutions: A Social History of American Family Life*. New York: Free, 1988.

Mitterauer, Michael. *The European Family*. Oxford: Blackwell, 1982.

Ozment, Steven. *When Fathers Ruled: Family Life in Reformation Europe*. Cambridge: Harvard UP, 1983.

Perdue, Leo G., et al. *Families in Ancient Israel*. Louisville: Westminster John Knox, 1997.

Pomeroy, Sarah B. *Families in Classical and Hellenistic Greece: Representations and Realities*. New York: Oxford UP, 1998.

Rawson, Beryl. *The Family in Ancient Rome: New Perspectives*. Ithaca: Cornell UP, 1986.

_____. *Marriage, Divorce, and Children in Ancient Rome*. New York: Oxford UP, 1991.

Seccombe, Wally. *Weathering the Storm: Working-Class Families from the Industrial Revolution to the Fertility Decline*. New York: Verso, 1993.

Stone, Lawrence. *The Family, Sex, and Marriage in England*. New York: Harper, 1977.

Familia Fictions: Writing the Family in Tomás Rivera's *... And the Earth Did Not Devour Him* and Sandra Cisneros's *Caramelo*

Catherine Leen

According to Latino writer Ilan Stavans, "geneology rules Latino literature tyrannically" and "fiction is a device used to explore roots" (54). While it is almost impossible to dispute the idea that the topic of the family is central to Chicana and Chicano writing, Stavans signals that such dominance must be weighed against authorial uses of the family motif as part of literary creations. The novels that will be examined in this chapter are very different. Tomás Rivera's *... And the Earth Did Not Devour Him* was originally written in Spanish in 1971. Set in rural Utah, this brief novel is a coming-of-age tale, or bildungsroman, that chronicles the experiences that will help the unnamed narrator make the transition from childhood to adulthood. *Caramelo*, a 2003 book by Sandra Cisneros, is a lengthy, fragmented novel divided into three parts. Beginning with the Mexican Revolution and ending sometime in the 1970s, *Caramelo* is also a bildungsroman, but the narrator finds her way in the world by rewriting the stories that comprise her family's history to create her own story.

These novels clearly reflect the very different times in which they were written. Rivera's almost exclusive concentration on male characters places his novel firmly within the first wave of Chicano nationalist writers, whose emphasis was on community and solidarity. As Santiago Daydí-Tolson suggests in his reading of the novel: "If the unidentified boy represents the collective mind of the group, it could be suggested that he does not constitute a truly individual character, but the representation of a whole generation. Rivera himself uses the singular to refer to the collective when he talks about the Chicano in general and says that 'this is the kind of character I tried to portray in my work'" (Daydí-Tolson 137).

In contrast, by focusing on the difficulties that the family creates for a young woman who longs to fashion her own identity, Cisneros calls into question the possibility that any individual can ever truly represent the whole collective and even whether they should be required to do so. Gabriela F. Arredondo has mentioned Cisneros as one of a number of Chicana writers who use the family motif not only to reflect on women's home lives, but also to rewrite the history of the Chicano movement: "By focusing on the centrality of home and providing critical perspectives on the family, these Chicanas 'talk back' to Chicano nationalist discourse and patriarchy" (8). Just as the young protagonists of the two novels in question interpret and unravel the family histories they are told, this chapter will seek to determine the ways in which each work represents very different perspectives on the Chicano family—perspectives that are profoundly shaped by the generational and gender differences between their authors.

In order to understand why the family is such an integral part of Chicano literature, we must briefly review the history of Mexicans and Mexican Americans in the United States. The American Southwest was originally settled in 1542 by Spanish colonizer Hernán Cortés in the name of the Spanish crown. Two centuries later, twenty-one Catholic missions were established along 500 miles of the Californian coast. Although some of the settlers at this time came from Spain, most were Mexicans recruited from the ranks of the desperately poor and lured with the promise of equipment, food, and cattle (Takaki 166–71). Mexicans initially welcomed immigrants from the United States, but this amicable acceptance came to an abrupt end in the 1840s, as settlers dreaming of wealth and land flooded into California during the gold rush. The state of Texas played a key role in the conflicts between American settlers and the Mexican government. Many of the North Americans who had settled in Texas during the 1820s were slaveholders, but in the 1830s, the Mexican government outlawed slavery and limited further emigration from the United States (Shorris 160). In response, a band of North Americans began an armed insurrection in

1836. The Mexican side was led by Mexico's President Santa Anna, who was later deposed, but served again as president from 1841 to 1844. According to a number of commentators, including John S. D. Eisenhower, it was the Mexican president's obstinacy in continuing the conflict with Texas that ultimately led to the Mexican-American War, which took place from 1846 to 1848:

> Santa Anna's worst mistake as president was to continue the Texas border war. The incursions, killings, and atrocities on both sides were lavishly reported in the United States—always from the Texan viewpoint. This constant flow of war news kept the people of the United States militantly sympathetic to their blood relations in Texas. Many Americans, most of them perhaps, were no longer in any mood to allow the rights of Mexico to have any influence upon the ethics of United States policy. (Eisenhower 15–16)

The defeat of Mexico was sealed in 1848 by the Treaty of Guadalupe Hidalgo, which forever changed the destiny of the Mexicans who remained in what had become the American Southwest. David C. Gutiérrez notes that this treaty provided for the payment of $15 million by the United States for over half of Mexico's lands—Texas, California, Arizona, Nevada, Utah, Wyoming, Colorado, Kansas, Oklahoma, and New Mexico. It formally granted the full protection of the United States Constitution and citizenship to all Mexicans who chose to remain in the territory north of the new international border (Gutiérrez 13). In practice, however, deeply ingrained racism toward Mexicans and their status as a minority in the new North American states meant that the new Mexican Americans were in no position to insist on their constitutional rights.

The early twentieth century saw the first wave of mass emigration to the United States as Mexico was in turmoil following the Mexican Revolution. Generally from the poorer echelons of society, these immigrants usually had little formal education in Spanish, or were illiterate altogether, and they did not speak English. Consequently, most secured poorly paid employment, lived in substandard housing, and frequently endured racism. Not only did Mexicans and Mexican Americans endure these hardships, but it was clear that they were only welcome in the United States if they assimilated. Attempts to deal with the presence of Mexicans concentrated on homogenizing them and insisting that they adopt what were, for them, Anglo customs: "Mexicans became a favorite target for assimilationists: they were expected to shed their cultural distinctiveness and adopt Anglo standards (household and family care practices, 'American' cooking, hygiene). These Americanization programs were generally unsuccessful, since they failed to deal with the hard economic and social realities faced by most Chicanos" (Camarillo 225–26). Ultimately, Americanization programs never had the chance to succeed, and when the Great Depression brought them to a sudden end, the government sought to get rid of immigrants altogether rather than assimilate them. Nonetheless, these programs had a profound effect on Mexican American communities, as many felt that the only way that they could successfully participate in North American society was to minimize their differences.

Given the suspicion with which Mexican customs were viewed, it is not surprising that the home is often presented as space of refuge and comfort in Chicano literature, as Pat Mora asserts in her 1997 novel *House of Houses*: "This is a 'world that we can call our own,' this family space through which generations move, each bringing its gifts, handing down languages and stories, recipes for living, gathering around the kitchen table to serve one another" (7). Mora's account stresses the persistence of traditions through the generations, rather than their abandonment, and presents the family as a repository of a unique identity signaled by its members speaking Spanish or indigenous languages, sharing stories, and enjoying their traditional foods.

Like Mora, Rivera has tended to represent the family as a very positive force against the pressures of a society that marginalized people of Mexican descent. In an essay on Chicano literature, he identifies three key themes that are characteristic of Chicano authors, beginning with the home: "*La casa, el barrio* and *la lucha* are constant elements in the ritual of Chicano literature.[1] I shall start with *la casa* as one of three parts in this ritual. *La casa* is to me the most beautiful word in the Spanish language. It evokes the constant refuge, the constant father, the constant mother. It contains the father, the mother, and the child" (Rivera 22–23). It is not surprising, given this decidedly idealistic view of the family, that the notion of familial bonds as an unwavering source of support and affection is a salient theme in Rivera's novel.

The protagonist of *. . . And the Earth Did Not Devour Him* is an unnamed young boy whose family members are impoverished Mexican American farm workers. Through his observations and experiences, the reader is drawn into the world of migrant farm laborers, who are paid poorly and forced to live in primitive conditions. Their degradation is such that in the episode entitled "The Children Couldn't Wait," the protagonist, his brothers, and his father—all of whom work the fields together—risk being fired merely for sneaking sips of water from a tank meant for cattle. Although at times this young boy rebels against his family, and particularly against his mother's faith in a God who seems indifferent to their suffering, he comes to understand that his family is his sanctuary. When he is refused service by a racist barber, for instance, his first thought is to turn to his father, certain that he will comfort him: "He crossed the street . . . but then the barber came out and told him to leave. Then it all became clear to him and he went home to get his father" (103).

The child is also aware that his father wants what is best for him and is determined that his son will finish school so that he can realize his dream of becoming a telephone operator—a job far removed from the backbreaking work of a farm laborer. His pride in his son's ambition is obvious when he talks to his friend: "I told the boss the other day and he laughed. I don't think he believes my son can do it, but that's 'cause he doesn't know him. He's smarter than anything" (95). In order to ensure that his son finishes the school year, his father pays a couple who are friends of the family to look after the boy while the rest of the family travels to another town to work. Unbeknownst to his father, this couple, Don Laíto and Doña Bone, are thieves who murder an old man to take his money and then force the boy to help them dispose of the body. The corruption and amorality of this couple again reinforces the idea of the boy's family as a positive element in his life, and he is desperate to be reunited with them. Even in his darkest moments with Don Laíto and Doña Bone, the boy takes comfort in the knowledge that he was sent to live with them because his parents wanted a better life for him: "I thought of how my Dad had paid them for my room and board and how even the Anglos liked them so much. All that my parents wanted was for me to finish school so I could find me some job that wasn't so hard" (101).

Cisneros's *Caramelo* also has a young person as its protagonist. Celaya, who is referred to as Lala, grows up in Chicago with her Mexican father and Mexican American mother. Like the young boy in Rivera's novel, Lala attempts to make sense of the world largely through the family dramas she witnesses and the stories that family members tell her. As the family moves from Mexico to Chicago and back on annual visits to her grandmother's home, she hears stories of wars, doomed love affairs, and family disputes, all of which are peppered with popular cultural references from both sides of the border. Often these stories are passed from generation to generation and exposed as myths or downright lies, but they still play an important part in her construction of her own identity. Lala, like the young boy in . . . *And the Earth Did Not Devour Him,* rebels against her family on occasion and often questions their versions of history; as she matures, however, she also learns to see her family as flawed human beings who, like her, face a barrage of conflicting messages as they attempt to negotiate the contradictions and tensions of living between Mexico and the United States.

As in Rivera's novel, the family is a primary source of consolation and protection for the young protagonist of *Caramelo.* The novel is dedicated to Cisneros's father, although she has noted in numerous interviews that it was her mother who encouraged her to get an education and become a writer. In fact, Cisneros's father only supported her decision to major in English at college because he saw college as a way for his daughter to marry well (Brackett 27). Despite her awareness of her father's limited ambitions for her, Cisneros has noted in an essay significantly titled "Only Daughter" that her work is largely inspired by her relationship with him, saying "I wanted my father to understand what it was I was scribbling, to introduce me as 'My only daughter, the writer.' Not as 'This is only my daughter. She teaches.'" She added that "in a sense, everything I have ever written has been for him, to win his approval even though I know my father can't read English words" (Castillo-Speed 157).

In *Caramelo*, the close relationship between Lala and her father, Inocencio, is one of the most touching aspects of the narrative. It is her father who teaches Lala Spanish, and he constantly calls her affectionate names such as *mi cielo*, or "my heaven." As the only daughter in a family with six sons, Lala faces repeated teasing from her brothers, but, like the model of Rivera's constant father, Inocencio is always there to defend her: "—Don't pick on Lalita, Father reminds Lolo. — She's your only sister and the baby" (241). Cisneros, like Rivera, presents a number of situations in *Caramelo* in which the outside world seems threatening to the young protagonist. When her father gets her a job helping the housekeeper at the local priest's house, Lala is overwhelmed by the unfamiliar work and terrified by the long journey home in the dark, and she refuses to return after her first day. Her father had arranged for her to take the job so that she could earn much-needed money to pay the tuition for her private Catholic school, but instead of worrying about the money that they will lose if she does not work, her mother and father immediately agree with her, and Inocencio reassures Lala that she does not have to go back: "Don't worry Lalita. We'll tell *el padrecito* that I don't permit you to return. It's too dark outside when you come home. How does he expect a young lady to be walking alone after dark? Doesn't he realize we are Mexican?" (322).

Although both novels cast the family in a positive light, the narratives nonetheless reflect the particular tensions experienced by the children of impoverished Mexican families. The protagonist of *. . . And the Earth Did Not Devour Him* is acutely aware that his family is poor. He and his younger siblings have to work in the fields with their parents and when both his father and his brother suffer from sunstroke, he vents his frustration at their circumstances: "Why Dad and then my little brother? He's only nine years old. Why? He has to work like a mule buried in the earth. Dad, Mom and my little brother here, what are they guilty of?" (111). Lala, meanwhile, experiences deep disappointment when the family finally manages to buy their own home, only to discover that it is decrepit and infested with mice and insects with no money for an exterminator: "It's always about cutting corners. Always about something shimmering on the wall when you turn off the lights. Or something creepy scurrying off along the floorboards. It's always, always about being afraid to get up in the middle of the night. And being scared to eat from a half-open box of corn flakes" (313).

Both of these young protagonists endure difficult living conditions and experience a sense of marginalization from the dominant society. While their families are presented as loving and supportive, belonging to these families can be, conversely, a cause for shame in the outside world. The young boy in *. . . And the Earth Did Not Devour Him* risks his father's wrath by defending himself in a fistfight against a racist schoolmate (92–3); likewise, Lala is embarrassed by her father's poor clothing and rumpled appearance when they meet the parish priest: "I wish Father hadn't insisted on coming straight from the shop. He's as nubby as a towel. Even his mustache has lint. When he sits down, I pick the bits of string and tufts of cotton off of him" (319). Lala is dominated by her awareness of the priest's superior status and therefore tries to make her father look less like a working man to lessen her sense of intimidation when meeting a father figure far more powerful than her own. Similarly, the young boy's fear of his parents is diminished by his need to defend himself against racist taunts at school.

Themes in the novels begin to diverge, however, when it comes to expressing gender roles within the family. Rivera presents the Mexican American family as an archetype—the boy's father is hardworking, authoritative, and loyal to his family. While his mother is also portrayed as an authority figure, she is predominantly cast in the typical role of the self-sacrificing angel who is the guardian of morality and religious tradition. The opening lines of the novel describe the mother's custom of leaving an offering for spirits, an act not only suggesting her superstitions and adherence to outmoded rituals, but one reflecting her obligations as a Mexican woman: "What his mother never knew was that every night he would drink the glass of water that she left under the bed for the spirits. She always believed that they drank the water and so continued doing her duty" (85).

For Lala, the close, protective relationship she enjoyed with her father as a young girl becomes stifling and repressive as she becomes a teenager. The Spanish language—once used to communicate love—has been transformed by the father's awareness of his daughter's physical maturation; it has become a language of patriarchal oppression that uses words of hatred to censure Lala for imagined indiscretions that she has not even thought to commit. When Lala innocently shares with her father her desire to live alone when she grows up, she is met with harsh condemnation: "If you leave your father's house without a husband you are worse than a dog. You aren't my daughter. You aren't a Reyes. You hurt me just talking like this. If you leave alone you leave like, and forgive me for saying this but it's true, *como una prostituta*. Is that what you want the world to think? *Como una perra*, like a dog" (360).

The issue of the ways in which Chicano culture has relegated women to a secondary role, both within the family and in society, has been much debated. In her seminal critical text *Borderlands/La frontera: The New Mestiza* (2007), Gloria Anzaldúa asserts that Chicano culture privileges the family unit and community ties at the expense of individual autonomy. She outlines the resulting repression that women have traditionally endured as follows:

The culture expects women to show greater acceptance of, and commitment to, the value system than men. The culture and the Church insist that women are subservient to males. If a woman rebels she is a *mujer mala*.[2] If a woman doesn't renounce herself in favour of the male, she is selfish. If a woman remains a *virgen* until she marries, she is a good woman. (39)

Cherríe Moraga, in her writings on the sexism that is endemic in Chicano culture, goes further, arguing that gender divisions within families weaken the community's ability to counter the oppression its members endure from the dominant white society: "We believe the more severely we protect the sex roles within the family, the stronger we will be as a unit in position to the Anglo threat. And yet, our refusal to examine all the roots of the lovelessness in our families is our weakest link and softest spot" (110).

Rivera has been criticized for the one-dimensionality of the female characters in . . . *And the Earth Did Not Devour Him* and their marginal status as mothers, daughters, and partners rather than central characters in their own right. In her analysis, Patricia de La Fuente notes that the novel reflects the society of its time and that Rivera's interest is not in foregrounding the experiences of the female characters but in depicting the viewpoint of his young male protagonist. Notwithstanding these qualifications, she is unambiguous in her critique of his presentation of the female characters: "Rivera's female characters are, with rare exceptions, stereotypical, totemic women, even caricatures, and contribute a muted, often inconsequential background to the male experience. Their humanity is arbitrarily submerged and at times trivialized" (De La Fuente 82). Rivera's novel never confronts the issue of gender oppression or the marginalization of women.

The vignette "The Night Before Christmas" uncharacteristically focuses on a female character, but the woman remains a shadowy presence defined by her roles as mother and wife. This woman suffers from agoraphobia but forces herself to go shopping to get Christmas presents for her children. Her outing ends in disaster when she is imprisoned after fleeing a crowded store in panic, unaware that she has not paid for the gifts. Her dilemma, which results from her desire to please her children, is resolved when her husband explains the situation to a notary public. The solution to her panic attacks is also provided by her husband: "Just stay here inside the house and don't leave the yard. There's no need for it anyway. I'll bring you everything you need" (Rivera 134). This episode both trivializes the woman's anxiety and infantilizes her; once her husband is in control of the situation, there is no need to examine the causes of her trauma or help her to regain some autonomy as an individual. This episode offers ample opportunity to explore the wider symbolism of this women's fear and dependence in a profoundly macho culture, yet Rivera presents it as a naturalistic portrait of a neurotic woman who is fortunate to have a husband who comes to her rescue.

Cisneros, in sharp contrast to this, continues the tradition of speaking out against the patriarchal nature of Chicano society pioneered by writers like Anzaldúa. The strongest point of Cisneros's largely sympathetic family saga—and the point that most marks a departure from Rivera's glorification of the family—is her capacity to confront the contradictions and hypocrisies of the Chicano family through Lala's story. What is most interesting about her reflection on this topic, moreover, is that Lala's rebellion against sexist mores is intertwined with her gradual realization that family stories may, in fact, be fictions or highly mediated versions of the truth. John V. Knapp has noted that families are marked by themes "that are present in the preceding generation and are transmitted from one generation to the next through narratives, family stories, assumptions of 'correct' behavior, etc.," and he adds that these themes can become family myths (Knapp 20). Lala, as the main narrator of *Caramelo*, proves adept at unravelling the different themes and myths that make up her family's narrative. She is a highly self-conscious narrator who underlines the fact that she is about to reveal her family's myths right from the beginning of the novel, as part 1 is preceded by the following disclaimer: "The truth, these stories are nothing but story, bits of string, odds and ends found here and there, embroidered together to make something new. I have invented what I do not know and exaggerated what I do to continue the family tradition of telling healthy lies" (Cisneros 1).

The opening section of *Caramelo* also introduces one of the key revelations in the novel: the fact that Inocencio had an illegitimate daughter called Candelaria with the family's servant when he was a young man, long before he moved from Mexico to the United States and married Lala's mother. This character's lack of innocence is underlined by the irony of his name, and his behavior is contextualized by the further revelation that it is part of a long list of sexual indiscretions by the male members of his family. Lala's formidable grandmother, Soledad, was also once a family servant and was only married to her much wealthier husband, Narciso, because his father, Eleuterio, demanded that his son face his responsibility when Soledad became pregnant (159). This intervention is decidedly hypocritical, as the Spanish heritage that the Reyes family is so proud of is marred by Eleuterio's own lack of responsibility to the wife he abandoned before making a new life in Mexico. In fact, Eleuterio's first marriage to a woman whose social standing outranked his own became a burden to him; the lineage he is so proud of in Mexico is not a reflection of his own social status, but a result of his first marriage, which did not last because of his sense of inferiority: "His first wife, a woman of exceptional memory, was especially adroit at reminding Eleuterio of his humble origin and his subsequent mediocrity. It was with no regret and only the clothes on his back that Eleuterio abandoned this wife, Seville, and that life without a life" (161). Eleuterio's name, which comes from the Greek meaning "freedom," is also seen to be ironic, as he takes decisive action to ensure his own freedom while insisting that his son face up to his responsibilities.

This catalogue of ironies is further compounded by the fact that when Lala, as a teenager, rebels against her father's restrictive control over her by running away to Mexico with her boyfriend, she is in fact replicating the behavior of both her father and her male ancestors. This rebellion is in turn inspired by the story of her Aunty Light Skin—the least conventional woman in Lala's immediate family. The family's reaction to Aunty Light Skin's marriage to a divorced man mirrors Lala's father's harsh words to his daughter many years later, when she expresses a desire to leave home: "And so, I was married, but what good did that do me when your grandmother found out? 'What, are you stupid or just pretending to be stupid? As long as his first wife is still alive, your marriage is just paper. You may think you are married, but in the eyes of God you're nothing but a prostitute.' Those words, they hurt me even now, Lalita" (271).

Despite his promise to disown his daughter, however, Lala's father is so distraught when she disappears to Mexico that he is overcome with emotion when she returns home: "Father holds me in his arms and sobs on my shoulder. —I can't, Father hiccups. —I can't. Even take care of you. It's all. My fault. I'm. To blame. For this. Disgrace" (395). While this heartfelt lament is undoubtedly genuine, it also suggests that Lala's father may indeed share some of the blame for his daughter's actions as she unconsciously emulates an experience of sexual rebellion not unlike his own youthful indiscretion. Moreover, the existence of a daughter whom he has never acknowledged casts doubt on his portrayal in the novel as a loving, devoted father.

The story of Candelaria, Inocencio's secret daughter, also calls attention to the ways in which Cisneros links the family's propensity for mythmaking to well-known Western fairytales. In part 1, Lala notes that Cinderella is her mother's pet name for her. The experience of Soledad—who was cast out by her father after her mother's death and his remarriage—also prefigures the Cinderella story involving Candelaria, though her situation is likened to a different fairytale: "It was like the fairy tale 'The Snow Queen,' a bit of evil glass no bigger than a sliver had entered into his eye and heart, a tender pain that hurt when he thought about his daughter" (95).

Like many of the other motifs in the story, the Cinderella symbol is multifaceted and shifts as the narrative progresses. Candelaria's story is also intertwined with the story of one of the most famous Mexican films of all time, Ismael Rodríguez's *Nosotros los pobres* (1948). As Soledad tells Lala the story of the hardship she endured after being banished from the family home, Lala immediately sees the connection: "If this were a movie from Mexico's Golden Age of cinema, it would be black-and-white and no doubt a musical. Like *Nosotros los pobres*" (98). *Nosotros los pobres* stars the Mexican heartthrob Pedro Infante, to whom Lala's father is often compared (3). This film is an enduringly popular musical that romanticizes poverty and stresses the importance of family and community. Infante plays Pepe el Toro, whose niece has been abandoned by her irresponsible mother; she is, however, unaware of this harsh reality and thinks that Pepe is her father and that her mother is dead. This popular Mexican cultural reference is grafted onto the family history, again suggesting the permeability of stories told over the years, as well as the habits of their tellers to embellish them with other stories far removed from the real-life events.

Although throughout the novel Lala calls into question the stories she hears and exposes the myths created to replace uncomfortable truths, she too has inherited a propensity for mythmaking. When she is bullied at school for not looking Mexican enough, she defends herself by citing a family history involving Nefertiti and Andalusian gypsies, which is even more fantastic than the myth propagated by her grandmother, much to her mother's disgust: "You're just like your father, Mother says.—A born liar. Nothing but a bunch of liars, from his mother all the way back to the great-grand-something-or-other who said he was descended from the king of Spain. Look, the Reyes are nothing but *mitoteros*,[3] and if they say they're not, they're lying" (353).

The novel ends with Lala's ultimate rebellion. As she dances with her father at her parents' anniversary celebration, he shares stories of his life, with the notable exception of the existence of her half-sister Candelaria. At the novel's conclusion, he urges her to keep this advice to herself and he especially stresses that it should not be spoken of outside the family circle, as the barbarians he calls Anglos would do:

Don't be talking such things like the barbarians, *mi vida*. To mention them makes our family look like *sinvergüenzas*, understand? You don't want people to think we're shameless, do you? Promise your papa you won't talk these things, Lalita. Ever. Promise. I look into Father's face, that face that is the same face as the Grandmother's the same face as mine. —I promise, Father (430).

Of course, the very existence of the novel is the negation of this promise. To return to the comparison between *Caramelo* and . . . *And the Earth Did Not Devour Him,* this concluding sentence can be interpreted less as a personal betrayal and more as a reflection of the chasm between writers like Rivera and contemporary writers like Cisneros. In terms of the novel's development, Lala's broken promise signals her desire to end a cycle of mythmaking and secrets that has done a great deal of damage to her family. In terms of the text's metanarrative, this exchange asserts the right of the Chicana writer to expose the negative aspects of Chicano family life, rather than concealing them out of a misguided sense of solidarity. Cisneros's insistence on the centrality of mythmaking to the particular family story she recounts ultimately exposes the idea of the Chicano family as the bedrock of Chicano society as a myth. While the myths perpetrated by the fictional Chicano family at the heart of the novel and by the extended family that is Chicano society can be consoling and nurturing, they can also be dangerously repressive when imposed as an unquestionable truth.

Notes

1. "The house, the neighborhood and the struggle." (Author translations throughout).
2. "Bad woman."
3. "Mythmakers."

Works Cited

Anzaldúa, Gloria. *Borderlands/La frontera: The New Mestiza.* San Francisco: Aunt Lute, 2007.

Arredondo, Gabriela F. "Chicana Feminisms at the Crossroads: Disruptions in Dialogue." *Chicana Feminisms: A Critical Reader.* Ed. Gabriela F. Arredondo. London: Duke UP, 2003.

Brackett, Victoria. *A Home in the Heart: The Story of Sandra Cisneros.* Greensboro: Reynolds, 2005.

Camarillo, Albert. *Chicanos in a Changing Society: From Mexican Pueblos to American Barrios in Santa Barbara and Southern California, 1848–1930.* Cambridge: Harvard UP, 1996.

Cisneros, Sandra. *Caramelo.* London: Bloomsbury, 2002.

_____. "Only Daughter." *Latina: Women's Voices from the Borderlands.* Ed. Lillian Castillo-Speed. New York: Simon, 1995. 156–60.

Daydí-Tolson, Santiago. "Ritual and Religion in Tomás Rivera's Work." *Tomás Rivera, 1935–1984: The Man and His Work.* Ed. Vernon E. Lattin. Tempe: Bilingual Rev., 1988. 136–49.

De La Fuente, Patricia. "Invisible Women in the Narrative of Tomás Rivera." *International Studies in Honor of Tomás Rivera.* Ed. Julián Olivares. Houston: Arte Público, 1986.

Eisenhower, John S. D. *So Far from God: The U.S. War with Mexico, 1846–1848.* Norman: U of Oklahoma P, 2000.

Gutiérrez, David C. *Walls and Mirrors: Mexican Americans, Mexican Immigrants, and the Politics of Ethnicity.* Berkeley: U of California P, 1999.

Knapp, John V., and Kenneth Womack. *Reading the Family Dance: Family Systems Therapy and Literary Study.* Newark: U of Delaware P, 2003.

Mora, Pat. *House of Houses.* Boston: Beacon, 1997.

Moraga, Cherríe. *Loving in the War Years: Lo que nunca pasó por sus labios.* Boston: South End, 1983.

Rivera, Tomás. *. . . y no se lo tragó la tierra / . . . And the Earth Did Not Devour Him.* Houston: Arte Público, 1995.

_____. "Chicano Literature: Fiesta of the Living." *The Identification and Analysis of Chicano Literature.* Ed. Francisco Jiménez. New York: Bilingual Rev., 1979.

Shorris, Earl. *The Life and Times of Mexico.* New York: Norton, 2006.

Stavans, Ilan. *A Critic's Journey.* Ann Arbor: U of Michigan P, 2009.

Takaki, Ronald. *A Different Mirror: A History of Multicultural America.* Boston: Little, 1993.

CRITICAL READINGS

An Evolutionary Approach to Shakespeare's *King Lear*

Joseph Carroll

What Can an Evolutionary Perspective Offer to Our Understanding of *King Lear*?

King Lear (1604 to 1605) is widely regarded as one of the greatest works of world literature, but also as one of the most challenging. The challenge is not just in the complexity of the language and the need for notes explaining obsolete terms and idioms—those problems are common to all of William Shakespeare's plays. Instead, *King Lear* is exceptionally demanding emotionally and imaginatively. An evolutionary perspective can help readers meet these challenges in three main ways: first, by offering a metaphysical vision that corresponds with that of the play; second, by providing ideas about human motives and values concordant with those in the play; and third, by integrating an awareness of universal aspects of human nature with a recognition of the historically specific features of the play.

Providence versus blind variation and selective retention

Efforts to interpret *King Lear* have often been distorted by trying to make the play fit the vision of a world in which good people are rewarded and evil people are punished. For more than a century and a half (from 1681 to 1834), the only version of the play produced on the stage was that of poet Nahum Tate, who revised it to produce a happy ending, interpolating a love story between Edgar and Cordelia and having all the protagonists live happily ever after. On the stage, the original form of the play was restored almost two centuries ago. Nonetheless, interpretation in the twentieth century often sought to emphasize redemption and consolation.[1]

At one time or another, characters including Lear, Kent, Edgar, Albany, and Gloucester all affirm that human lives are governed by divine justice. The action of the play, though, gives no evidence that a just providence watches over the fate of individuals. The antagonists unleash violence that rebounds lethally against themselves, but that same violence takes the lives of Cordelia, Lear, Gloucester, Cornwall's servant, and likely the Fool as well (he disappears after the third act). Kent, too, declares he will soon be dead. Among the major characters, only Albany and Edgar remain standing. A naturalistic view of human social relations can easily enough make sense of these outcomes. A providential world view cannot. Hence Tate's feeling that the play needed to be rewritten.

Within the framework of evolutionary theory, life is a mechanical and blindly developing process. More organisms are born in any generation than can survive and reproduce; organisms vary in the traits for survival and reproduction; the organisms that possess more favorable variations reproduce at a higher rate and also transmit their more favorable characteristics to their offspring. This simple causal sequence entails no cosmic purpose for the evolution of life. Nor does it entail a divine source for human motives and values. From an evolutionary perspective, if people wish to justify ethical values, they can look for justification only within a purely human context.

Many characters in *King Lear* make broad general statements about the human condition. All but one such statement either conflict with the action of the play or exceed the evidence it affords. Admonishing Gloucester to keep up his spirits after Lear and Cordelia have been defeated in battle, Edgar declares, "Men must endure / Their going hence, even as their coming hither; / Ripeness is all" (Shakespeare 5.2.9–11).[2] This statement stands apart from Edgar's affirmation of a just providential order. After having defeated Edmund, Edgar declares that "the gods are just" (5.3.168) because they mete out appropriate punishments for vice. Gloucester's vice was adultery: "The dark and vicious place where thee he got / Cost him his eyes" (5.3.170–71). This kind of Draconian moralism would be at home in a rigidly moralistic theocracy, but it is not characteristically Shakespearean. The appeal to "ripeness," in contrast, has no moralistic overtones. The metaphor is taken from plant life and thus says nothing about the specific characteristics that ripen into fulfillment in human beings. An image of that kind of fulfillment nonetheless emerges from the action of the play.

The lag between literary criticism and modern psychology

Evolutionary psychologists have a term for common human intuitions about the motives and emotions of other people; they call such intuitions folk psychology, and they argue that folk psychology converges closely with evolutionary psychology. Since human beings are highly social, being able to understand the character and purposes of other human beings has always had adaptive value.[3] Literature gives the fullest possible expression to intuitive folk psychology. Indeed, until very recently, fictional depictions offered much more adequate insights into human nature than any psychological theory could offer. Professional psychology is now finally catching up with the insights of novelists and playwrights, but many literary theorists and critics have not kept up with modern psychology. Instead, they have continued to use Freudian psychoanalytic theory, which is in basic ways simply wrong. Freudian conceptions of the stages of development have long since been abandoned by most serious psychologists, and the oedipal theory, at the heart of Freudian developmental psychology, has been empirically disconfirmed in multiple ways. Freudian theory can thus give no reliable account of the true nature of bonding between parents and children. That bonding is central to all human experience and is foregrounded in *King Lear*. The Freudian emphasis on purely sexual motives also limits the understanding of romantic love, which includes admiration and respect along with sexual desire—as it does, for instance, in the King of France's response to Cordelia. A similar limitation in critical perspective—blindness to mutuality in relationships between men and women—hampers the feminist criticism that focuses exclusively on male dominance.[4]

Modern literary critics now typically blend Freudian concepts of family relations with feminist concepts of gender and with Marxist concepts of social dynamics. Like Freudianism, Marxism is obsolete in its own field and produces interpretive ideas that fit poorly with Shakespeare's depictions of human behavior. The Marxists identify economic class as the chief constituent in social relations. That preconception blocks insight into *King Lear* in two important ways: it gives no adequate access to the feelings of reverence associated with Renaissance conceptions of royalty, and it obscures the sense of a common humanity.[5]

Archetypalism and biocultural critique

The historical period is notoriously vague in *King Lear*. The source story is set in a pre-Christian era. Except for one glancing reference to God in the singular, Shakespeare's characters refer only to pagan deities. However, the ranks, titles, military accoutrements, and matters of daily life depicted or mentioned in the play are more appropriate to the sixteenth century than to a barbarous British antiquity. By blurring historical period while simultaneously invoking multitudinous images of nature, animals, and the human body, Shakespeare directs attention away from any culturally specific setting and directs it instead toward human universals—toward physical sensations (especially pain), basic motives, basic emotions, intimate family relationships, and elementary principles of social organization.[6]

In the earlier decades of the twentieth century, some of the best and most influential criticism of *King Lear* was produced by critics who emphasized universal themes and images—often designated *archetypes*.[7] The archetypal critics have made it easier to understand why Shakespeare has been admired in widely different cultures all over the world, and why, in our own time, despite political and religious institutions radically different from those of Elizabethan England, works like *King Lear* still elicit awe and wonder. However, the archetypal critics make little or no effort to link universal themes and images with a biologically grounded understanding of human nature. As a consequence, archetypal criticism lacks the dimension of causal explanation made possible by integrating literary study with biology and psychology. It also lacks a comprehensive model of human motives and emotions.

G. Wilson Knight, following Bradley, declares that *King Lear* depicts "not ancient Britons, but humanity, not England, but the world" (Knight 202; see Bradley 240). This claim for universality is overstated. The religion depicted in *King Lear* is pagan and polytheistic, not Christian, Muslim, or Buddhist. The political organization is monarchical and feudal, not tribal, republican, capitalist, or socialist. The characters are aristocrats, servants, soldiers, or peasants, not hunter-gatherers, tribal warriors, imperial administrators, salaried workers, or bourgeois merchants. The culturally specific religious and sociopolitical conditions in *King Lear* limit the forms of value and belief possible for the characters. They can imagine the gods intervening directly in human affairs—for either good or ill—but they cannot imagine a mythology in which the Son of God redeems the world from sin and offers salvation to all who acknowledge his divinity. They can envision more equitable distributions of material goods, and they can cast doubt on the legitimacy of political authority, but they cannot envision a teleological historical progression concluding in the triumph of the proletariat.

Biocultural critique versus New Historicism

Over the past thirty years, the idea of human universals has been roundly rejected by historicist critics who insist that human beliefs and values are wholly constituted by specific cultures. The chief theoretical source for New Historicist criticism, cultural historian Michel Foucault, presupposes that power is the sole determining influence on the beliefs and values within any given culture.[8] The leading New Historicist practitioner, Stephen Greenblatt, argues that *King Lear* is "part of an intense and sustained struggle in late sixteenth- and early seventeenth-century England to redefine the central values of society" (95). That struggle, as Greenblatt envisions it, involves "rethinking the conceptual categories by which the ruling elites constructed their world and which they attempted to impose on the majority of the population"

(95). This top-down model of beliefs and values registers an important aspect of social interaction: dominance and subordination. Like the view of social relations in Marxist and feminist theory, though, the top-down model eliminates any generous or sympathetic understanding of shared interests, values, and beliefs. In the New Historicist vision of culture, the feeling of belonging to a community, so crucial to most actual human experience, is reduced on the one side to cynical manipulation and on the other to foolish credulity.

In affirming that values and beliefs are wholly "constructed" by culture, the New Historicists obscure a deeper truth: that beliefs, values, and social practices originate in evolved and adapted features of human nature. It is from those features that cultural constructs ultimately derive their passion and imaginative force. This argument—that cultural images articulate natural passions—can be sharply contrasted with Greenblatt's concept of culture. In his essay on *King Lear*, Greenblatt argues that theater empties life of its content and then replaces life with its own purely cultural form of reproduction. The theater "signifies absence" and "evacuates everything it represents"; it is, nonetheless, able to "reproduce itself over generations" (127). From a biocultural perspective, in contrast, the theater comes alive precisely because it grounds itself in the reproductive cycle of human life. [9]

Human Nature

Life history theory is a comprehensive biological conception that organizes ideas about the nature of all species. Each species has a life history consisting in a reproductive cycle—birth, mating, reproduction, growth, maturity, and death. The life cycle for humans includes intense and prolonged parental care; it thus requires bonding between parents and children and cooperative parental effort. Adult pair-bonding is a trait humans share with many species of birds, but not with most mammals. Like wolves and chimpanzees, but unlike tigers and orangutans, humans are highly social animals. That is why solitary confinement is such a severe form of punishment. Social life among humans, like social life among wolves and chimpanzees, is hierarchical. Some people hold higher status and exercise more power than others. But humans display an exceptional capacity for concerted, collective action, and they have strong impulses toward egalitarianism. All human social organization thus involves a dynamic tension between dominance and affiliation.[10]

Because evolutionary psychology converges with folk psychology, a modern evolutionary conception of human nature looks very much like what ordinary people have in mind when they say, "Oh, that's just human nature." Phrases like that usually refer to basic motives and passions: the instinct for survival, the urge to seek sexual intimacy, companionship, the deep attachment between children and parents, and the driving need to belong to a social group. Common ideas about human nature also include the desire to get ahead, to take advantage of others, to think a little better of one's self than one deserves, and to indulge in envious spite against people who are better off. Because human nature includes deviousness, hypocrisy, and manipulation, the phrase "that's just human nature" sometimes has a cynical tinge, but the concept also includes values like honesty, justice, gratitude, charity, and community. An evolutionary perspective systematizes these elements and encompasses them within a causal explanation.

The characteristic that most distinguishes humans from other species is a highly developed mental life made possible by a large and highly structured brain. People have a sense of personal identity as a continuously unfolding sequence of experiences, and they project that sequence into the future. They connect their own identities with those of other people, and they create mental images of themselves located within a social order, within the natural world, and within any spiritual world they might envision. They engage in collective action on the basis of shared images of social identity and shared norms of behavior. Since they have the power to direct their actions in accordance with consciously held goals, they often feel a need for "meaning" in their lives; that is, they feel a need for a sense of value and purpose in their connection with the world around them.

In the dominant forms of academic literary theory and criticism, the various theoretical schools—Marxism, psychoanalysis, feminism, and New Historicism—all blend together within an overarching set of theoretical ideas commonly designated poststructuralism. These overarching ideas derive chiefly from deconstruction, a form of skeptical epistemology that purports to disclose the instability and incoherence of all knowledge.[11] Jonathan Culler, a chief proponent of poststructuralism, rightly observes that its main characteristic is "the disputing of 'common sense'" (4). There are three chief bits of common sense disputed by the poststructuralists: the ideas that authors and readers share experience within a real, physical world; that authors intend to say specific, definite things about this world; and that readers can more or less accurately understand what authors mean to say. Evolutionary critics typically reaffirm these bits of common sense. They argue that language is an evolved and adapted feature of human nature and that it serves vital functions in communicating information and creating shared experience.[12]

When readers seek to identify what Shakespeare means, they are not looking only for the moral—a theme or idea—that the writer is trying to convey. Shakespeare's plays are not arguments. They are depictions designed to have an emotional, imaginative effect on an audience. From an evolutionary perspective, there are three main ways we can identify the effect Shakespeare meant to have on his audience: first, recognizing universal motives and emotions; second, comparing the cogency of the characters' interpretations of events; and third, following the guidance of the more reliable characters.

Shakespeare can be fairly confident that most of his audience will feel with him in detesting hypocrisy; recoiling from psychopathic cruelty; and responding favorably to honesty, kindness, and loyalty. Basic emotions are human universals (Brown; Ekman). That does not mean that every reader will feel precisely the same way in responding to a play. After all, psychopaths like Edmund and Goneril do exist, though they evidently constitute a small percentage of the total population

(Baumeister; Grossman). A human universal is not a form of behavior or judgment that appears in all individuals; it is a form of behavior or judgment that appears in all known cultures (Brown). Because universals appear in all known cultures, we can reasonably infer that they are not a product of any specific culture. They are built into human nature.

For forms of behavior that constitute the dominant pattern of value, belief, or behavior in all known cultures, we can use the term *normative universals*. For instance, incest between fathers and daughters is taboo in all known cultures. That taboo is thus a normative universal. Normative universals typically reflect and reinforce adaptive mechanisms such as the psychological inhibition against sexual behavior that produces inbreeding. Most, but not all, members of a community feel revulsion against incest. Culture turns this common feeling into a rule of behavior enforced by social sanctions ranging from disapproval and shunning to execution.

Normative universals include horror at the murder of kinfolk and respect for honest dealing. When Edmund announces that his sole motive in life will be to gain power and rank denied him by the rules of inheritance, many readers feel sympathy for a disadvantaged young man who is determined to make his own way in the world. Protagonists in literature often fit that pattern. But when Edmund conspires to have his brother Edgar executed on false charges, and when he turns his father over to be tortured by Cornwall, most readers feel their sympathy fade. Edmund's patently hypocritical language in justifying his behavior—declaring that his love for his father must yield to his loyalty to Cornwall and his party—demonstrates that his motives will not bear public scrutiny. He cannot speak the truth about himself without anticipating public revulsion. In this respect, the audience of the play merges with the public mind from which Edmund feels it necessary to hide his true character.

Edmund's duplicity and hypocrisy stand in sharp contrast to the honesty of Kent, Cordelia, and the Fool. Shakespeare could with confidence anticipate that readers would admire these characters for speaking truth to power. Because they thus establish their reliability as witnesses, they can also help guide readers' responses to Lear. Despite Lear's freak of impulsive rage at the beginning of the play, Kent must be right in characterizing him as "the old kind king" (Shakespeare 3.1.28). Otherwise, Lear could not have won the devotion of characters such as Cordelia, Kent, the Fool, and Gloucester. Once Lear completes the mental collapse heralded in his initial act of folly, the shock and pity felt by Edgar, Gloucester, and Cordelia help guide the audience to the response intended by Shakespeare.

When Kent and Gloucester declare that the stars govern the human condition, readers can remain agnostic; the action of the play gives no evidence either way. When any of the characters make declarations about the gods—declaring either that they kill for sport or that they are the instruments of cosmic justice—readers can infer the arbitrariness of such judgments by comparing them with the varied outcomes of the play: some of the good characters die, and some remain alive. But when Gloucester and Kent denounce the older sisters for parricidal cruelty, when Edgar and Albany declare that Edmund is a villain and a liar, when Edgar praises Kent as an honest and loyal man, or when Kent praises Cordelia for wisdom and truth, the play gives readers good evidence in support of such contentions.

Playwrights reflect the ethos of their communities and also help shape that ethos. Since communities depend on prosocial dispositions, it is not surprising that audiences usually respond with revulsion to Machiavellian personalities like those of Edmund, Goneril, and Regan. In literature across the world, more often than not, antagonists are actuated chiefly by a desire for power and personal gain; protagonists tend to form prosocial clusters by helping kin, creating friendship groups, and exercising magnanimity toward the less fortunate. Empirical evidence for those trends has been gathered on a large set of British novels in the nineteenth century (Carroll, Gottschall, Johnson, and Kruger), and the pattern is also evident in the plays of Shakespeare.

Lear, Gloucester, and Edgar all experience the world as outcasts, and all three, as a consequence, expand in general human sympathy. When Lear is cast out into the storm, deprived of all social standing and power, he recognizes the plight of "poor naked wretches" (Shakespeare 3.4.28) who have no protection from the elements. Gloucester, after he is blinded, takes comfort in the thought that his misfortune will benefit a mad beggar. When Gloucester asks Edgar who he is, Edgar describes himself as a man whom sorrow has made "pregnant to good pity" (4.6.219). These statements are made by Shakespeare's characters; they are not his own direct pronouncements. Nonetheless, it can be said with confidence that the ethos of the play—Shakespeare's own ethos—includes a sense of universal human compassion. *King Lear* contains a great deal of cruelty, violence, and treachery, but it does not invite its audience to share vicariously in the enjoyment of sheer malevolence. It inclines readers instead to join Edgar, Lear, and Gloucester in sympathy for the wretched of the earth.

The Central Theme of *King Lear*

The central theme of the play is announced in Cordelia's first speech to Lear, refusing his demand for flattery:

> I love your majesty
> According to my bond, no more nor less. . . .
> You have begot me, bred me, loved me: I
> Return those duties back as are right fit,
> Obey you, love you, and most honour you.
> Why have my sisters husbands, if they say
> They love you all? Haply, when I shall wed,
> That lord whose hand must take my plight shall carry
> Half my love with him, half my care and duty. (1.1.92–102)

Had Cordelia thought ahead, she might have added that once she had children, she would have to further subdivide her love, leaving a third, or perhaps less than a third, for Lear. She could also have added something about her engagement with the wider social world. Though her statement is schematic and incomplete, Kent is right to praise it for justness of thought. Cordelia here enunciates the central principle that is violated in the play: due proportions in the phases and offices of life, the balance in attention and concern distributed among parents and children, marital partners, and the larger community.[13]

Cordelia is not, of course, an evolutionist. Nor is Shakespeare. They are both intuitive folk psychologists. Nonetheless, the wisdom of their intuitive moral sense depends on its insight into human life history. On the level of moral principle, it might not be possible to improve on their judgment. But by invoking human life history, readers can locate this judgment within a larger explanatory context and can confirm its wisdom.

At Dover, speaking with Cordelia, Lear acknowledges his folly in dividing his kingdom and disinheriting Cordelia, but he does not achieve the kind of balance implicit in Cordelia's statement about a due proportion in "bonds." He had been violently angry at her because he had wanted her love all to himself. At Dover, when he and Cordelia are being led to prison, he is delighted with the outcome of the events he set in motion. He has what he had wanted all along—Cordelia all to himself, and with no further social responsibilities to trouble him. "We two alone will sing like birds i' the cage" (5.3.9). Cordelia is not here called upon to remind him of the due proportions of human life, but she is a married woman, young, and with her whole adult life ahead of her. Being a caged bird, having only her father as company, could hardly make her as happy as it makes Lear. He asks, "Have I caught thee?" (5.3.21). He has indeed, and he is perfectly satisfied to let the rest of the world go its own way. For Cordelia, as it turns out, the rest is silence.[14]

As king, Lear is supposed to be a living personification of the body politic. The reverence due to royalty, though perhaps seldom earned in practice, depends on that personification. A king, then, needs to be wise. The Fool puts it mildly when he teases Lear about having been old before he was wise. Kent is more incisive: "be Kent unmannerly / When Lear is mad" (1.1.146–47). Lear is mad long before his wits begin to turn in the storm. When Goneril and Regan say they love him more dearly than life itself, he actually believes them. At Dover, he announces to Gloucester that they were untruthful in telling him he was everything. This discovery, he feels, is significant; he cites his experience in the storm as empirical evidence confirming it: "I am not ague-proof" (4.6.104). Lear's first onset of madness is an eruption of narcissism coupled with delusions of grandeur.[15] The astonishment expressed by Kent in the first scene implies that Lear has not always been like that. Evidently, a sudden onset of senile dementia has collapsed the rational constraints that in healthy minds regulate the claims of the self in relation to other people.[16]

In the first phase of his madness, Lear fails as a king because he fails to embody the shared norms that form a community. He identifies his own desires as ultimate and non-negotiable assertions of his regal authority. His narcissistic impulses become one, in his own mind, with his authority as king. On the heath, confronting Edgar, and again at Dover, speaking with Gloucester, he goes to an opposite extreme. As soon as Goneril provokes a quarrel and begins treating him with contempt, his fragile sense of personal identity, too heavily invested in his public persona, begins to dissolve: "Does any here know me? Why, this is not Lear. . . . Who is it that can tell me who I am?" (1.4.217–21). On the heath in the storm, he begins to tear off his clothes, aiming at discovering "the thing itself," "unaccommodated man" (3.4.104, 105). In casting off his clothes, he is symbolically casting off convention. In this respect, he makes a mistake similar to the mistake Edmund makes in his first soliloquy: "Thou, Nature, art my goddess" (1.2.1). Edmund takes Nature to be pure egoistic energy, without regard to human bonds. Lear takes a mad beggar—"a poor, bare, forked animal" (3.4.105–06)—as the paradigmatic human form. Edmund and Lear both make false reductions, stripping away essential features of human nature. At Dover, Lear comes still closer to Edmund's cynicism.

Evoking the image of a dog barking at a beggar, he declares, "there thou mightst behold the great image of authority: a dog's obeyed in office" (4.6.153–55). This repudiation of all authority might resonate with readers who equate cynical skepticism with intellectual sophistication, but it is not the ethos that actually governs the play.

Kent, in disguise, tells Lear that he seeks service with him because he sees in his countenance what he would "fain call master": "Authority" (1.4.28, 30). And yet, Kent has severely rebuked Lear precisely for failing to embody the wisdom that is the legitimate ground of authority. Kent himself makes an appropriate distinction when contrasting himself with Oswald. "Such smiling rogues as these," he says, serve all their master's lusts and impulses, "knowing naught, like dogs, but following" (2.2.71, 78). Loyalty to legitimate authority is part of the basic ethos of the play. The play is a tragedy precisely because authority, first in Lear and then in the Machiavellian antagonists, fails to sustain its legitimacy.

The hypocrisy in the speeches made by the antagonists reflects the bad faith in their claim to political authority. Though purely egoistic, the antagonists realize they must at least pretend to embody the moral sense of the community. Oswald is merely a dog, loyal but without principles. Edmund, Goneril, and Regan can claim even less authority than that which could be claimed by a loyal dog. They are monsters in human form. In place of the bonds that form the basis of community, their only relation to others is envy, resentment, ravenous lust, jealousy, and murderous deceit. The imagery of fierce wild animals that pervades the play evokes the quality of their inner lives. The human wreckage that litters the stage exemplifies the consequences of life conducted without legitimate forms of authority.

Tragic Vision in *King Lear*

King Lear tacitly affirms an ethos of domestic and social order grounded in a sane understanding of the due proportions in human life, but that ethos makes itself felt less in its positive manifestations than in its violations. Despite moments of humor and tenderness, the dominant emotions in *King Lear* are rage, venomous resentment, cruel vindictiveness, hatred, outrage, anguish, remorse, and grief. The storm scene at the center of the play provides a dramatic symbol for the play as a whole. Lear does not embody the positive ethos of the play. Kent and Cordelia come closest to that. But Lear is nonetheless the central figure in the play that bears his name. Shutting the gate against him, Goneril declares, "Tis his own blame; hath put himself from rest, / And must needs taste his folly" (2.2.479–80). And he does taste it. The disintegration of his mind is the chief medium through which the audience feels the stress of the destructive forces he has himself unleashed.

Though he is a vessel for suffering on a grand scale, Lear does not embody the full tragic vision of the play. He never achieves the balance and wisdom necessary for that. Indeed, no character in the play fully encompasses its tragic scope. That is in part because the play involves so many phases and offices of life: troubled relations between aging parents and adult children, sibling conflict, marital strife, sexual jealousy, violent conflict between servants and masters, political dissension, and war between nations.

Compared to the scope of conflict in *King Lear*, Shakespeare's other major tragedies are relatively simple. *Othello* (1603), in particular, has only one chief tragic subject—the murderous jealousy of Othello. Othello commits a rash act, tastes his folly, and then dies. *Macbeth* (1603 to 1606) contains family grief, but its main subjects are political: ambition, loyalty, and betrayal. *Hamlet* (1604 to 1605) includes the metaphysical dimension—the quest for meaning in life—that also distinguishes *King Lear*, but it is essentially a family drama. Social and political conflicts are marginal to Hamlet's resentment at the murder of his father and his revulsion against his mother's unseemly remarriage. Othello, Macbeth, and Hamlet all have imaginations adequate to the scope of the tragic action in which they are involved.[17]

The action of *King Lear* is unified, so that each scene contributes ultimately to the catastrophic culmination, with wrecked families on a field of battle amidst a "gored state" (5.3.319). Individual characters, though, are caught up in different parts of the "general woe" (5.3.318). Cordelia, held captive after the battle, is focused on Lear's suffering. After her death, Lear is indifferent to everything except his grief for her. Gloucester is already dead, somewhere offstage. Albany has to deal with Edmund and Goneril, who have plotted against his life, and he must also work out a new distribution of political power. Kent is too emotionally shattered even to live much longer; he expresses only grief. Edgar waxes moralistic over his own family drama, and then Albany and Edgar, responding to the death of Cordelia and Lear, express simple sorrow.

King Lear, then, issues a double challenge to the imagination of its audience: requiring that the audience be responsive to passions and concerns in diverse phases and offices of life, including those of old age, and demanding that the audience achieve a full tragic understanding greater than that achieved by any individual character in the play. Adopting a life history perspective can help readers avoid falsely reducing the concerns of the play to any one issue—to relations between the sexes, for instance, parent-offspring conflict, or social dominance. By providing a thematic framework adequate to the whole scope of the play, a life history perspective can also help to more closely approximate Shakespeare's own encompassing vision of human life.

Though no single character fully embodies the tragic vision of *King Lear*, several characters rise to high poetry in the midst of violent emotional turmoil. The specific imaginative effect of *King Lear* depends in part on the way its brilliantly figurative language interacts with the speed and ferocity of its depicted events. Amid a chaos of false appearances and turbulent relationships, the characters use highly wrought rhetoric to capture fleeting insights or create powerfully synoptic images of human life. Lear is duped by the flattery of his older daughters and fails to see the inner truth in his youngest daughter. But he does not merely bellow in rage; he constructs an elaborate curse so that he can create an emotional barrier between himself and Cordelia. Then, in calling on nature to blight Goneril's womb, he rises to a magnificent height of sustained rhetoric, encapsulating a whole lifetime of maternal misery in his curse. The simplicity of Kent's rebuke to Lear—"What wouldst thou do, old man?" and "thou dost evil" (1.1.146, 167)—has a massive force. In a different rhetorical mode, Kent's extravagant diatribe against Oswald outlines by contrast his own sense of honor. Edmund, too, attributing his "composition and fierce quality" to "the lusty stealth of nature" (1.2.12, 11), uses powerful rhetoric to affirm his identity. Albany is the least of the major characters, but there is fierce poetic power in his repudiation of his wife: "O Goneril, / You are not worth the dust which the rude wind / Blows in your face" (4.2.30–32). Few readers sympathize with Goneril and Regan, but most readers register the force and pith of utterances such as "he hath ever but slenderly known himself" (1.1.294–95) and "must needs taste his folly" (2.2.480). Cornwall's brutality excites universal horror, but readers still feel the evocative power of his gloating sneer at Gloucester's eye, "Out, vile jelly, / Where is thy lustre now?" (3.7.82–83). When Edgar depicts Gloucester's fall from an imaginary cliff at Dover, his word painting is so vivid that it compels his father's belief. That scene is only the most extreme instance of a pervasive theme: that we live in images, often delusive, but nonetheless so powerful that they can overmaster even our physical sensations.

More than in any of Shakespeare's other plays, even *Hamlet*, the characters in *King Lear* display the common human need to encompass their own experience within some cosmic scheme of things, characterized variously as the gods, the stars, or nature. After Gloucester is blinded and discovers that Edmund has betrayed him, he exclaims, "As flies to wanton boys are we to the gods, / They kill us for their sport" (4.1.38–39). Taken merely as a philosophical proposition, this declaration has no more general validity than Edgar's affirmation that "The gods are just" (5.3.168). Gloucester's utterance nonetheless has a powerful poetic effect. In this his highest moment of imagination, he takes in human life at a single glance, with all its turbulence, torment, and ultimate helplessness. The dizzying height from which Gloucester sees his own bitter experience puts him on the same visionary level as that which Lear achieves on the heath, bidding the heavens to "smite flat the thick rotundity o' the world" (3.2.7); it is of a piece, too, with Edgar's admonition, "Ripeness is all" (5.2.11); with Edmund's vow to a universal predatory force, "Thou, Nature, art my goddess" (1.2.1); and with Kent's characterization of the world as a scene of torment: "O, let him pass. He hates him / That would upon the rack of this tough world / Stretch him out longer" (5.3.312–14).

The experience of reading or watching *King Lear* is not just the effect of observing passions and actions in the commonplace matters of family strife and political intrigue. Such passions and actions intertwine with the characters' struggles to encompass the whole scope of human life within their own minds. The audience feels sympathy, pity, horror, and revulsion, but it also shares with the characters—good and bad alike—the sensation of minds expanding to the grandest possible scale.

Grand rhetoric and visionary expansion contribute to the total impression made by *King Lear*. The play does not, though, suggest that poetic imagination is an ultimate, final good. The ethos of the play is essentially moral, not aesthetic. It points away from art and back toward the world of ordinary human relationships. Shakespeare depicts a world gone mad, but he does not generalize madness as the essence of the human condition. Sanity, decency, and charity exist all around the fringes of the madness. The play points its audience toward restoring those qualities to the center of the world.

Notes

1. Major redemptive readings include those by Dowden, Bradley, and Knight. For critical accounts of such readings, see Everett; Foakes 45–54. On specifically Christian interpretations, see Vickers, chapter 7.

2. Like most modern editions of *King Lear*, the text cited here conflates the Quarto and Folio versions.

3. For evolutionary concepts of folk psychology, see Geary; Mithen; Sterelny.

4. On the decline of Freudian psychoanalysis in professional psychology, see Crews; Eysenck; Webster. On the empirical disconfirmation of Freudian oedipal theory, see Degler. On evolutionary developmental psychology, see Bjorklund and Pellegrini. For an evolutionary commentary on romantic love, see Gottschall and Nordlund; on both romantic and filial love, see Nordlund. For a critical account of Freudian readings of Shakespeare, see Vickers, chapter 5; on feminist readings, see Levin; Vickers, chapter 6.

5. The last Marxist economist of note in the United States was Paul M. Sweezy. His magnum opus (co-authored with Paul A. Baran), *Monopoly Capital*, was published nearly half a century ago. For a critical commentary on Marxist readings of Shakespeare, see Vickers, chapter 7. On Renaissance conceptions of royalty, see Headlam Wells, *Shakespeare's Politics*, chapter 4.

6. On the animal imagery, see Bradley 244–45; Holloway 80–84; Knight 205–11; Spurgeon 342.

7. Major universalizing readings include those by Bradley, Knight, and Mack. For a more recent "archetypal" commentary, see Boose.

8. For a critique of Foucault from an evolutionary perspective, see Carroll, *Evolution and Literary Theory*, 32–40, 411–35, 445–48.

9. For a critical commentary on several New Historicist readings of *King Lear*, see Foakes 65–68. For an extended critique of Greenblatt on Shakespeare, see Vickers 231–71. On the history of historical criticism of Shakespeare, see Headlam Wells, *Shakespeare's Politics*, 184–215.

10. On human life history theory, see Kaplan and Gangestad; Low; MacDonald. On the prosocial elements in human nature, see Goleman; Keltner; Wilson. On the tension between dominance and affiliation, see Boehm. On the correlation between conceptions of human nature in Shakespeare and those in evolutionary psychology, see Headlam Wells, *Shakespeare's Humanism*.

11. For critical commentaries on Jacques Derrida, the chief deconstructive theorist, see Carroll *Evolution and Literary Theory*, 390–409; Searle.

12. For comparisons of poststructuralist and evolutionary perspectives, see Boyd; Carroll, *Evolution and Literary Theory*, 49–95; Carroll, *Reading Human Nature*, 71–87, 271–77; Headlam Wells, *Shakespeare's Humanism*.

13. Holloway (94–95) makes a similar argument, though without reference to evolutionary theory.

14. Boose makes a similar argument and locates it within an archetypal analysis of the marriage ritual.

15. For an examination of narcissistic personality disorders in several modern tyrants, see Barbara Oakley, *Evil Genes*.

16. In his biocultural analysis of Lear's character (chapter 3), Nordlund rightly places a strong emphasis on Lear's senile dementia.

17. For an evolutionary perspective on Hamlet, see Carroll, *Reading Human Nature*, 123–47. For a comparison of the history of responses to Hamlet and King Lear, see Foakes.

Works Cited

Baumeister, Roy F. *Evil: Inside Human Cruelty and Violence.* New York: Freeman, 1996.

Bjorklund, David F., and Anthony D. Pellegrini. *The Origins of Human Nature: Evolutionary Developmental Psychology.* Washington: APA, 2002.

Boehm, Christopher. *Hierarchy in the Forest: The Evolution of Egalitarian Behavior.* Cambridge: Harvard UP, 1999.

Boose, Lynda E. "The Father and the Bride in Shakespeare." *PMLA* 97 (1982): 325–47.

Boyd, Brian. "Getting It All Wrong." *The American Scholar* 75.4 (2006): 18–30.

Bradley, A. C. *Shakespearean Tragedy: Lectures on Hamlet, Othello, King Lear, and Macbeth.* 1904. London: Penguin, 1991.

Brown, Donald E. *Human Universals.* Philadelphia: Temple UP, 1991.

Carroll, Joseph. *Evolution and Literary Theory.* Columbia: U of Missouri P, 1995.

_____. *Reading Human Nature: Literary Darwinism in Theory and Practice.* Albany: SUNY P, 2011.

Carroll, Joseph, Jonathan Gottschall, John A. Johnson, and Daniel J. Kruger. "Human Nature in Nineteenth-Century British Novels: Doing the Math." *Philosophy and Literature* 33 (2008): 50–72.

Crews, Frederick, ed. *Unauthorized Freud: Doubters Confront a Legend.* New York: Viking, 1998.

Culler, Jonathan. *Literary Theory: A Very Short Introduction.* Oxford: Oxford UP, 1997.

Degler, Carl. *In Search of Human Nature: The Decline and Revival of Darwinism in American Social Thought.* New York: Oxford UP, 1991.

Dowden, Edward. *Shakespeare: A Critical Study of His Mind and Art.* 3rd ed. New York: Harper, 1918.

Dunbar, Robin. "Why Are Good Writers so Rare? An Evolutionary Perspective on Literature." *Journal of Evolutionary and Cultural Psychology* 3 (2005): 7–22.

Ekman, Paul. *Emotions Revealed: Recognizing Faces and Feelings to Improve Communication and Emotional Life.* New York: Holt, 2003.

Everett, Barbara. "The New *King Lear.*" *Critical Quarterly* 2 (1960): 291–384.

Eysenck, H. J. *Decline and Fall of the Freudian Empire.* London: Penguin, 1991.

Foakes, R. A. *Hamlet versus Lear: Cultural Politics and Shakespeare's Art.* Cambridge: Cambridge UP, 2004.

Geary, David C. *The Origin of Mind: Evolution of Brain, Cognition, and General Intelligence.* Washington: APA, 2005.

Goleman, Daniel. *Emotional Intelligence.* New York: Bantam, 1995.

Gottschall, Jonathan, and Marcus Nordlund. "Romantic Love: A Literary Universal?" *Philosophy and Literature* 30 (2006): 450–70.

Grossman, Dave. *On Killing: The Psychological Cost of Learning To Kill in War and Society.* Rev. ed. New York: Little, 2009.

Headlam Wells, Robin. *Shakespeare's Humanism.* Cambridge: Cambridge UP, 2005.

_____. *Shakespeare's Politics: A Contextual Introduction.* London: Continuum, 2009.

Holloway, John. *The Story of the Night: Studies in Shakespeare's Major Tragedies.* London: Routledge, 1961.

Kaplan, Hillard S., and Steven W. Gangestad. "Life History Theory and Evolutionary Psychology." *The Handbook of Evolutionary Psychology.* Ed. David M. Buss. 68–95. Hoboken: Wiley, 2005.

Keltner, Dacher. *Born To Be Good: The Science of a Meaningful Life.* New York: Norton, 2009.

Knight, G. Wilson. *The Wheel of Fire: Interpretations of Shakespearean Tragedy.* 4th ed. 1949. London: Routledge, 1989.

Levin, Richard. "Feminist Thematics and Shakespearean Tragedy." *PMLA* 103 (1988): 125–38.

Low, Bobbi S. *Why Sex Matters: A Darwinian Look at Human Behavior.* Princeton: Princeton UP, 2000.

Mack, Maynard. King Lear *in Our Time.* Berkeley: U of California P, 1965.

Mithen, Steven. *The Prehistory of the Mind: The Cognitive Origins of Art, Religion, and Science.* London: Thames and Hudson, 1996.

Nordlund, Marcus. *Shakespeare and the Nature of Love: Literature, Culture, Evolution.* Evanston: Northwestern UP, 2007.

Oakley, Barbara. *Evil Genes: Why Rome Fell, Hitler Rose, Enron Failed, and My Sister Stole My Mother's Boyfriend.* Amherst: Prometheus, 2007.

Searle, John. "The Word Turned Upside Down." *The New York Review of Books* 30.16 (1983): 74–79.

Shakespeare, William. *King Lear.* Ed. R. A. Foakes. London: Arden Shakespeare, 1997.

Spurgeon, Caroline. *Leading Motives in the Imagery of Shakespeare's Tragedies.* London: Oxford UP, 1930.

Sterelny, Kim. *Thought in a Hostile World: The Evolution of Human Cognition.* Malden: Blackwell, 2003.

Sweezy, Paul M., and Paul A. Baran. *Monopoly Capital: An Essay on the American Economic and Social Order.* New York: Monthly Rev., 1966.

Vickers, Brian. *Appropriating Shakespeare: Contemporary Critical Quarrels.* New Haven: Yale UP, 1993.

Webster, Richard. *Why Freud Was Wrong: Sin, Science, and Psychoanalysis.* New York: Basic, 1995.

Wilson, David Sloan. *Evolution for Everyone. How Darwin's Theory Can Change the Way We Think about Our Lives.* New York: Delacorte, 2007.

Order Restored: Conventional Family as Model of Governance in Shakespeare's *The Tempest*_____

Thomas M. McCann

Some post-colonial readings of *The Tempest* (1610 to 1611) suggest that the play reveals William Shakespeare's questioning of a predominantly paternal and Eurocentric view of the rule of nations and, in some instances, critics celebrate Caliban as a hero of resistance to the conventional order. While Shakespeare was likely aware of the abuses of colonizers and exposes his audience to the views of challengers to the dominant order, he responds by representing the image of a stable family as the appropriate model for ruling and functioning in a civilized society.

Aimé Césaire's reimagining of the play as *A Tempest* (1969) places Caliban at the center of the work. In this rendering of the narrative, Caliban represents the indigenous people of an island subject to the colonial rule of a European despot. In Césaire's version, Caliban reminds Prospero that without the European's incursion, "I'd be the king, that's what I'd be, the King of the Island. The king of the island given me by my mother, Sycorax" (17). He goes on to embrace his connection to Sycorax, even in the face of Prospero's attack: "Dead or alive, she was my mother, and I won't deny her!" (18). Caliban insists that Sycorax remains alive as a spirit that visits his dreams and imbues the natural elements of the island. According to Caliban, then, Prospero's denial of the living spirit of Sycorax on the island allows him to justify his disrespect and pollution of the island.

Césaire's argument in his version of the play posits that Caliban has rightful claim to the island. Upon Prospero's arrival, Caliban welcomes him and helps him to adjust to his new environment. Over time, Prospero teaches Caliban his European language in order to command him as a servant to do his bidding. Césaire invites sympathy for Caliban and solicits admiration for his resistance to tyranny and injustice: "Every time you summon me it reminds me of a basic fact, the fact that you've stolen everything from me, even my identity!" (20).

While Césaire clearly saw Caliban as representative of the plight of colonized people throughout the world, and depicts Prospero as the oppressive colonizer, the reader of Shakespeare's *The Tempest* has to wonder if Shakespeare shared to some degree the sympathy for Caliban and the indictment of Prospero. Such a reading of Shakespeare's play assumes that he was aware of the brutal acts of oppression committed by colonizers in Ireland and in the New World, and that he questioned the policies that directed the actions of the colonizers.

Stephen Greenblatt suggests that it is possible that Shakespeare was aware of the brutality of colonizers and also sympathetic toward Caliban and other indigenous people who had fallen victim to the incursions of Europeans. He insists that "it is very difficult to argue that *The Tempest* is *not* about imperialism" Greenblatt, in his reaction to George Will's warning about attempts by literature professors to read contemporary political statements into the works of Shakespeare, reminds the reader that Shakespeare would likely have been familiar with the writings of Bartolome de Las Casas and Montagne. Las Casas characterizes the native peoples of the New Worlds as gentle and civil, describes the abuses at the hands of the European oppressors, and pleads with the king of Spain to end the colonizing of new lands as a hopeless and immoral venture. Montagne, in language echoed by Gonzalo, describes the indigenous people of the Americas as naturally gentle, civil, and noble. In observing these people, Montagne notes, "There is perfect religion, perfect policy, perfect and complete use of all things." He observes that the characterization of such people as "barbarous" or "savage" is to impose a foreign standard in judging things that appear strange or out of the ordinary. But, he argues, there is no more "savagery" or "barbarity" than there is in a pristine natural setting, untainted by the reordering at the hands of foreign powers who do not understand nor appreciate the innate qualities (102).

In *The Tempest*, Shakespeare represents these ideas and arguments—that the indigenous people in new lands might not be savage and barbarous and that these people perhaps should be left to their own devices—but he stops short of challenging the presumption of European leaders to colonize and rule foreign lands. He is not likely to condemn King James I for imposing his will on the native inhabitants of Ireland, nor for settling new lands in North America. Shakespeare's apparent argument in *The Tempest* is that educated, civil, and enlightened people have a right to govern more naive and less nurtured people and to advance their state so that it approximates more closely the state of the more developed societies of Europe. Shakespeare would have seen this arrangement as the natural order of things, following the example of the structure and traditions of family as understood by aristocracy in western Europe.

Lawrence Stone describes the Elizabethan conception of family in this way:

> This sixteenth-century aristocratic family was patrilinear, primogenitural, and patriarchal: patrilinear in that it was the male line whose ancestry was traced so diligently by the genealogists and heralds, and in almost all cases via the male line that titles were inherited; primogenitural in that most of the property went to the eldest son, the younger brothers being dispatched into the world with little more than a modest annuity or life interest in a small estate to keep them afloat; and patriarchal in that the husband and father lorded it over his wife and children with the quasi-absolute authority of a despot. (271)

Stone's representation of the family in Shakespeare's time suggests an unambiguous image, which Steven Ozment disputes as too simplistic. According to Ozment, the organization of the family was experiencing some change: "As a general rule, all household members remained subordinate to the paterfamilias, whose strong leadership was deemed essential to household unity, security, and success" (48). At the same time, in some households the wife might have begun to take on greater responsibility and there was some movement toward equality. Yet the Elizabethan notion of the family structure derives from a presumption that the arrangement followed a natural order, which few questioned (Kahn). The arrangement for the family derives from divine right, and the structure of the family suggests a natural order for the structure of a state: the head of state, like the head of the family, rules subjects as a god would rule mortals. From a common Elizabethan perspective, it is difficult to question the authority that derives from divine will, even if some subjects suffer under the arrangement. The patriarchal image suggests that just as a god would know more than mere mortals, royalty would be far more enlightened than their subjects; just as a king would know more than his subjects, a father would know better than his spouse or his offspring.

The Tempest begins with images that affirm a presumed natural patriarchal order, which was most accurate in representing the families of the aristocracy. A furious storm with its attendant terror and chaos opens the action. The chaos of the storm suggests that elements are out of their natural order, with a mere boatswain ordering and insulting the aristocratic passengers: "What cares these roarers / for the name of king? To cabin: silence! trouble us not" (1.1.15–16). When nature imposes its will, it matters little what title or status one holds in civilized society. The boatswain again advises Gonzalo:

> You are a councillor; if you can command these elements to silence and work the peace of the present, we will not hand a rope more. Use your authority. If you cannot, give thanks you have lived so long, and make yourself ready in your cabin for the mischance of the hour, if it so hap. (1.1.18–23)

To those on board, the storm is a terror, threatening violent destruction and the loss of friends and family. But to Prospero, the force behind the storm, the tempest is merely a device to set in motion a grand plan of recovery and retribution that only he understands. For the audience of Shakespeare's time, the storm would signal the disruption in the natural order of the affairs of society and serve as a warning against challenges to that order. According to Wolfgang H. Clemen,

> In *The Tempest*, the actual catastrophe is at the beginning, and not at the end or in the middle of the play. And everything derives and develops from this beginning. Thus the images from this first scene that act as links from the previous events have not the function of preparing or foreboding what is to come; they are rather a reminiscence, an echo, an afterthought, they keep awake our remembrance of what has happened. (182–83)

Just as storms tumble chimneys when Macbeth slaughters Duncan or follow King Lear's alienation from his family, the opening tempest signals a fissure in the divinely ordained arrangement. For those who do not understand the plan behind the storm, it is a malevolent torment. From Ferdinand's perspective in the midst of the storm: "Hell is empty / And all the devils are here!" (1.2.213–14).

Miranda witnesses the storm from a distance and feels for the terrorized wretches aboard the stricken ship:

> O, I have suffered
> With those that I saw suffer! A brave vessel,
> Who had, no doubt, some noble creature in her,
> Dashed all to pieces. O, the cry did knock
> Against my very heart! Poor souls, they perished.
> Had I been any god of power, I would
> Have sunk the sea within the earth or ere
> It should the good ship so have swallowed and
> The freighting souls within her. (1.2.5–13)

Prospero calmly reassures Miranda that no harm is done. He knows that the terrifying storm is mere fabrication:

The direful spectacle of the wreck, which touched
The very virtue of compassion in thee,
I have with such provision in mine art
So safely ordered that there is no soul—
No, not so much perdition as an hair
Betid to any creature in the vessel
Which thou heard'st cry, which thou saw'st sink. (1.2.26–32)

Prospero, from his elevated and enlightened perspective, knows that the tempest is a mere artifice—a product of his craft, designed for the purpose of accomplishing a greater end. While the victims and naive viewers of the storm perceive it as a hellish terror, Prospero, the ruler of the island and the rightful ruler of Milan, knows that it is all show and the necessary means toward his ends. Prospero reminds Miranda, condescendingly, how ignorant she is:

I have done nothing but in care of thee,
Of thee, my dear one, thee, my daughter, who
Art ignorant of what thou art, nought knowing
Of whence I am, nor that I am more better
Than Prospero, master of a full poor cell,
And thy no greater father. (1.2.16–21)

He reminds her that the current display of terror and all that he has done in the conduct of his life on the island was done with the welfare of Miranda foremost in mind. According to Prospero, Miranda—with her limited understanding—cannot begin to comprehend his actions. In a similar way, the victims aboard the storm-tossed ship, from their narrow vantage, cannot begin to understand the true nature of the storm and the purpose for its unleashing. For her part, Miranda does not even understand who she is, nor does she know or appreciate the true stature of her father.

In an extended exchange between Miranda and Prospero, he recounts the events that brought them to their current condition. He faults himself on two grounds. First, he neglected his temporal duties as the head of state; he neglected his responsibility to preserve the natural order of things by abdicating his rule to a less worthy person. Furthermore, he fell victim to deception. Like an indulgent parent, he placed too much trust in someone who may have appeared capable, but proved not to be in the proper position to govern:

> I, thus neglecting worldly ends, all dedicated
> To closeness and the bettering of my mind
> With that which, but by being so retired,
> O'er-prized all popular rate, in my false brother
> Awaked an evil nature; and my trust,
> Like a good parent, did beget of him
> A falsehood in its contrary as great
> As my trust was; which had indeed no limit,
> A confidence sans bound. (1.2.89–97)

Throughout the interchange, Prospero scolds Miranda and prompts her attention: "Thou attend'st not." "I pray thee, mark me." "Dost thou hear?" The promptings suggest that Prospero doubts that Miranda has full apprehension and appreciation for the significance of the events that he recalls and evaluates.

Ariel is the agent of Prospero's biddings, and executes all orders with proper dispatch. But Ariel voices the challenge to authority and reminds Prospero about a promise of liberation: "Let me remember thee what thou hast promised / Which is not yet performed me" (1.2.243–44). This challenge prompts Prospero to recall how he had released Ariel from Sycorax's much narrower confinement, making Prospero the benefactor for Ariel's liberty:

And, for thou wast a spirit too delicate
To act her earthy and abhorred commands,
Refusing her grand hests, she did confine thee,
By help of her more potent ministers
And in her most unmitigable rage,
Into a cloven pine; within which rift
Imprisoned thou didst painfully remain
A dozen years; within which space she died
And left thee there; where thou didst vent thy groans
As fast as mill-wheels strike. (1.2.273–82)

Prospero recalls that it was "mine art" that freed Ariel, and he fully intends to release Ariel from further obligations after Prospero's current plan is complete. Ariel, forgetting his miserable condition upon Prospero's arrival, lacks the ruler's understanding and seeks only his further comfort, which Prospero grants in increments.

Caliban insists on his own sovereignty, usurped from him by Prospero: "This island's mine, by Sycorax my mother, / Which thou tak'st from me" (1.2.334–35). He advances his argument by insisting on the basic injustice of Prospero's rule:

For I am all the subjects that you have,
Which first was mine own king: and here you sty me
In this hard rock, whiles you do keep from me
The rest o' the island. (1.2.344–47)

At the same time, Caliban admits that the relationship was initially symbiotic, and he derived tangible benefit and made no complaint:

When thou cam'st first,
Thou strok'st me and made much of me, wouldst give me
Water with berries in't, and teach me how
To name the bigger light, and how the less,

That burn by day and night: and then I loved thee
And showed thee all the qualities o' the isle,
The fresh springs, brine-pits, barren place and fertile.
(1.2.335–41)

Prospero reminds Caliban that he was treated as a member of the family until his attempted rape of Miranda required his separation and restrictions. Miranda reports that she and her father had attempted conscientiously to teach Caliban and to improve his condition on the island, including introducing him to language, not supplanting his own:

When thou didst not, savage,
Know thine own meaning, but wouldst gabble like
A thing most brutish, I endowed thy purposes
With words that made them known. (1.2.358–61)

The model for the relationship comes from a patriarchal vision of the family, yet Prospero and Miranda initially treated Caliban as an equal, sharing their humble cell, without the intention to exploit him for their own advantage. It is only when Caliban attempts, through his own admission, a rape of a member of the household that he is rejected, separated, and reduced to the status of servant.

If there is an argument for the dissolution of a social hierarchy on the island and a defense of living within the untamed conditions in which the Europeans find it, Gonzalo voices the argument. He describes an Eden:

I' the commonwealth I would by contraries
Execute all things; for no kind of traffic
Would I admit; no name of magistrate,
Letters should not be known; riches, poverty,
And use of service, none; contract, succession,
Bourn, bound of land, tilth, vineyard, none;

No use of metal, corn, or wine, or oil;
No occupation; all men idle, all;
And women too, but innocent and pure;
No sovereignty— (2.1.144–53)

Although Prospero regards Gonzalo as a kindly old gentlemen, he also appears as naive and bombastic, the subject of Sebastian's and Antonio's ridicule. If Gonzalo's vision of an unspoiled state has merit, the balance of the play puts the proposal to the test, with evidence of the duplicity of Sebastian and Antonio and the treachery of Caliban, Stephano, and Trinculo when these usurpers maneuver unchecked.

The missteps of Antonio and Sebastian and the foolish attempts by Stephano and Caliban underscore the implied argument that only a designated few deserve to bear the mantle of responsibility as head of state. Usurpers might assume the trappings of leadership, but lack the substance. Antonio notes, "And look how well my garments sit upon me, / Much feater than before" (2.1.26–68). He refers to the garments he assumes as the usurping Duke of Milan, suggesting that in looking the part ("executing th' outward face of royalty") he has become the real thing, "Absolute Milan" as Prospero reports. The image repeats in act 4, when Prospero's hanging garments distract Stephano and Trinculo from their dark design: "O King Stephano! O peer! O worthy Stephano! Look what a wardrobe here is for thee!" (4.1.221–22). Prospero had directed Ariel to display the garments, knowing that this would distract the fools from their purpose, seeing only the trappings of leadership and not owning the substance. Even Caliban warns that the garments are "such luggage" and "trash," recognizing that Prospero's powers derive from his superior knowledge represented by his books. Without the books, according to Caliban, Prospero would be "but a sot, as I am" (3.2.88). Caliban suggests that all of the inhabitants of the island would be equal in being mere fools if not for possession of some superior knowledge.

Trinculo acknowledges, perhaps unwittingly, that not everyone is equally capable of governance and that a state cannot function when those subjects who are incapable of leadership must manage for themselves: "They say there's but five upon this isle. / We are three of them; if th' other two be brained like us, / the state totters" (3.2.4–6). The state would be in perilous condition if ignorant subjects would recognize the likes of Stephano as a "noble lord," a god, or a "wondrous man." Caliban later admits his error in presuming superior qualities in Trinculo and Stephano when he acknowledges "What a thrice-double ass / Was I to take this drunkard for a god / And worship this dull fool!" (5.1.296–98)

In act 5, with Prospero's tempest-initiated plans having played out, he reminds the characters and the audience about his conception of the natural order of things—that God rules mortals as a father rules his family and as a king rules his subjects. *Natural* in this context means as nature or God intended, not in the sense of untamed or instinctive. Unlike the unnatural Antonio, Prospero allows reason and compassion to guide his actions. He acknowledges to Ariel that it is natural for a human being to feel compassion for the suffering of a fellow human being, and that mercy is the human command over passion and instinctive impulses:

> Though with their high wrongs I am struck to the quick,
> Yet with my nobler reason 'gainst my fury
> Do I take part. The rarer action is
> In virtue than in vengeance. They being penitent,
> The sole drift of my purpose doth extend
> Not a frown further. (5.1.25–28)

Prospero's condemnation of Antonio emphasizes his violation of the natural bond and affection between brothers, and between subjects and their divinely ordained head of state:

You, brother mine, that entertained ambition,

Expelled remorse and nature; whom, with Sebastian,

Whose inward pinches therefore are most strong,

Would here have killed your king, I do forgive thee,

Unnatural though thou art. (5.1.75–79)

Prospero notes that Antonio suppressed ("expelled") conscience and any natural affection he should have toward a brother and head of state. He continues by insisting that his conspiracy to kill a king was hideous in its being "unnatural."

In introducing Miranda to Alonso, her new father-in-law, Ferdinand acknowledges that his bond to Miranda is an act of providence; he notes that he was so bold to choose her as a wife without seeking the counsel and permission of his father only because Ferdinand assumed his father to be dead:

But by immortal Providence she's mine.

I chose her when I could not ask my father

For his advice, nor thought I had one. (5.1.189–91)

Ferdinand goes on to acknowledge that the marriage makes Prospero his "second father," and Miranda becomes daughter to Alonso, if he will have her. He replies, "I am hers." Recalling his part in the plot that placed both Prospero and Miranda in peril, Alonso reverses the natural order of things and notes: "But, O, how oddly will it sound that I / Must ask my child forgiveness!" (5.1.197–98).

Gonzalo summarizes the restored order, which is the proper ending of the comedy:

Was Milan thrust from Milan, that his issue

Should become kings of Naples? O, rejoice

Beyond a common joy, and set it down

With gold on lasting pillars: In one voyage

Did Claribel her husband find at Tunis,

And Ferdinand, her brother, found a wife

Where he himself was lost; Prospero his dukedom

In a poor isle; and all of us ourselves

When no man was his own. (5.1.205–13)

The tempest recalls past actions and represents the state at the beginning of the play when the providential order had been disrupted. With order restored, it is possible to return to Milan and to Naples to live in harmony.

Of course, with Shakespeare, affairs are never neatly tied up, and the prospects for harmonious living remain tenuous. While harmony requires honoring the natural or divine order—based on the model of a patriarchal family—the preservation of harmony requires constant diligence and reliable recognition of the true nature of matters, if that is ever possible. Prospero did not fall from power because he was an unjust and intolerable ruler. If readers are to believe his testimony, his subjects held him in high esteem: "Prospero the prime duke, being so reputed / In dignity, and for the liberal arts / Without a parallel" (1.2.72–74). According to Prospero, Antonio would not go so far as to assassinate the Duke because "So dear the love my people bore me, nor set / A mark so bloody on the business, but / With colors fairer painted their foul ends" (1.2.141–43). Prospero's crime was twofold. First, he did not recognize the potential for evil within his brother and placed complete trust in him, like a parent who cannot conceive of his child capable of wrongdoing:

Like a good parent, did beget of him

A falsehood in its contrary as great

As my trust was; which had indeed no limit,

A confidence sans bound. (1.2.94–97)

Prospero tells Miranda that he placed complete trust in Antonio, "he whom next thyself / Of all the world I loved" (1.2.68–69). If Prospero could not trust his own brother and neglected to perceive his falsehood, there remains the prospect that he can fall victim again. There is, however, no guarantee that Prospero will see matters for what they really are and will not fall victim to deception again.

Prospero's second failing was his negligence: turning his attention to the "liberal arts," "those being all my study, / The government I cast upon my brother / And to my state grew stranger, being transported / And rapt in secret studies" (1.2.74–77). The abdication of duty and the transfer of power to a subordinate would be akin to a father devoting his attention to his golf game while the other members of the family take responsibility for earning incomes and managing the affairs of the household. Prospero has not learned his lesson entirely. He starts from his viewing of the pageant of spirits that he conjures for Ferdinand's and Miranda's entertainment, when he recalls: "I had forgot that foul conspiracy / Of the beast Caliban and his confederates / Against my life: the minute of their plot / Is almost come" (4.1.139–42). Fortunately he has Ariel to serve as spy, advising him about plots and serving as agent to thwart those plots. As Prospero returns to Milan, he frees Ariel and no longer can rely on his service and must remain vigilant himself at a time when "Every third thought shall be my grave" (5.1.312).

Prospero expresses little sympathy for Caliban. He suggests that Caliban is inherently corrupt, and the efforts of Prospero and Miranda have failed to change him:

> The form reveals the diseased mind within.
> A devil, a born devil, on whose nature
> Nurture can never stick; on whom my pains,
> Humanely taken, all, all lost, quite lost;
> And as with age his body uglier grows,
> So his mind cankers. (4.1.188–92)

Prospero suggests that Caliban's outward appearance reveals his diseased nature, both of which grow worse as he ages. Miranda suggests that physical appearance reveals moral character: "There's nothing ill can dwell in such a temple. / If the ill spirit have so fair a house, / Good things will strive to dwell with't" (1.2.461–63). This complicates matters, for Prospero's poor judgment based on the outward appearance of things led to his ouster from Milan. If he continues to embrace the idea that things are what they appear to be, he remains vulnerable when he and his family return to Europe.

For all of his disdain for Caliban, Prospero acknowledges the basic humanity within his subordinate: "This thing of darkness I / Acknowledge mine" (5.1.275–76). This assertion admits a connection to Caliban and a responsibility for what Caliban has become. While Prospero refers to Caliban as "thou earth," "thou tortoise," and "thou poisonous slave" (1.2.322), he still acknowledges him as "mine." In a similar way, Prospero demeans Miranda in asking, "My foot my tutor?" (1.2.473). The corporal metaphor suggests that while he is the head, she is the lowly foot, which should be governed by the head. He also calls her "advocate for an impostor" and "foolish wench" (1.2.481). These belittling terms might be the expression of an exasperated parent who cannot fathom the foolish actions of his children, yet acknowledges them as his own, and his own responsibility.

If Prospero has any sympathy for Caliban, it is revealed in his decision to leave him behind on the island. The less cultured Stephano would bring Caliban to Europe where he could win courtly favor by presenting him as a gift to the King, or could display him as a curious sideshow for profit. Shakespeare would have been familiar with the fact that European explorers to the New World had captured indigenous people and brought them to England for display. In the play, such a plan is the notion of only a drunken sot like Stephano.

In revealing his plan to return all the Europeans to Naples and Milan, Prospero is not heeding the advice of Las Casas that the attempt to colonize the indigenous people of the New World is both futile and inhumane and therefore should be abandoned. The removal from the island of Sycorax and the return to Europe is more of an artistic necessity than a political statement. Prospero projects the outcome:

> And in the morn
> I'll bring you to your ship and so to Naples,
> Where I have hope to see the nuptial
> Of these our dear-beloved solemnized;
> And thence retire me to my Milan (5.1.307–11)

As Frye notes, the return to civilized society is part of the argument of comedy. The problems of the families—the intrigue, political corruption, neighbor against neighbor, and brother against brother—derive from the affairs of the developed society and have become so entrenched and entangled, that the players in the political and familial dramas must abandon that society and enter a more pristine world in order to correct themselves and restore natural affections and order. But, realistically, the green world is a temporary retreat, and the responsible characters must return to their own society. While harmony has been restored, there remains the threat that the problems can emerge again, with humans subject to misapprehension and neglect.

It is likely that Shakespeare was aware of the abuses that European colonizers committed in subjecting indigenous people in the Americas to their rule. He may have been sympathetic. While he may have disdained the abuses of power, he does not use *The Tempest* to argue against the right of Europeans to colonize new lands. The play argues for supporting the status quo, founded on the Elizabethan era conception of family—suggesting that a natural and divine order calls for a patriarchal structure within the family, analogous to the relationship between God and humans, between King and subjects.

Works Cited

Bevington, David, ed. *The Complete Works of Shakespeare,* 5th ed. New York: Longman, 2003.

Césaire, Aimé. *A Tempest.* Trans. Richard Miller. New York: Theatre Communications Group/TGC Translations, 2002.

Clemen, Wolfgang H. *The Development of Shakespeare's Imagery.* London: Methuen, 1951.

Frye, Northrop. "The Argument of Comedy." *Shakespeare, Modern Essays in Criticism,* Ed. Leonard F. Dean. London: Oxford UP, 1967.

Greenblatt, Stephen. "Turning Literature Into a Celebration of New World Order." *Chronicle of Higher Education.* Chronicle of Higher Education, 12 June 1991. Web. 24 May 2011.

Kahn, Coppèlia. "The Absent Mother in King Lear." *Rewriting the Renaissance: The Discourses of Sexual Difference in Early Modern Europe.* Ed. Margaret Ferguson, Maureen Quilligan, and Nancy Vickers. Chicago: U of Chicago P, 1986. 33–49.

Ozment, Steven. *Ancestors: The Loving Family in Old Europe.* Cambridge: Harvard UP, 2001.

Stone, Lawrence. *The Crisis of the Aristocracy, 1558–1641.* Abr. ed. New York: Oxford UP, 1967.

Takaki, Ronald. "The *Tempest* in the Wilderness: The Racialization of Savagery." *Journal of American History* 79.3 (1992): 892–912.

The Power of Story to Shape Lives in Lorraine Hansberry's *A Raisin in the Sun*_____

Susan Callahan

In his introduction to *How to Read Literature Like a Professor* (2003), Thomas Foster tells his students that experienced readers will recognize Karl Lindner, the mild-mannered white representative of the Clybourne Park Improvement Association, is meant to represent the devil. He explains that Lindner fits within the tradition of satanic tempters, citing the work of Christopher Marlowe, Johann Wolfgang von Goethe, Stephen Vincent Benét, and even the author of *Damn Yankees* (xii). He does not mention the Bible or John Milton, but he certainly could have. In the remainder of his highly readable text, Foster proceeds to demonstrate how to become highly skilled readers of literature by reading a great deal and learning to recognize the echoes of previous texts in the one currently being read. In short, one learns to read like a professor by reading like a professor—something that is easier said than done. This approach to literature can be very frustrating to readers who do not yet have a large bank of previously read texts upon which to draw. So what are these readers to do while they gain the intertextual knowledge that is essential for a sophisticated reading of literature?

Probably the most useful thing readers can do is to look closely at the text before them—in this case Lorraine Hansberry's 1959 play *A Raisin in the Sun*—while attempting to place it within the wider historical context in which it is set. There are numerous ways that close reading can provide insight into this powerful drama of a working-class Chicago family's response to the long-awaited arrival of a life insurance payout for the death of the family patriarch. Steven Carter, for instance, looks closely at the way Hansberry creates a variety of "meticulous and lively delineations of . . . widely contrasting speech patterns" (26–27) and uses them to reveal differences in class and social experiences, while J. Charles Washington argues that Walter can be viewed as both "a tragic hero who is elevated by his growth from ignorance to knowledge, and . . . a realistic hero whose transcendence involves a tremendous sacrifice" (123).

The approach here, however, is to examine some of the key stories the characters in the play tell each other and tell themselves. These stories, called "doubly embedded narratives" by literary theorist Alan Palmer, reveal that "versions of characters [versions of themselves as well as versions of other characters] exist within the minds of characters" and can show "the whole of a character's various perceptual and conceptual viewpoints, ideological worldviews, and plans for the future" (15). All stories are important because, as psychologist Jerome Bruner reminds us, they are one of the primary methods humans use to make sense of their own actions and the actions of others. Bruner, in fact, suggests that "stories create a reality of their own—in life as in art" (43), concluding that "our sensitivity to narrative provides the major link between our own sense of self and our sense of others in the social world around us" (69). Thus, a focus on the stories told within *A Raisin in the Sun* not only provides insight into the motives and emotions of individual characters, but also establishes the content of the powerful Younger family story that Walter finally tells Lindner at the end of the play. Moreover, an analysis of the little stories told within the wider narrative of the play highlights the overarching social and political message of the play.

Before focusing on some of the individual stories within *A Raisin in the Sun*, however, it is best to have a clear sense of the context in which the play was written and first performed. As more than one writer has noted, "*Raisin* is far more than an abstract comment on black life in mid-twentieth-century America" (M'Baye 173). Hansberry acknowledged that she drew upon her own experience with housing discrimination in Chicago for the scene in which the Youngers' neighbor, Mrs. Johnson, stops by to see whether they had "read 'bout them colored people that was bombed out their place" (Hansberry 100) and to predict, "I bet this time next month y'all's names will have been in the papers plenty" (102). Hansberry had been a child in the late 1930s when her father challenged real estate practices that kept blacks out of certain neighborhoods by moving his family into a house near the University of Chicago, where the family encountered violence and was forced to move back to a black neighborhood for safety. The situation had become even more violent by the 1950s. Critic Kristin L. Matthews suggests that "both the volatility of the issue and its commonplace nature" (556) in 1959 meant that Hansberry could assume her audience would understand that Walter's casual comment early in the play in response to a newspaper article—"Set off another bomb yesterday" (Hansberry 26)[1]—was a reference to a similar incident. Her audience would also be familiar with the ongoing Civil Rights Movement.

Ever since Lorraine Hansberry's *A Raisin in the Sun* was first produced, audiences have responded to the story of the Youngers' individual and collective struggle for fulfillment and financial stability. This is not to say that the play initially met with universal critical acclaim or that all audience members were satisfied with Hansberry's depiction of African American life. In a recent volume dedicated to the American dream in literature, Barbacar M'Baye notes that early "critical reaction was ambivalent" with mixed reactions among both white and black critics, most of whom "tended to be more concerned with the racial background of the dramatist than with the complex work she created" (171, 173). Although the New York Drama Critics Circle honored *A Raisin in the Sun* as the Best Play of the Year in 1959 and most black audience members were pleased to see black life depicted in a realistic manner, one prominent black critic scoffed that the play was merely a "cleverly written piece of glorified soap opera" (Cruse 278). Other African American theatergoers felt the play did not address the economic and social oppression of the Younger family in explicit enough terms.

In response to critical reviews, Hansberry expressed astonishment that "some writers" ignored the "purely *class* aspirations" at the heart of her play and described Walter Lee Younger's final decision to accept his mother's plan to move the family into a hostile white neighborhood as an act "quite as small as it seems and quite as significant"

("An Author's" 195, 199). Accepting that move and all it would entail was both an acknowledgment of the system of oppression that kept most African Americans in poverty and an indication that that system could and should be challenged. When Hansberry said "some writers" seemed incapable of seeing her play in terms of a human desire to overcome oppression and poverty, Hansberry was referring to the white critics and audiences who saw *A Raisin in the Sun* in 1959 and in the early 1960s. Because white audiences liked Hansberry's characters and admired the close-knit family, they often ignored or simply did not see elements of the play that were particularly working-class African American, mentally creating an "acceptably 'middle class' family" whose desire for a house of their own "became a desire to 'integrate'" rather than a need to move out of a cramped apartment in a rat-infested neighborhood (Nemiroff 9). This inability of white audiences to see the play except through the unacknowledged racial lenses of the time has been explored in some detail by Robin Bernstein, who suggests that "the play's realism satisfied its white viewers in much the same way that minstrelsy satisfied its viewers by providing them with easy access to consumable, perceived 'Negro culture'" (18). Bernstein goes on to say that this ability to see the black culture on the stage as non-threatening and understandable also allowed white audiences to experience it as something "collectable," a form of knowledge they could show off to their friends in the same way they could show off an exotic painting that they had collected. This response to *A Raisin in the Sun* thus reinforced a sense of white superiority while allowing the viewer to admire the play as a piece of art.

With this general sense of the play's historical context and its initial reception, it is now possible to turn to some of the smaller narratives that exist within it with an eye to seeing how they help to construct the wider narrative. These mini narratives meet the basic identifying features of stories as defined by Seymour Chatman: They have "order and selection" and are intended as a form of "communication" requiring interpretation by the one who hears or reads the story (28). That is,

these little stories are told to someone—in this case to another character and to the wider audience for the play—and they follow a beginning, middle, and end sequence of events, using details that have been
carefully selected by the teller. These stories, like more polished literary narratives, are designed to have an intended effect. Some of them
are the short, everyday stories characters tell about where they have
gone and what they have done, which serve to provide insight into the
speaker while moving the action of the play forward. Others, generally
more significant, consist of retellings of past events, events that have
been reshaped and focused by the teller to convey a specific message,
to paint a very particular portrait of reality. A third type, a story created
totally out of the teller's imagination, also occurs, serving to highlight
the contrast between the Youngers' reality and their ability to envision
other possibilities. All three types of stories are necessary for the overall impact of the play.

The first mini-story, a retelling of past events, occurs early in act
1. Ruth has roused Travis from his bed on the couch in the living
room and started the family's regular morning routine, which involves
shifts in the communal bathroom in the hall and conflicts about small
amounts of money. Once Travis has left for school, Walter tries to convince his wife to talk to his mother about using the $10,000 life insur-
ance check from his father's death to invest in a liquor store, clearly
something neither Ruth nor Mama Lena wishes to do. In response to
Ruth's complaint that the anticipated partner in the liquor store deal,
a man named Willy Harris, is a "good-for nothing loudmouth," Walter responds: "Charlie Atkins was just a 'good-for-nothing loudmouth'
too, wasn't he! When he wanted me to go in the dry-cleaning business
with him. And now—he's grossing a hundred thousand dollars a year.
A hundred thousand dollars a year! You still call *him* a loudmouth!"
(Hansberry 32).

Clearly Charlie's success, and the fact that Walter was not a part of
it, rankles. Walter's brief story about Charlie Atkins' economic success
encapsulates his dream that a working-class man can become wealthy

---

if only he is able to make the right investment. Walter sees Charlie as the man he might have been, the man he might yet still become. The story is intended to convince Ruth she was wrong about Charlie, and, by extension, that she must also be wrong about Willie. Walter must reject Ruth's criticism of Willie Harris because it is also an implied criticism of himself. He needs to convince Ruth that none of these three black men—Charlie, Willie, and Walter—are good-for-nothing loudmouths. This little story that reveals much about Walter's dreams and frustrations is followed shortly by another story that says even more about how Walter views himself. This second story also establishes the importance of stories and storytelling within the context of the play.

Walter tells Ruth, "I'm thirty-five years old; I been married eleven years and I got a boy who sleeps in the living room—(*very, very quietly*)—and all I got to give him is stories about how rich white people live" (34). In saying that stories about how white people live is "all" that he has to give his son, Walter establishes two beliefs: first, that he has no story about himself and his life that is worth passing on to Travis and second, that stories themselves are not very important. As a chauffeur, Walter admires his employer's home, polishes and drives his car, and closely observes his clothing and business meetings. He is, indeed, well-qualified to describe how rich, white people live. He is less qualified, though, to describe what he does offer his son. Because he defines himself as a financial failure, Walter fails to see the importance of his steady job and his loving presence in Travis's life. He dismisses these intangible gifts and focuses on the material goods he wishes he could provide. His sense of himself comes from his belief that a man is defined by his economic status, a belief that is reinforced by the white world in which he works.

The power of this external, white world to shape Walter's sense of himself and his place in society cannot be underestimated. The post–World War II culture, which is the wider context for the play, was dominated by images of the cars, refrigerators, houses, and other material goods that the American middle class was purchasing in unparalleled abundance. The Youngers, clinging to the lowest rungs of the working class, however, are not participants in this buying spree. The apartment in which they live has seen better days. It is part of an old mansion that has been subdivided to create the type of apartments that poet Gwendolyn Brooks describes as "kitchenette building"[2]—living spaces with very basic kitchen requirements wedged into one end of the living room, two small bedrooms, and a shared bathroom down the hall. Walter's parents moved into this apartment when they were first married, planning to live in it no longer than a year while they saved enough for a small house. Decades later, the family is still there, still using the same well-worn furniture and barely surviving on the salaries of three working adults. Walter is fully aware that their collective, ceaseless toil will never be enough to lift the family into the middle class. Although he understands his financial position and his limited options for fulfilling his economic aspirations, Walter does not see that, in focusing so intently on material possessions, he has accepted a value system that could prove anathema to his survival as a decent human being.

Painfully aware of his status in relation to his wealthy employer and the power of money to purchase the things he wants to provide for his family, Walter dismisses stories as having no value. He does not yet know what most psychologists know: that a "story has a peculiar kind of power" when it "passes on values," or when it "provides us with role models to validate our views and guide our conduct" (Randall 98–99). Walter does not yet realize that the story he should tell his son is the story of the Younger family's survival. Instead, at the end of act 2, scene 2, he tells Travis a story based on his dream of financial success. He describes an idyllic scene in which he earns a large salary in a downtown office for going to conferences and dealing with multiple secretaries. He returns to a large home, complete with gardener. He continues:

I'll go inside and Ruth will come downstairs and meet me at the door and we'll kiss each other and she'll take my arm and we'll go up to your room to see you sitting on the floor with the catalogues of all the great schools in America around you . . . All the great schools in the world! And—and I'll say, all right son—it's your seventeenth birthday, what is it you've decided? . . . Just tell me where you want to go to school and you'll *go*. Just tell me, what it is you want to be—and you'll *be* it [. . .] You name it, son [. . .] and I hand you the world! (Hansberry 109)

Walter's love for his wife and son shines through this fantasy. The story also shows his understanding that an education from a "great" school is connected to a parent's wealth and a child's success. At the end of the story, Travis—responding to the love in his father's voice more than to the content of the story, which probably means little to him—leaps into the open arms that Walter holds open for him.

Walter's fantasy builds upon the simple dream his father had for him and Beneatha: a life without exhausting physical toil. Walter has achieved that dream by securing a service job that does not involve backbreaking labor. But he also knows that a better life is possible for his son and wants to give it to him, using the only method he sees available. Investing in a liquor store is very risky, not only because his partners seem to be as poorly educated and inexperienced as he is, but because it will mean ignoring his mother's strong religious objections to that type of business. In addition, unlike the dry cleaning store provided by Charlie Atkins, which would provide a real service to the African American community, the liquor store has the potential to harm the community by encouraging liquor consumption as an avenue of temporary escape from reality. This destructive power of alcohol is demonstrated in act 2 when Walter begins visiting the Green Hat instead of going to his job. At that point in the play, Walter is not considering the needs of his family, only his own misery and his desire to escape it. Alcohol has the potential to destroy families, and selling liquor encourages that possibility. Even if Walter were able to make his liquor store investment pay off financially, it is doubtful it would bring the kind of satisfaction and status he is seeking. It would sow discord within his own family and engender disapproval from a significant proportion of the wider black community.

Mama Lena is the other significant storyteller in the play. The ghost of Big Walter Younger hovers over the entire play, conjured by the stories she tells about him. We first catch a glimpse of him in the first act after Mama, talking with Ruth, describes the dream she and Big Walter shared when they were newlyweds. They would buy a small house, fix it up, and have "a little garden in the back" (45). This memory leads her to recall how exhausted Big Walter would be after a hard day of physical labor for minimal pay, how he "would slump down on that couch there and just look at the rug, and look at me and look at the rug and then back at me—and I'd know he was down then . . . really down" (45). She also remembers the death of a baby and says, "I almost thought I was going to lose Big Walter too. Oh, that man grieved hisself! He was one man to love his children" and adds "I guess that's how come that man finally worked hisself to death like he done. Like he was fighting his own war with this here world that took his baby from him" (45). Thus, the first things readers learn about Big Walter are that he had a dream of homeownership, that he worked incredibly hard, that he loved his children, and that he felt that life was a battle for mere survival. These four traits become the cornerstones of the picture of Big Walter that is told at the end of the play.

Big Walter was not, however, a perfect man. Mama acknowledges that he was "hard-headed, mean, kind of wild with women" (45), but these traits are never mentioned outside this one brief passage of "girl talk" with Ruth. Mama quickly returns to Big Walter's love of his children and the fact he "wanted them to have something—be something." She describes how "he'd get right wet in the eyes sometimes, lean his head back with the water standing in his eyes and say, 'Seem like God didn't see fit to give the black man nothing but dreams—but He did give us children to make them dreams seem worth while'" (45–46). The picture she focuses on in her story about Big Walter is that of a loving father who hopes his dreams will be realized in the lives of his children. It is this image of Big Walter that she evokes later in the act when she tells Walter, "I'm waiting to hear how you be your father's son. Be the man he was. . . . I'm waiting to see you stand up and look like your daddy and say we done give up one baby to poverty and that we ain't gong to give up nary another one" (75).

Later in act 1, eleven-year-old Travis also tells a story, one that illuminates the reality in which the Youngers live. He has been sent outside to play while the women clean the apartment and spray for roaches. He has nowhere to play except in the street outside the apartment building, and when Beneatha sees that her nephew and some other boys are chasing a rat, she calls for him to come inside. When Travis enters he is filled with the excitement of the rat hunt. He tells Ruth:

Mama, you should of seen the rat . . . Big as a cat, honest! *(He shows an exaggerated size with his hands)* Gaaleee, that rat was really cuttin' and Bubber caught him with his heel and the janitor, Mr. Barnett, got him with a stick—and then they got him in a corner and—BAM! BAM! BAM!— and he was still jumping around and bleeding like everything too—there's rat blood all over the street! (59)

His dramatic rendition of events makes it clear that he sees nothing wrong with killing rats as blood sport. It is simply an aspect of his environment that he accepts and enjoys. The three women, though, are appalled. His mother *"clamps a hand over his mouth and holds him to her"* and Mama Lena says, "You hush up now . . . talking all that terrible stuff" (59). They see what he does not—that a story about rat blood all over the street is not a good thing. It is a demonstration of their poverty and the potential violence inherent in the neighborhood. They fear for Travis and what he might become if they continue to live in the apartment.

In the first act, neither Beneatha nor Ruth tells stories about people or events in their lives that possess the vivid detail of Walter, Lena, and Travis's stories. Beneatha makes wisecracks, insults her brother, criticizes a black college boy she has been dating, justifies her constant flitting from one hobby to another, and finally pushes her mother's indulgent nature too far when she claims that she does not believe in God. Her constant stream of opinions seems intended partly to provoke, partly to try out potential roles for herself, and partly to create an identity separate from the rest of her family. She is inconsistent about nearly everything except her intent to become a doctor. It is not until act 3 that Beneatha finally tells a story that reveals why having a medical career is so important to her. She is speaking with her African suitor, Asagai, telling him how angry and hurt she is that Walter has lost the money that was to pay for her schooling. Abruptly, she begins telling him why she wanted to be a doctor in the first place:

> When I was very small . . . we used to take our sleds out in the wintertime and the only hills we had were the ice-covered stone steps of some houses down the street. And we used to fill them in with snow and make them smooth and slide down them all day . . . and it was very dangerous, you know . . . far too steep . . . and sure enough one day a kid named Rufus came down too fast and hit the sidewalk and we saw his face just split open right there in front of us . . . And I remember standing right there looking at his bloody open face thinking that was the end of Rufus. But the ambulance came and they took him to the hospital and they fixed the broken bones and they sewed it all up . . . and the next time I saw Rufus he just had a little line down the middle of his face . . . I never got over that . . . (132–33)

Suddenly, just for a moment, the audience sees a Beneatha who is not sharp-tongued, frivolous, and changeable. The audience instead sees a Beneatha who has a warm heart and a serious goal born of genuine concern for others. When she goes on to say, "I always thought it was the one concrete thing in the world that a human being could do. Fix up the sick, you know . . . make them whole again" (133), readers believe her because the story she has told about Rufus rings true. That belief in Beneatha's genuine compassion has been established so that when she explodes with newfound cynicism and a determination to turn her back on a career in medicine because it "was a child's way of seeing things—or an idealist's" (133), there is hope that the idealist is not really gone for good. And indeed, at the end of the play, the optimistic Beneatha is back, talking about possibly marrying Asagai and going to Africa to practice medicine.

Ruth is by far the quietest member of the family and, until Mama announces that she has bought a house, she seems almost too tired to say much. She is the family peacekeeper and go-between, who spends most of the play cooking, ironing, or cleaning—working as hard inside the apartment as she does in her job as a domestic servant outside. Ruth's story, as Hansberry tells it, begins when Ruth abruptly faints at the end of the first scene in act 1, shortly after Mama has told the story of Big Walter's response to the death of one of their children and seems to end when Ruth tells Walter in act 2, "I guess maybe I better go on and do what I started" (87), suggesting that she had hoped he would say something to change her mind about the abortion. In between these two points, Ruth's story is told primarily through the facial expressions and speculative comments of Mama and Beneatha, culminating in the fact that it is Mama, not Ruth, who tells Walter that Ruth has consulted an abortionist.

When Mama announces that she has bought a house, however, Ruth's despair turns to happy anticipation and she speaks with passion and fluency about leaving the cramped apartment for a place with more bedrooms and "a whole lot of sunlight" (94), making it clear to Mama that the house is what she needs in order to welcome a second child. It is only at this point, when the Younger family's joy is at its height, that she volunteers to tell Beneatha a story demonstrating that her husband shares this new attitude. At this point in the play Walter believes they can have the house and his investment in the liquor store as well. Unlike in her painfully sparse telling of her trip to the doctor earlier in the play, Ruth now provides many details:

> RUTH. You know—you know what we did last night? Me and Walter Lee?
> [. . .]We went to the movies. (*Looking at Beneatha to see if she understands*) We went to the movies. You know the last time me and Walter went to the movies together?
> BENEATHA. No.
> RUTH. Me neither. That's how long it been. (*Smiling again*) But we went last night. The picture wasn't much good but that didn't seem to matter. We went—and we held hands.
> BENEATHA. Oh Lord!
> RUTH. We held hands—and you know what?
> BENEATHA. What?
> RUTH. When we came out of the show it was late and dark and all the stores and things was closed up . . . and it was kind of chilly and there wasn't many people on the streets . . . and we was still holding hands me and Walter (111–12)

This story lets Ruth tell Beneatha, and the audience, that because things are finally right between Walter Lee and herself, she will have the baby and move forward with their lives together.

Later, however, when Mama says it is no longer possible for them to move into the house, Ruth refuses to let go of the dream that means not only a home but a new baby. She says, "I'll work . . . I'll work twenty hours a day in all the kitchens in Chicago . . . I'll strap my baby to my back if I have to and scrub all the floors in America and wash all the sheets in America if I have to—but we got to MOVE! We got to get OUT OF HERE!!" (140). Ruth's story of her pregnancy is so personal and so painful that Hansberry cannot have Ruth tell it directly. Instead, the playwright lets the story and its meaning emerge through others and through Ruth's statements about her relationship with Walter and her need for a house. This fragmented, elliptical telling creates a narrative of silences and implications, one with wider gaps for interpretation than the inevitable gaps in the stories that are told more directly. In a play filled with powerful stories, Ruth's story is one of the most affecting, perhaps because the audience is forced to piece it together, becoming in effect, co-creators of her story.

There is one more painful short story near the end of the second act, and that is the story that Bobo eventually manages to tell Walter about the loss of their money and their dreams. From his entrance, when Hansberry introduces him as *"a very slight little man in a not too prosperous business suit and with haunted frightened eyes and a hat pulled down tightly brim up, around his forehead"* (125), it is obvious that Bobo is not the bearer of good news. His frightened eyes give him away. Ruth instantly recognizes that he has something terrible to say, but Walter is at first oblivious to the truth staring him in the face and then frantic to avoid the words that Bobo is trying to force out. After a painful number of obvious delays and false starts, Bobo finally chokes out that he did not go to Springfield to arrange the agreed-upon bribes for a liquor license because Willy never showed up with the money Walter and Bobo had given him. When Walter, trying desperately to create a different ending to the story, suggests that they go looking for Willy, who may be sick or off doing something else, Bobo finally cries, "What's the matter with you, Walter! *When a cat takes off with your money he don't leave you no road maps!"* (128). At this, Walter finally breaks and acknowledges that the money is gone, saying, "I trusted you . . . Man, I put my life in your hands [. . .] THAT MONEY IS MADE OUT OF MY FATHER'S FLESH" (128). He interprets Bobo's story only in terms of what it means to him, ignoring Bobo's attempt to communicate his own loss. Ruth stands *"with her face covered with her hands"* and Beneatha *"leans forlornly against a wall"* (129), seeing the end of their individual dreams. A devastated Walter must then face his mother's fury and disappointment as she strikes him over and over and then reiterates part of the story of Big Walter, ending with "working and working like somebody's old horse . . . killing himself . . . and you—you give it all away in a day" (129). At this moment Mama can understand the content of Bobo's story only in terms of her own story, which focuses on the suffering of her husband and his sacrifices for their family. No longer do they share a story in which Big Walter's sacrifice leads to economic security for his family and the possibility of happiness for each family member. All their stories of self-identity, relationships, and dreams come together in loss at this point, and there is great potential for the characters and their dreams to irretrievably fly apart.

Act 3 begins with the conversation between Beneatha and Asagai in which Beneatha tells the story about the genesis of her plan for a medical career and her anger at having to give up that dream. Asagai responds to her cynicism by imagining his own future in Nigeria, including several ways he might die in pursuit of his desire to transform his country. In spite of the potential for violence and death, he encourages Beneatha to consider marrying him and moving to Africa with him, but Beneatha is in no condition to give his suggestion serious consideration. Instead, when Asagai exits, she turns on Walter and heaps insults on him for his dreams of financial success and his inability to fulfill them.

When Mama reenters from the bedroom, she is ready to give up on the idea of moving to Clybourne Park and questions herself and Big Walter, saying, "Me and Big Walter just didn't never learn right [. . .] Just aimed too high" (139–40). She begins to talk about making some minor improvements to the apartment, adding "Sometimes you just got to know when to give up on some things . . . and hold on to what you got" (140). At this point Walter returns and reveals that he has invited Mr. Lindner back to tell him that Walter will take him up on his offer for the house. He breaks into a parody of slave talk to show that he now believes his relationship to the white world of money and power is still that of slave and master and that the only way to survive is to lie and steal as Willie Harris has done.

Horrified, Mama retells and interprets a bit of the family story: "Son—I come from five generations of people who was slaves and sharecroppers—but ain't nobody in my family never let nobody pay 'em no money that was a way of telling us we wasn't fit to walk the earth. We ain't never been that poor. [. . .] We ain't never been that—dead inside" (143). Up until this moment, Mama has believed that, although her family may have been poor in worldly goods, they remained rich in human dignity. At this point in the play, Walter has lost all dignity. He no longer values himself at all, so he is, indeed, dead inside—as poor as a man can be. Mama senses that the only way to snap Walter back to her vision of who he really is requires him to face himself in his son's eyes. Thus, when Mr. Lindner arrives, Mama insists that Travis stay to hear what Walter will say so he can see "where our five generations done come to" (147). At this point, Walter finally discovers the story that he needs to tell. He begins, speaking as much to Travis as to Mr. Lindner, and gathers strength and conviction as the story develops:

WALTER. Well—we are very plain people . . .

LINDNER. Yes—

WALTER. I mean—I have worked as a chauffeur most of my life—and my wife here she does domestic work in people's kitchens. So does my mother. I mean—we are plain people . . . .[. . .] And—uh—well, my father, well he was a laborer most of his life . . .

LINDNER. *(Absolutely confused)* Uh, yes—yes, I understand. *(He turns back to the contract)*

WALTER. *(A beat; staring at him)* And my father—*(With sudden intensity)* My father almost *beat a man to death* once because this man called him a bad name or something you know what I mean?

LINDNER. (*Looking up, frozen*) No, no, I'm afraid I don't—

WALTER. *(A beat. The tension hangs, then WALTER steps back from it)* Yeah. Well—what I mean is that we come from people who had a lot of *pride*. I mean—we are very proud people. And that's my sister over there and she's going to be a doctor—and we are very proud—

LINDNER. Well—I am sure that is very nice, but—

WALTER. What I am telling you is that we called you over here to tell you
is that we are very proud and that this—*(Signaling to TRAVIS)* Travis,
come here. *(TRAVIS crosses and WALTER draws him before him facing
the man)* This is my son, and he makes the sixth generation of our family in this country. And we have all thought about your offer—

LINDNER. Well, good . . . good—

WALTER. And we have decided to move into our house because my father—my father—he earned it for us brick by brick [. . .] We don't want
to make no trouble for nobody or fight no causes, and we will try to be
good neighbors. And that's *all* we got to say about that. *(He looks the
man absolutely in the eyes)* We don't want your money. (147–48)

He begins with "We are plain people" so that he can justify their
need for the money and then adds the fact that his father was a laborer, something that seems totally irrelevant to Mr. Lindner. But his
father's hard physical work is part of the family story that Walter has
absorbed, and Walter is shifting into that story. The idea that Big Walter
once almost beat a man to death is new—at least it has not been mentioned elsewhere in the play—and it is an idea that clearly frightens
Mr. Lindner because it suggests that Walter, too, might be dangerous.
Walter immediately changes directions because it is not his father's
temper, but his pride, that he wants Lindner and Travis to understand.
Six generations of pride and hard work and the fact that they are not
troublemakers but good neighbors—this is the Younger family story
that Walter wants his son to understand and continue. It is the story that
Walter wants to be true for himself as well, and it finally is. In Mama
Lena's words, he has "come into his manhood" (151) and acknowledged that the love that he has for Travis and the other members of the
family and his willingness to do what is necessary to keep the family
together is what makes him a worthwhile human being. The life that
they face will definitely not be an easy one. Keeping the new house
will require every ounce of energy and luck that each member of the

family possesses, but it is a possibility, a chance for a real future. The Youngers, as individuals and as a family unit, will move ahead, creating a new chapter in the story of their struggle for survival in a hostile world.

Notes

1. All quotations from *A Raisin in the Sun* are taken from the 1994 Vintage edition. Ellipses within speeches are the author's unless placed in brackets. Italics, too, are represented as they occur in the original.
2. It is not necessary to know Gwendolyn Brooks' poem "kitchenette building" in order to appreciate the cramped and dreary nature of the Youngers' apartment, but the poem was written as a vivid counterpoint to the Langston Hughes' excerpt from "Harlem" which Hansberry drew upon for her title, and Brooks' poem complements Hansberry's depiction of kitchenette building life and the dreams of her various characters.

Works Cited

Bernstein, Robin. "Inventing a Fishbowl: White Supremacy and the Critical Reception of Lorraine Hansberry's *A Raisin in the Sun.*" *Modern Drama* 42 (1999): 16–27.

Brooks, Gwendolyn. "kitchenette building." *Selected Poems.* New York: Harper, 1963.

Bruner, Jerome. *Actual Minds, Possible Worlds.* Cambridge: Harvard UP, 1986.

Carter, Steven R. *Hansberry's Drama: Commitment amid Complexity.* Urbana: U of Illinois P, 1991.

Chatman, Seymour. *Story and Discourse.* Ithaca: Cornell UP, 1978.

Cruse, Harold. *The Crisis of the Negro Intellectual.* New York: Morrow, 1967.

Foster, Thomas C. *How to Read Literature Like a Professor.* New York: Harper, 2003.

Hansberry, Lorraine. "An Author's Reflections: Willy Loman, Walter Younger, and He Who Must Live." *The Village Voice Reader.* Garden City: Doubleday, 1962. 194–99.

_____. *A Raisin in the Sun.* New York: Vintage, 1994.

Hughes, Langston. "Harlem." *Collected Poems of Langston Hughes.* Ed. Arnold Rampersad. New York: Vintage, 1995. 426.

Mathews, Kristin L. "The Politics of 'Home' in Lorraine Hansberry's *A Raisin in the Sun.*" *Modern Drama* 51 (2008): 556–78.

M'Baye, Babacar. "Discrimination and the American Dream in Lorraine Hansberry's *A Raisin in The Sun.*" *Bloom's Literary Themes: The American Dream.* Ed. Harold Bloom. New York: Infobase, 2009. 171–86.

Nemiroff, Robert. Introduction. *A Raisin in the Sun*. By Lorraine Hansberry. New York: Vintage, 1994. 5–16.

Palmer, Alan. *Fictional Minds*. Lincoln: U of Nebraska P, 2004.

Randall, William Lowell. *The Stories We Are: An Essay on Self-Creation.* Toronto: U of Toronto P, 1995.

Washington, Charles T. "A Raisin in the Sun Revisited." *Black American Literature Forum 22* (1988): 109–24.

A Very Wild Dance Indeed: Family Systems in Henrick Ibsen's *A Doll's House*_____

Beth McFarland-Wilson and John V. Knapp

Since its premiere in Copenhagen in 1879, Henrik Ibsen's *A Doll's House* has provoked impassioned debate about the nature of the marriage relationship, the duties of a wife and mother, Nora Helmer's function and moral bearing as a character, and Ibsen's reasons for ending the play so ambiguously.[1] Many in society, and especially the church, have considered the play an open attack on marriage (Zucker 167). Other discussions have addressed the play's dramatic and thematic credibility because Nora and Torvald Helmer seem so thoroughly mismatched in marriage and because Nora undergoes an extraordinary emotional transformation in the space of a few acts (Marker and Marker 85; Durbach 16). Indeed, in act 1 she appears to be a silly, frivolous, and yet loveable woman, but by the time she walks out of and slams the door to her home in act 3, she appears to have thoroughly transformed into someone self-centered and defiant. Given the dramatic intensity of Nora's character, one well-regarded early twentieth-century scholar considered *A Doll's House* a comedy and argued that Nora would in time return to her husband, children, and home, all in keeping with conventions of the genre (Weigand 52–53).

After more than a century of debate, there seem to be few satisfying conclusions about *A Doll's House*, and primarily about Nora. She has been considered a monstrous child, a lying manipulator, an irresponsible cheat, a hysterical neurotic,[2] and a woman without principle for walking away from her husband and children[3] (Coontz 169–70). Alternately, she has been sympathetically considered a creative problem solver and a woman willing to sacrifice her own reputation for the sake of her family. Feminist scholars and proponents, even contemporary with Ibsen, have considered her a heroine and responded strongly to the diminution of her character and her womanhood (Finney; Garton 11, 48). Some critics contend that Ibsen is not writing about the women's issue at all (Meyer 266; Templeton 30–31; Neserius 35–37), while others believe that Nora's character has been reduced to a metaphor of oppression. However, speaking at the Banquet of the Norwegian League for Women's Rights on May 26, 1898, Ibsen did not claim to focus upon women's issues, but rather upon issues of humanity ("Speech" 437; Sprinchorn 337).

Of the other characters in the play, Torvald has been criticized for his ignorance of his wife's goodness to him and is described as a "boob" who has no sense of why he faces the situation he is in (Clurman 110). His authenticity and credibility as a character and good husband have been questioned, even in the earliest years of the twentieth century (Roberts); further, Torvald is despised for his harsh and hypocritical judgment of his wife, but then others have admired him for his strong sense of duty. Besides Nora and Torvald, the characters Kristine Linde, Nils Krogstad, and Dr. Rank complicate the plot of the play, and therefore the Helmer home, but seem to suffer far less notoriety than Nora and Torvald for their own vulnerabilities. Through the lens of family systems theory (FST), however, these three become essential characters, not incidental or minor ones, and paradoxically they will affirm Nora. Nora's children, undeveloped characters as they may be in and of themselves, still carry great dramatic and thematic weight both because their mother chooses to leave them and because Torvald convinces Nora that she is an inadequate mother.

Those who have discussed *A Doll's House* have long relied upon important questions to understand what has happened in Ibsen's play: What should Nora have done?[4] Was she right in doing what she did?[5] Why are Mrs. Linde, Krogstad, and Dr. Rank relevant characters? What is Ibsen telling his audiences through and beyond the play?[6] Traditional approaches to the play have helped address these questions. For example, biographical and historical approaches have helped explain Ibsen's cultural perspective in writing the play. A formal approach helps identify how specific literary and dramatic elements like plot, character, point of view, setting, irony, mood, tone, and theme help define the play's structure and meaning. Another approach, FST, can help explain how dynamic interactions within the family, either holistically, or interdependently, construct a literary work[7]; a family systems approach can also help illumine the influence of the play's structure, characters, and themes.

Considering Nora and Torvald's interactions with each other—and with other characters—from a family systems perspective can also help readers to better understand the deeper dramatic structures in *A Doll's House* and express a more coherent, truthful explanation of how and why Ibsen introduced the Helmer household, and especially Nora, to the world. This essay will show that the family system in *A Doll's House* is rich with complexities of character and situation that evoke consideration of the emotional processes, actions, and impacts of human relationship.

Just as some elements of fiction particularly stand out in a literary work—for example, irony in William Shakespeare's *Romeo and Juliet*, setting and point of view in William Faulkner's "A Rose for Emily," or theme in Ernest Hemingway's *The Old Man and the Sea*—certain dynamics of the family system get foregrounded in a given literary and/or dramatic work. In *A Doll's House*, six prominent family systems concepts are addressed—parentification, triangulation, homeostasis, transgenerational processes, differentiation, and morphogenesis. For example, the homeostatic balance[8]—the default assumptions of power and control of the Helmer family system—has relied upon Torvald's assuming the role of parent to Nora, who acts like a child and thus helps turn her husband into a kind of parent (Papero 51–60; Finney 58). Even so, Nora fundamentally influences the balance in the family because she has long hidden her secret of securing a loan without her husband's approval and of forging her father's signature on the note for the loan. As Nora protects and exploits these secrets within and beyond the Helmer family system, she will establish multiple and shifting relational triangles in an attempt to control, diminish, and redistribute the distress she feels.

Another systemic phenomenon can be seen as Ibsen incorporates the relationship between Nora and her father into the dramatic structure of the play. The relationship Nora has shared with her father reveals a powerful intergenerational influence upon the Helmer family system. When Nora realizes how her father's behavior toward her has influenced Torvald's treatment of her, and when she realizes that she has in turn treated her children the same way,[9] she sets boundaries to protect herself from a family system that is dysfunctional. This transgenerational phenomenon may be seen also in Ibsen's portrayal of Dr. Rank, who suffers ill health and ultimately death because of his own father's wantonness.

A family systems approach would suggest that when Nora makes the momentous decision to leave her husband and children, she affords herself the positive distance from her family that she needs in order to experience autonomy and maturity. However, in differentiating herself from the family's dysfunction, Nora risks all. Perhaps her willingness to do so is what audiences and critics most likely do not understand about the play or her character. Thus, Nora's final action in the play, the "door slam heard around the world" (Heiberg 208),[10] offers a focal point for discussing both the Helmer family system and the decision she makes to leave home.

Parentification and Intergenerational Influences

In the earliest actions and dialogue of the play, the family systems concept of parentification can be observed. Parentification is a dynamic in which a family member is systemically, rather than biologically, designated to fulfill a parental role. Commonly, an older child is required by a family to function emotionally as a parent to siblings. In the case of *A Doll's House*, a husband systemically behaves as a parent would to his wife instead of as a spouse.[11] Readers immediately sense this departure from the marital norm in the first scene of act 1, where Torvald speaks more like a father than a husband to Nora. His first words to his wife are "Is that my little sky-lark chirruping out there?" (*Doll's House* 1),[12] an endearment that, spoken by itself, could be considered an expression of simple affection by a husband for his wife. However, Torvald calls his wife such names repeatedly in subsequent lines, and indeed throughout the play. The excess in just the first scene of the play is notable as he calls her "my little squirrel," "the little spendthrift," "my little singing bird," and "my pretty little pet" (2–4).

From a relational point of view, and in their unusually repetitive use, Torvald's silly, childish names for his wife throughout the play do not establish her as an equal partner in the marriage; rather, they are diminutives and reveal her dependent and childish status in the family. His use of these names also reveals his inability to respond seriously to his wife (Jakovljevic 437). Even when he correctly reads Nora's guilt for sneaking macaroons, Torvald is directed by Ibsen to wag his finger at his wife as he interrogates her: "My little sweet-tooth surely didn't forget herself in town today?" (*Doll's House* 5). It is no surprise when Nora lies to him, a natural response to a simpering parental figure who dresses such an accusation in the form of a playful question.

Nora's interaction with Torvald reveals her own complicity in positioning herself emotionally as a child within the family. Just as she will through most of the play, Nora entertains Torvald as she justifies her need for money. She begs, pouts, plays with his buttons, and cajoles like a child who is determined to have what she wants. As Torvald has done to her, she has also placed her spouse in a position of inequality. Rather than interacting with him in a relationship where there is equity between two mature individuals (cf. Yarhouse and Sells 348), Nora manipulates Torvald to get what she wants. Thus, Torvald's parental treatment of Nora and her childish responses to him reveal the lack of intimate, mutually edifying interaction within their relationship. Although the relationship they share is symbiotic, it is a dysfunctional association contrasted to a healthy family system where the biological parent or legal guardian functions to nurture, protect, teach, discipline, and encourage his or her child.

Readers also need to consider how Nora's relationship with her father during her childhood influenced her present behavior. Significantly, because Nora has been treated and behaved like a doll-child in her father's home, she acts like a doll-child with Torvald. It is also significant that Nora and her husband give their daughter Emmy "a doll and doll's cot" (*Doll's House* 3) for Christmas; in this action, Emmy's parents have, in effect, passed down a significant emblem of family dysfunction. In these contexts, a clear picture is shown of how a particular role or expectation of behavior within a family is transmitted from one generation to the next.

The effect of Nora's relationship with her father can be fully felt in act 3 when she and Torvald finally sit together to discuss what has happened in their relationship. Here, Nora's sense of her father's influence upon on her is keen:

> NORA. At home, Daddy used to tell me what he thought, then I thought the same. And if I thought differently, I kept quiet about it, because he wouldn't have liked it. He used to call me his baby doll, and he played with me as I used to play with my dolls. Then I came to live in your house. . . . (80)

Astonished, Torvald asks Nora if she's ever been happy with him, and she responds:

> NORA. No, just gay. And you've always been so kind to me. But our house has never been anything but a play-room. I have been your doll wife, just as at home I was Daddy's doll child. And the children in turn have been my dolls. I thought it was fun when you came and played with me, just as they thought it was fun when I went and played with them. That's been our marriage, Torvald. (81)

When Nora realizes the generational impact that her family has had on her, and the impact that she will have on her children, she is finally able to articulate what has happened to her. Also, she is better able to decide about how to release herself from the constraints both her father and husband have placed upon her by making her their doll.

Family Secrets, and Triangulations, and Homeostatic Imbalance

Another significant influence upon the Helmer family system is Nora's secret. Toril Moi explains that Nora's secret is her substance (232). Systemically, however, it is the central point of dysfunction in the family, driving the dramatic progression of the play and the primary reason Nora has co-opted her husband to act as a parent. Further, the secret is the fundamental source of tension within the Helmer family and what draws others into the family's anxiety.

When such secrets are brought into the family system, family members interact with one another, and also with others outside the family system, without the essential information they need to participate fully and authentically within it (Knapp 18). Consequently, the secret that is kept to preserve both the appearance and the homeostatic balance of a family system can cause great dysfunction within that family. To protect her secret and maintain her family's appearance of propriety, then, Nora participates in multiple relational triangles. In doing so, she works to maintain the family's equilibrium, dysfunctional as it is.

Nora plants the secret early in her marriage. When her husband became ill and needed to move to Italy for a period of time to recover, she secured a loan. However, because a wife needed her husband's permission to take out a loan at that time (Durbach 29), because Torvald would not agree to taking out a loan himself, and because Nora knew that her husband's life was at risk, she arranged to take out a note for 4,800 crowns (kroner) with Nils Krogstad, an unscrupulous lawyer (*Doll's House* 10). This act alone was sufficient to affect the Helmer family negatively; Nora tells Kristine that it would be "terribly embarrassing and humiliating for Torvald if he thought he owed anything to me" for saving his life (15).

The greater impact of Nora's secret comes to light when Krogstad, who was willing to draft the note as long as Nora's father countersigned the loan (27), reveals to Nora that he knows of a further deception in the matter: when Nora's father died before she could get his signature, she forged it and dated the document three days after his death (27–28). Thus, Krogstad threatens to expose Nora's original deception and what he claims is her own fraudulent treatment of him if she does not use her influence to help him keep his job at the bank (28–29). Ironically, Krogstad himself had been caught forging documents when he was younger and lost his job and his reputation. Now employed in a low-level position at Torvald's bank, he knows that Torvald will be ethically and morally compromised if Nora's dishonesty is revealed. Torvald will also lose his work and reputation.

Hence, in an ironic shift of Nora's triangulation with Krogstad against Torvald, Krogstad has aligned with Torvald against Nora to achieve his own ends: "if I am pitched out a second time, you are going to keep me company" (29). Now triangulated by Krogstad through the act of blackmail, Nora stands decorating her Christmas tree, chanting: "Candles here . . . and flowers here.—Revolting man! It's all nonsense! There's nothing to worry about. We'll have a lovely Christmas tree. And I'll do anything you want me to, Torvald; I'll sing for you, dance for you. . . ." (30). In what becomes one of the most disheartening scenes in the play, it is apparent that just as Nora will ultimately sing and dance for Torvald to protect him from her secret and herself from his disapproval, Nora must sing and dance for Krogstad for the same reasons.

Nora's interactions with Kristine Linde are also dramatically and systemically important. As a foil to Nora's already strong characterization, Kristine is characterized through her own depressive, but highly rational, demeanor and dialogue. She is a widow who has moved back home and needs work. As soon as Nora shares the good news of Torvald's new position with Kristine, Kristine seizes upon the opportunity and then upon Nora's offer of help (12). When Kristine meets

Torvald, Nora manipulates the introduction sufficiently to secure the probability of Kristine's employment at the bank (20–21). This progression of the plot, which is systemically developed through the triangulation between Nora and Kristine against Torvald, becomes dramatically important because Kristine's employment at the bank will cause Krogstad to lose his position. It also creates the conflict establishing the turning point of the dramatic action, the moment when Krogstad gives Torvald the letter exposing Nora's actions. And, ultimately, it will be Kristine's pursuit of a new relationship with Krogstad that will help bring Krogstad to his senses.

Kristine's presence also allows Nora to distribute the distress she has experienced within the imbalance of her relationship with Torvald. Often, when married couples experience conflict, a third party is triangulated into the relationship to stabilize the marriage (Klever 244). Subsequently, Nora tantalizes Kristine with the "big thing" (*Doll's House* 12), her secret in her taking out a note by herself. Nora tells Kristine that "nobody must know about it [. . .] nobody but you" (13), and then she leads Kristine through a child's guessing game about how she got the money to take care of Torvald when he was so ill. In this confession, Nora renegotiates some level of psychological and emotional status in her family by proving that she could make money, that what she had done "was almost like being a man" (16). And while Nora lies to Kristine about how she got the money, she is honest and perceptive in one point: she tells Kristine that paying the money back to Krogstad has been "a lot of worry" (15). Indeed, Nora's secret is a worry that has driven the Helmer family system now for eight years.

A third significant triangulation can be identified in act 2. Just after Torvald tells Nora that he has sent Krogstad his dismissal, and as Nora psychologically spirals deeper into her fearful conflict with Krogstad and husband, Dr. Rank walks on stage. Nora welcomes her friend, who is terminally ill, only to learn of his worsening health. Even so, Nora demands that the mood of Dr. Rank's conversation should change, whereupon Dr. Rank acquiesces with banter. Nora flirts back, with humorous comments about asparagus, *paté de foie gras*, truffles, oysters, port, and champagne—all sensual, seductive foods. Seductively taunting the doctor with her silk stockings (Durbach 46–47), Nora tells him that she will dance for him—and her husband (*Doll's House* 47).

When Nora then intimates that she needs something from Dr. Rank, he tells her that he is in love with her, keeping a promise to himself that she should know of his love before he dies. Just as Krogstad has reversed a triangle Nora constructed with him against Torvald, Dr. Rank reverses the triangle Nora engineered with him against her husband. In response to his revelation, Nora authentically responds, "Oh, my dear Dr. Rank, that really was rather horrid of you" (49). She has realized that Dr. Rank cannot help her and understands that she is now very much on her own. Her words reveal her disappointment, confusion, and sense of loss: "Oh, how could you be so clumsy, Doctor Rank! When everything was so nice!" (49). Her words also reflect her own clumsiness and regret both about her conduct toward him and the impending changes in her own life (Meyer 49–50).

Differentiation and Morphogenesis

Ibsen was sensitive to the possibility of positive change in the Helmer family. At the same time that the playwright recognized his individual character's need for freedom, he did not forget that the individual was a part of society (Hageberg 15–16; *Cambridge Companion* 76). Ibsen also intensely focused his writing upon ideas of individual freedom and human will (Jacobs 425). From a family systems perspective, it is understood that neither an individual nor a family can enjoy optimal freedom or expression of will within the constraints of a dysfunctional family system. However, through the process of differentiating from such a system, an individual gains the opportunity to search for his or her authentic self. This process, called morphogenesis, occurs when an individual changes the way he or she functions within a family system to achieve freedom from that system's dysfunctionality. Through morphogenesis, an individual and a family may pursue systemic change despite the difficulty of the process, and that individual and family have a greater chance of becoming more functional (Napier and Whitaker 184).

The seduction scene between Nora and Dr. Rank, then, stands as a psychological turning point in Nora's life. In professing his love for Nora, in claiming that she can trust him in a way she can trust no one else, and in offering to do for her whatever a man can do, Dr. Rank has sounded the death knell of Nora's willingness to continue in her role as the family doll. By this time, Nora has become emotionally aware of the entanglements she has participated in with the men in her house—her father, her husband, Dr. Rank, and even Krogstad—and from this point on, she will begin to assert her independence from them all.

Over the next several scenes, and because of her desperation, Nora even considers suicide to free herself from suffering once the secret is exposed, at least until she realizes that there is another option. To keep her husband from discovering her secret, she begs him to play the tarantella for her on the piano so that she can practice and then dances "as though [her] life depended on it" (59). Her hair is wild, her actions are wild, and her soul is on display (Moi 238). Thus, the dance may be seen as a reflection of the distress of Nora's soul, the disarray and dysfunction of the Helmer family,[13] and Nora's need to free herself from it.

Her need for freedom is fully revealed when Torvald finally retrieves Krogstad's letter from the mailbox and also Dr. Rank's cards. When Nora explains the meaning of Dr. Rank's cards, Torvald declares, "Now there's just the two of us" (*Doll's House* 74). That statement ultimately motivates Nora to act against the dysfunction of which she is now fully aware. Thus, when Torvald tells her that he will never be able to hold his darling wife close enough (74), Nora "[*tears herself free and says firmly and decisively*] Now you must read your letters, Torvald" (74). Upon reading Krogstad's letter, Torvald, like Nora, dances:

HELMER. (*walking up and down.*) Oh, what a terrible awakening this is. All these eight years . . . this woman who was my pride and joy . . . a hypocrite, a liar, worse than that, a criminal! Oh, how utterly squalid it all is! (75)

And just as Nora has been frantic to cover up her secret, Torvald demands that "the thing has to be hushed up at all costs" so that "things must appear to go on exactly as before" (76). Indeed, once change occurs in a system, the first response by many is, all too often, to change back to maintain homeostasis.

Paradoxically, the secret that has kept Nora entangled within her family system is what will release her from it. As soon as Torvald verbally attacks her, Nora is fully able to articulate her father's and her husband's limiting influence upon her. She calls Torvald to sit down at the table and talk with her, something they have never done in their marriage: "We have now been married eight years. Hasn't it struck you this is the first time you and I, man and wife, have had a serious talk together?" (79). When she comes to realize that she and her husband have never shared a truly equitable marital relationship, that Torvald has wanted only to preserve his honor, Nora understands that she is not the wife for him: "When you had got over your fright—and you weren't concerned about me but only about what might happen to you—and when all danger was past, you acted as though nothing had happened. I was your little sky-lark again, your little doll, exactly as before" (84). Soon thereafter, she leaves, slamming the door.

Audiences can only speculate about whether or not Nora will return to her family. Certainly the cultural and legal constraints of the time could have placed her in a double bind and kept her from any opportunity to free herself from her husband. Both her conduct and the action of divorce would have been scandalous and resisted by the community and the law. But contemporary critics dismissing this possibility as a kind of presentism, or an anachronistic approach to the text, should note that social mores and legal practices regarding divorce and separation were also actively in flux at the time Ibsen wrote the play. In 1883, Theodore Woolsey and John A. Jameson described the variety of legal considerations and treatments of divorce that were debated throughout America and Europe at the time. Woolsey, writing separately, specifically reported that separations and divorces were on the increase in populations throughout America and Europe as marriages were declining. In either case, he attributed these phenomena to the decline of morality in the community (310–11). Further, Jameson, again separately, pointed out that one of the reasons immigrants from Europe, including Scandinavia, came to the United States was to seek a divorce where it was easier to dissolve a marriage. In coming to America, these individuals could preserve their social and business integrity, which would have been suspect had they pursued divorce in their countries of origin (320). Jameson then reported that because of the social consequences, couples who were quite well-off rarely divorced (320). Finally, he explained that many divorces resulted when a wife or husband in a poorer home became tired of the marriage and simply left. In these instances, the wife would take what she could materially and the husband would take what he could monetarily, and neither would return (320). Lawrence Stone, discussing divorce reform between 1857 and 1987, identifies the shift of opinion on divorce and separation that took place during the last half of the nineteenth century as a result of people's and the court's recognition that some marriages were "disastrously failed" and that equitable legal remedy was needed even for cases of incompatibility (391). That remedy would come in the Royal Commission of 1912 (392). Hence, *A Doll's House* reflects Ibsen's awareness that marriages were not only devastated by infidelity, but also by a couple's inability to establish a mutually satisfying marital relationship.

From what Woolsey and Jameson report, Torvald Helmer could have had grounds for separation or possibly divorce, but, unless she left the country, Nora would have had no legal remedy at the time for her distress within the marriage. Thus, readers are still unable to determine what Nora would have done. She was neither poor nor rich. She was independent enough to desire new experiences, and she left asking nothing from the marital estate. Clearly, Nora's strength in refusing to participate in the Helmer family system gives readers reason to believe that she would not return to the family as it was. But just as clearly, Torvald has sat down and talked with her.

Conclusion

Henrik Ibsen's *A Doll's House* illuminates how individuals in a family system work within and against relationships as they try to establish, preserve, or limit power and prominence in a family. Specifically, the play dramatizes a woman's recognition of the emotionally limiting boundaries of her own family system and her willingness to move beyond it. Nora Helmer's desire to resist, and even walk out of, the position she has assumed within her family, as well as her ability to resist her husband's and father's limiting influences upon her, exemplify the dynamics of a family system in which one of its members becomes unwilling to tolerate its systemic forces.[14] Because Nora lived during an age that considered marrying only for love and happiness wrong-minded, marriage was often considered a familial and corporate obligation. People feared that if a marriage were based in love rather than family and gender roles, then a couple would have every reason to separate if the love was not sustained (Coontz 174–75). Throughout the play, then, Nora's actions reveal her attempts to recalibrate the unlivable imbalance in her relationship with her husband and family to find some measure of freedom in living. In doing so, she resists the Helmer family system to the point that even Torvald is freed enough to consider the need for change.

A Doll's House shook European society in 1879 when it was first performed in Copenhagen. The play and its slammed door continue to shake even contemporary sensibilities. While there has been a sea change in regard to the cultural concept of marriage since this play was first performed, there is something still commonly held to be sacred about the relationship between a woman and her young children. But

Nora needed to leave.[15] She desired a marriage based in mutual respect and emotional intimacy between equal individuals, not convenience or utilitarian purposes, in her relationships with Torvald and her family. Given the constraints of her society, her final action may be argued by some as more genuine and moral than if she had stayed in the home and passively participated in, or resented, the destructiveness of the Helmer family system. Nora's action, fully removed from the sentimental, comic ending Ibsen's contemporary audience desired, allows her to remove herself from damaging social forces that inhibited her personal freedom (Lord 59) and would affect her children. Like other Ibsen characters, Nora is "destroyed [as she affirms] something special about the potential of the human spirit" (Northam 226).

From a systemic view, Nora's ability to differentiate herself from the Helmer family system affords her at least the possibility of reestablishing a functioning marital relationship with her husband and becoming her children's psychological mother, rather than their emotional sibling. David Gaunt and Louise Nyström note that because of the changing Nordic society at that time, some "people hoped that the traditional bonds uniting husbands and wives, parents and children, would disappear to allow the whole person to flourish" (485). But the authors also note that "the family is not a thing but a network of human relations, which survive even when their forms change" (486). With Nora's departure and Torvald's willingness to acknowledge his wife's influence upon him, Ibsen offers his audiences some small hope. In fact, a family systems perspective would suggest that, for the Helmers and the play, Nora's departure is the turning point.[16] Paradoxically, when an individual rejects his or her role in the family system, as Nora has done in refusing to be or perpetuate the role of the family doll (Thomas 72), a family has already gained a potential for functioning more effectively. Thus, while FST cannot finally put Nora back into her home,[17] it can help illuminate why she felt compelled to leave it, and it can suggest that the hope Ibsen incorporates in his stage directions to Torvald just before Nora slams the door is not empty.

Notes

1. See Archer 212; Meyer 263–68; Rosenberg and Templeton; Templeton; Marker and Marker; and especially Durbach 13–23. Importantly, the woman about whom Ibsen developed his idea for *A Doll's House*, Laura Kieler, was most unhappy that he had written about her life, even though his play vindicated her actions on behalf of her husband (Meyer 266).

2. See Showalter 5; Kaufmann 237; and Finney 98.

3. See McCarthy; Crawford; and Zucker.

4. See Roberts.

5. See Lee.

6. See Shaw; Hageberg; and Lee.

7. See Knapp, *Striking*; and Knapp and Womack.

8. In FST, homeostasis is the systemic dynamic by which a family preserves its patterns of behavior. When the family undergoes change, its members may not adapt to the change (negative feedback loop); consequently, the family system functions less efficiently and effectively. If members of the family are willing to make changes to accommodate change (positive feedback loop), the family system functions more efficiently and effectively.

9. Yarhouse and Sells provide a helpful summary of the Bowenian Family Therapy approach, which places significant emphasis on understanding the generational influences of the family. Specifically, they refer to Murray Bowen's study of the intergenerational influences of alcoholism, in which Bowen explains how anxiety in a family influences a family member's drinking. Theodore Jorgenson explains that Ibsen understood that "hereditary implications and the restrictions of a mass society seemed to drive every man and woman into the herd" (347). George B. Bryan, in *An Ibsen Companion: A Dictionary-Guide to the Life, Works, and Critical Reception of Henrik Ibsen,* also notes the significance of "heredity and environment as determinants of character" (79).

10. When *A Doll's House* was first performed in 1879, the audience's shock at Nora's leaving was so great that her slamming the door was described as "the door slam heard around the world."

11. Phillip Klever explains that individuals can be extraordinarily immature in marriage and develop patterns that distress a relationship. In addition to acting immaturely, these individuals will often triangulate with others to alleviate their distress (243), i.e., as Nora has done with her friends, Kristine and Dr. Rank. In this immaturity and social expectation, we find irony in that Torvald is as self-centered as Nora is accused of being by her audiences. Ronald Gray points out that Torvald's conduct helps justify Nora's departure (58).

12. While a number of translated texts may be used reliably to cite lines and passages from *A Doll's House*, including those by Archer (authorized translation), Fjelde, Le Galienne, McFarlane, Meyer, and Watts, this essay uses the 1998 McFarlane and Arup translation of the play found in the Oxford World's Classics

Four Major Plays. For direction in this matter, we referred to Egil Törnqvist's bibliography in *Ibsen: A Doll's House* (196) and then noted McFarlane and Arup's collaboration in revising McFarlane's earlier translation.

13. John V. Knapp reiterates the metaphor of the family dance in *Reading the Family Dance* as he defines and describes the dynamics of the family system (1–25). Also, Durbach explains that the impact of the Norwegian words expressing Nora's curse in front of Kristine and Dr. Rank (*Doll's House* 20), *død og pine*, the death and pain she felt in her home, were dramatically translated through her dance (Durbach 38).

Stephanie Coontz explains that when Ibsen was writing *A Doll's House*, cultural change was occurring, even if it was not of a large scale; marriage was being reconsidered as a relationship of intimacy and satisfaction, not a relationship of domination and submission (182). However, Coontz notes that the voice of this change was "well published" (183), and when we consider that Ibsen was a significant voice for this change, we understand that Nora reflected it.

Coontz also explains that in the early nineteenth century, and against the consideration of women's rights that had made strides in the late eighteenth century, a cultural return to a focus upon women's domesticity and moral position within the family characterized European society (162–65). By the late nineteenth century, the family in Europe and the United States had become so exclusive that it removed itself from the community (167). Paradoxically, the harm of such exclusiveness pervades Nora's thinking and behavior. When she dances the tarantella, she wants to be seen, and her sensuality is expressed in her dance though not consummated, given Torvald's commitment to maintaining her as a child. Also by this time, if an engaged or married woman participated in intimate behavior that others considered improper, she would have no opportunity to recover herself into respectable social standing (169). While Nora unfairly and thoughtlessly flirts with Dr. Rank for a moment, she ultimately declines his advances and his declaration of love.

14. John Gottman et al., in their study of marital happiness and stability in newlyweds, explain that when husbands refuse to share power with their wives and also refuse their wives' influence, the marriage is more likely to be unhappy. The men who are willing to be influenced by their wives, on the other hand, are more likely to live in happy and stable marriages (18).

15. In writing this play, Ibsen did not seek to give individuals an excuse for divorce. In one instance, a woman who had left her husband for another man approached the playwright to tell him that she had done what Nora had done. Ibsen reminded her that his "Nora went alone" (Meyer 471).

16. This ambivalence is in keeping with Ibsen's ability to impose a sense of contradiction and opposition, or *tvertimod*, into what he wrote (Durbach 6).

17. Ibsen wrote a second ending to *A Doll's House* that kept Nora in the home; however, the play with this ending did not run for very long (Meyer 266–70; *Ibsen: Letters and Speeches* 183–84, 301; *Letters* 325–26).

Works Cited

Archer, William. "*A Doll's House.*" Ed. Thomas Postlewait. *William Archer on Ibsen: The Major Essays, 1889–1919.* Westport: Greenwood, 1984.

Bowen, Murray. "Alcoholism as Viewed through Family Systems Theory and Family Psychotherapy." *Annals of the New York Academy of Sciences* 233 (1974): 115–22.

Bryan, George B. *An Ibsen Companion: A Dictionary-Guide to the Life, Works, and Critical Reception of Henrik Ibsen.* Westport: Greenwood, 1984.

Cambridge Companion to Ibsen. Ed. James McFarlane. Cambridge: Cambridge UP, 1994.

Clurman, Harold. *Ibsen.* New York: Macmillan, 1977.

Contemporary Approaches to Ibsen: Proceedings of the Second International Ibsen Seminary. Oslo: Universitetsforlaget, 1970.

Contemporary Approaches to Ibsen: Reports from the Fourth International Ibsen Seminar. Vol. IV. Oslo: Universitetsforlaget, 1978.

Coontz, Stephanie. *Marriage, a History: From Obedience to Intimacy or How Love Conquered Marriage.* New York: Penguin, 2005.

Crawford, Oswald. "The Ibsen Question." *Fortnightly Review* 55 (1891): 727–40.

Durbach, Errol. *A Doll's House: Ibsen's Myth of Transformation.* Boston: Twayne, 1991.

Finney, Gail. "Ibsen and Feminism." *Cambridge Companion to Ibsen.* Ed. James McFarlane. Cambridge: Cambridge UP, 1994.

Garton, Janet. *Norwegian Women's Writing: 1850–1990.* London: Athlone, 1993.

Gaunt, David, and Louise Nyström. "The Scandinavian Model." *A History of the Family.* Vol. II: The Impact of Modernity. Eds. André Burguiçre, Christian Klapisch-Zuber, Martine Segalen, and Françoise Zonaben. Trans. Sarah Hanbury Tenison. Cambridge: Harvard UP, 1996. 476–501.

Gottman, John M., James Coan, Sybil Carrere, and Catherine Swanson. "Predicting Marital Happiness and Stability from Newlywed Interactions." *Journal of Family and Marriage* 60.1 (1998): 5–22.

Gray, Ronald. *Ibsen: A Dissenting View: A Study of the Last Twelve Plays.* London: Cambridge UP, 1977.

Heiberg, Hans. *Ibsen: A Portrait of the Artist.* Trans. Joan Tate. London: George Allen and Unwin, 1969.

Ibsen, Henrik. *A Doll's House. The Oxford Ibsen.* Vol. 5. Trans. and ed. James W. McFarlane. London: Oxford UP, 1961.

_____. *A Doll's House and Other Plays.* Trans. Peter Watts. New York: Penguin, 1965.

_____. *Complete Major Prose Plays.* Trans. Rolf Fjelde. New York: NAL-Dutton, 1978.

_____. *Four Major Plays.* Trans. James W. McFarlane and Jens Arup. New York: Oxford UP, 1998.

_____. *The League of Youth: The Pillars of Society: A Doll's House.* Ed. William Archer. 3rd ed. London: Walter Scott, 1904.

_____. Letters of Henrik Ibsen. Trans. John Nilson Laurik and Mary Morison. New York: Duffield, 1908.

_____. *Plays*. Trans. Michael Meyer. London: Methuen, 1990.

_____. "Speech at the Banquet of the Norwegian League for Women's Rights *Ibsen's Selected Plays*. Ed. Brian Johnston. New York: Norton, 2004. 437.

Jacobs, Elizabeth. "Henrik Ibsen and the Doctrine of Self-Realization." *The Journal of English and Germanic Philology* 38.3 (1939): 416–30.

Jakovljevic, Branislav. "Shattered Back Wall: Performative Utterance of *A Doll's House*. 54.3 (2002): 431–38.

Jorgenson, Theodore. *Henrik Ibsen: Life and Drama*. Northfield: St. Olaf Norwegian Inst., 1963.

Kaufmann, F. W. "Ibsen's Search for the Authentic Self." *Monatshefte* 45.4 (1953): 232–39.

Klever, Phillip. "Triangles in Marriage." *Triangles: Bowen Family Systems Theory Perspectives*. Ed. Peter Titleman. New York: Haworth P, 2008. 243–64.

Knapp, John V. "Family Systems Therapy and Literary Study: An Introduction." Ed. John V. Knapp and Kenneth Womack. *Reading the Family Dance: Family Systems and Literary Study*. Newark: U of Delaware P, 2003. 13–26.

_____. *Striking at the Joints: Contemporary Psychology and Literary Criticism*. Lanham: UP of America, 1996.

Knapp, John V., and Kenneth Womack, eds. *Reading the Family Dance: Family Systems and Literary Study*. Newark: U of Delaware P, 2003.

Lee, Jennette. *The Ibsen Secret*. New York: Putnam's, 1907.

Le Galienne, Eva, trans. *Six Plays by Henrik Ibsen*. New York: Random, 1957.

Lord, Henrietta Frances. "Henrietta Frances Lord on *A Doll's House*." *Ibsen: The Critical Heritage*. Ed. Michael Egan. London: Routledge, 1972. 59.

Marker, Frederick, and Lise-Lone Marker. "The First Nora: Notes on the World Premiere of *A Doll's House*." *Contemporary Approaches to Ibsen: Proceedings of the Second International Ibsen Seminary*. Oslo: Universitetsforlaget, 1970. 84–100.

_____. *Ibsen: A Biography*. New York: Doubleday, 1971.

McCarthy, Mary. "The Will and Testament of Ibsen." *Partisan Review* 23 (1956): 74–80.

McFarlane, James Walter, ed. and trans. *The Oxford Ibsen*. Vol. 5. London: Oxford UP, 1961.

Meyer, Michael. *Henrik Ibsen: A Farewell to Poetry*. London: Hart-Davis, 1971.

Moi, Toril. *Henrik Ibsen and the Birth of Modernism: Art Theater, Philosophy*. Oxford: Oxford UP, 2006.

Napier, Augustus Y., and Carl Whitaker. *The Family Crucible: The Intense Experience of Family Therapy*. New York: Harper, 1978.

Neserius, Philip George. "Ibsen's Political and Social Ideas." *The American Political Science Review* 19.1 (1925): 25–37.

Northam, John. *Ibsen: A Critical Study*. London: Cambridge UP, 1973.

The Oxford Ibsen. Ed. James W. McFarlane. Vol. V. London: Oxford UP, 1961.

Papero, Daniel V. *Bowen Family Systems Theory*. Boston: Allyn, 1990.

Postlewait. Thomas, ed. *William Archer on Ibsen: The Major Essays, 1889–1919*. Westport: Greenwood, 1984.

Roberts, R. Ellis. *Henrik Ibsen: A Critical Study*. London: Secker, 1912.

Rosenberg, Marvin, and Joan Templeton. "Ibsen's Nora." *PMLA* 104.5 (1989): 894–96.

Shaw, Bernard. *The Quintessence of Ibsenism*. New York: Hill, 1913/1958.

Showalter, Elaine. *The Female Malady: Women, Madness, and English Culture*. New York: Pantheon, 1985.

Sprinchorn, Evert, ed. *Ibsen: Letters and Speeches*. New York: Hill, 1964.

Stone, Lawrence. *Road to Divorce: England 1530–1987*. Oxford: Oxford UP, 1990.

Templeton, Joan. "The *Doll's House* Backlash: Criticism, Feminism, and Ibsen." *PMLA* 104.1 (1989): 28–40.

Thomas, David. *Henrik Ibsen*. London: Macmillan, 1983.

Titleman, Peter, ed. *Triangles: Bowen Family Systems Theory Perspectives*. New York: Haworth, 2008.

Törnqvist, Egil. *Ibsen: A Doll's House*. New York: Cambridge UP, 1995.

Weigand, Hermann J. *The Modern Ibsen: A Reconsideration*. New York: Holt, 1925.

Woolsey, Theodore, and John A. Jameson. "Divorce." *The North American Review* 136.317 (1883): 305–25.

Yarhouse, Mark A., and James N. Sells. *Family Therapies: A Comprehensive Christian Appraisal*. Downers Grove: InterVarsity, 2008.

Zucker, A. E. *Ibsen: The Master Builder*. New York: Henry Holt, 1929.

Robert Frost and the Absent Child: Valuing Loss in "Home Burial" and "The Death of the Hired Man"_____

James Postema

Many people know Robert Frost's poetry, but few readers know he was a battered child. Growing up in San Francisco, he suffered both physical and emotional abuse, lived with fear and uncertainty, and had no stable structure in his home. While these experiences would hurt him for the rest of his life, they also helped him become one of America's most profound and beloved poets. Still, they caused enough pain that Frost had to find a way to re-value himself as a child, which he did by considering what it means to lose a child.

Unsound Parenting

Robert Frost's father, William Prescott Frost Jr., was an alcoholic who could explode violently at any time, especially when drinking. One time Will Frost whipped young Robbie's legs repeatedly with a dog-chain (Thompson 24). On several occasions Robert's mother, Isabelle Moodie Frost, took her son and fled the house; things were so bad that when Robbie was two years old, Belle Frost decided to leave her husband, fleeing across the country, first to Massachusetts and then to relatives in Ohio. She did go back to San Francisco, but only with a friend whose presence in the Frost household might serve as a buffer against Will Frost's violence (15, 33). Still, biographer Lawrance Thompson writes that Robbie and his sister Jeanie "were nurtured on fear; they drank it with the mother's milk" (10–11, 18).

Partly to compensate for their father's violence, Belle Frost "smothered" Robbie and Jeanie with love, indulging them to excess (18). Robert was always extremely and painfully sensitive as a child, possibly a result of living in constant anxiety. Yet when stomach pains (conveniently) flared up whenever he was asked to go to school, Isabelle gave in to her son's complaints and kept him home, where she home-schooled both children (21). William died of tuberculosis in 1885 and

Belle Frost was left to care for the children on her own. She had only $8 to her name, and so William Frost's parents paid for her and the children to move east to Massachusetts ("Chronology" 931). Robert was told that now he was "the man of the family" (Thompson 48).

Such an upbringing would have significant effects on any child's life. According to experts in child development, the quality of a child's early home life can greatly influence his or her future: "Because of the continuity between early experiences and subsequent relationship expectations, child maltreatment can exert a devastating impact on the quality of relationships across the life course" (Toth, Pickreign, and Gravener). Indeed, according to Janet Geringer Woititz, sometimes an alcoholic and abusive household can rob a person of any true childhood: she asks the rhetorical question, "When is a child not a child? When the child lives with alcoholism" (1). In her widely read book, *Adult Children of Alcoholics*, Woititz reports that people suffering the effects of a toxic childhood have repeatedly told her that, although they looked like children to other people, they were not as lighthearted or spontaneous as other children: "Whatever others saw and said, the fact remains that you didn't really feel like a child" (1).

While readers cannot "diagnose" any specific adult problems that Robert Frost had, it is nevertheless true that both his and Jeanie's lives followed a pattern consistent with those of other abused children of alcoholics. Woititz has created a list of thirteen patterns that show up repeatedly in her treatments of adults who survived alcohol-driven abuse as children. Most statements in her list would accurately describe Robert Frost's life. He could be incredibly harsh on himself and always needed approval from others; he had "difficulty with intimate relationships"; he could feel guilty for things he did not cause, but could also act irresponsibly or impulsively; Woititz says that children of alcoholics "tend to lock themselves into a course of action without giving serious consideration to alternative behaviors or possible consequences. This impulsivity leads to confusion, self-loathing and loss of control over their environment" (xix).

One particular event illustrates most of these characteristics. Robert Frost was often insecure about many things, especially his relationship with his fiancée, Elinor White. In 1894, when Elinor was away at Saint Lawrence University, Frost was overtaken by fear and jealousy, thinking that she was paying attention to other men, even though she had promised to marry him. Robert rushed to Canton, New York, and demanded to talk with her. However, rather than receiving him with romantic joy, Elinor told him to go home—in part because he was breaking college rules about men visiting women (Thompson 175–76). Stunned by what he saw as rejection from Elinor, Robert decided he would flee to Virginia's Dismal Swamp, where he would die from a broken heart, causing Elinor to regret her actions forever. And in fact he did make his way to Virginia and tromped off into the swamp, but after stumbling through wetlands for hours he finally asked a group of duck hunters for a ride out. Frost eventually had to write his mother for money to pay his way home (Thompson 176–88).

Though this whole episode is a bit surreal in how improbable it seems, that is exactly the point: though extreme, it does reflect Frost's patterns of harsh self-judgment, depression, insecurity, and sometimes rash actions. In fact, in Frost's life as a whole, almost all of the behavioral patterns that Woititz associates with children of alcoholics are present. While he was often genial, and he seems to have been a good father (Francis 257), Frost would suffer much, and sometimes he would cause others to suffer; it seems reasonable to conclude that his rough childhood had something to do with these patterns.

Sensitivity to Sound

But Frost's adult problems are only one legacy of his childhood. Thompson thoroughly documented Frost's personal issues (perhaps too thoroughly), but Thompson himself observed, "the simple fact remains: Frost was a neurotic, most of his life, *and* he did make some extremely useful demands on his own fantasies for purposes of creating literary art" (qtd. in Sheehy 403; emphasis added).

His mother's influence was crucial: while Isabelle Frost had her weaknesses as a parent, she did fire Robert and Jeanie's imaginations by reading and telling romantic stories to them. Frost's love for literature started there. And Frost's father, despite his faults, passed on to his son a remarkable way with words: William Frost had made his living as a writer, and while most of what he wrote was hack journalism, he could be eloquent and persuasive when he wished. He used these skills, in fact, to convince Isabelle Moodie to marry him, despite her serious (and justified) qualms (Thompson 4–5).

So some of Frost's skills were genetic, but other aspects of his early family life also have intriguing correlations to his poetic career, some of them directly related to his abuse. According to Woititz, children of alcoholic parents often have to "guess at what normal behavior is" (xix). They can never be sure that what they are doing is right because they have been punished too many times for incomprehensible reasons. The flip side of this uncertainty and insecurity, however, is that Frost as a writer was not accustomed to making pat judgments about situations, which in turn helped him observe people's behaviors closely and insightfully. As Mark Richardson writes, "Persistent insecurities bred in him a certain tentativeness, which in turn kept him from ever becoming dogmatic, defensive, or especially contentious about being a poet in America" (Richardson).

One other aspect of Frost's abused childhood is significant for the nature of his poetry—an awareness of sound and voice. Any battered child has to be very alert to what is going on with his or her parents, and must be able to read nuances in voice and gesture that might signal an ensuing explosion. Robert Frost has always been famous for that kind of sensitivity, and in turn for his ability to reproduce natural-sounding speech; even when he is using quite rigorous meters and rhyme schemes, his poems do not become sing-songy, but rather have a clear and natural voice. Indeed, one of his most important contributions to contemporary poetry was an awareness of language that he called "the sound of sense," which he explained using the analogy of "voices behind a door that cuts off the words" (Frost 664). To further illustrate this concept, in a letter to former student John T. Bartlett, Frost wrote a few lines from seemingly mundane conversations, saying,

> Ask yourself how these sentences would sound without the words in which they are embodied:
>> You mean to tell me you can't read?
>> I said no such thing.
>> Well read then.
>> You're not my teacher. (Frost 664–65)

He went on to say, "The reader must be at no loss to give his voice the posture proper to the sentence": the language that comes through in the poem must sound like it comes straight out of readers' own everyday experiences. Frost's poems grew out of the inflections he heard around him, with "an ear and an appetite for these sounds of sense" (665). In his adult life, the sounds he heard were New England voices, and he became famous as "the New England poet." But he first began listening to that "sound of sense" in San Francisco, as a battered child.

Missing Children

Especially given Frost's own childhood context, it is interesting to note that there are almost no children in his poetry—among hundreds of poems by Frost, perhaps a handful contain realistic portrayals of a child, and in most of those poems the child's role is minimal. Even the most famous poem involving childhood, "Birches," does not actually portray a real boy so much as the memories of an older man about one childhood activity. In this poem, as in others, Frost more typically writes about elements of childhood rather than actual children. And even though adult couples, typically married, appear again and again in Frost's work, they rarely have children present, nor do the couples' activities or discussions usually involve even the suggestion of a family. The children just are not there.[1]

However, two of Frost's more famous poems involve couples dealing with the absence of a child: "Home Burial" presents a couple trying to cope with the recent death of an infant son, while "The Death of the Hired Man" features a husband and wife who have taken a hapless old man into their family, somewhat in the role of a child. Each poem appeared in Frost's second book, *North of Boston* (1914), which uses several dramatic dialogues to explore the sound of sense in many different voices. In these poems, readers hear and see a single scene in the lives of the poems' characters, moments that are isolated and held up for examination. The audience can often learn indirectly about the characters' lives, based on what they say. But in those isolated scenes, readers must rely most heavily on the characters' voices—how the men and women speak about their relationships, and what they do while they're speaking. While both poems have semi-omniscient narrators, the narration is minimal: its purpose is to provide a framework for the couples' voices of the characters who live the scenes out loud.

This dramatic structure has particularly interesting implications if viewed in the context of the lives of battered children, for the poems give readers an experience that is somewhat parallel to the moment-to-moment life of a child in an abusive relationship. Battered children cannot possibly understand their overall family situation, so for their very survival they must read the nuances of their situation in any given moment, to predict what might be coming at them. While obviously the stakes are not as high, readers of dramatic dialogues must also rely on the nuances of voice and scene as they listen to both speakers, trying to understand what is going on.

Further, when considering the idea that Robert Frost did not have a childhood, the dramatic structure of each of these poems can embody a kind of psychological drama. One could argue that in these poems Frost is exploring the implications of his own lost childhood indirectly, after the fact and from the points of view of parental figures. The couples in "Home Burial" and "The Death of the Hired Man" did have "children"—in the past tense—whose earlier presence underscores their current absence. Although the child figure in each poem was perhaps taken for granted while alive, neither seen nor understood nor valued fully, his absence now helps parents understand what it meant to have him present. Frost can thus use this structure to explore what his own childhood presence or absence might have meant to his parents, particularly his father. By constructing scenes in which a child's loss is significant to his parents, perhaps Frost can recoup some of what was valuable about himself in his parents' eyes—and thus his own. It is a desperate attempt—but then, Frost's early life was also desperate.

The Unhappy Couple: "Home Burial"

In "Home Burial" the parents feel the loss of their child deeply. This poem reveals an argument between a husband and wife that takes place relatively soon after the death of their first child. Each parent is grieving, though they grieve in different ways, and neither can let him- or herself understand the other's way. Their perspectives are mutually incompatible, so they conflict with each other, and as a result neither husband nor wife can alleviate their joint grief. The absence of the child, and their reactions to the loss, set up an extraordinarily precise and symmetrical balancing of opposing forces in their marriage.

It seems the husband tried to work out his pain using forceful activity: the wife says that he made "the gravel leap and leap in air" (Frost line 79) as he dug his own child's grave. The intensity of his actions suggests an intensity of feeling in his grief. He may also be immersing himself in mundane chores as a way to avoid thinking about the loss—again, the wife notes that very soon after digging the grave, he was talking with a neighbor about birch fences. For the husband, talking provides relief from emotional pain.

For her part Amy, the wife, is repeatedly drawn to a stairwell window, where she stands gazing at the grave of her son. She does not use words to express herself—at least, not to her husband. She has apparently found consolation with someone outside their home, perhaps a sister or friend. It is unclear whether she talks with others, but it is clear that at least in the home she does not want to speak about her loss. When the husband realizes—and says—what she is looking at, she uses a single repeated word to try to silence him: " 'Don't, don't, don't, don't,' she cried." (32). Then she physically distances herself from the husband: "She withdrew shrinking from beneath his arm" (33). Distance is her way to alleviate the pain of her loss, leaving the scene of the child's life.

Amy seems to be practiced at putting space between herself and her husband, for an unfortunate reason that he himself acknowledges indirectly. As he is imploring her not to leave, he says, "Listen to me. I won't come down the stairs" (42), but the next line notes that his hands have formed fists. In fact, he does not move from that position throughout the poem, but at the end threatens to do so: if she leaves, he says, "I'll follow and bring you back by force. I *will!*—" (120). Force is the mode he used when digging the child's grave, and it seems that sometimes he has resorted to force when talking with his wife.

Unlike the stereotypical wife-beater, however, the husband seems to be quite savvy about what their relationship needs. He asks his wife to share her grief with him in words: "Tell me about it . . . . / Let me into your grief" (61–62). He even asks her to help him how to talk with her: "My words are nearly always an offense. / I don't know how to speak of anything / So as to please you. But I might be taught" (48–50). In these requests, the husband is making what psychologist John M. Gottman calls "repair attempts," seeking to repair the damage that grief has caused in their relationship (39).

The problem is that the wife simply does not trust speech. She repeatedly discredits her husband's very right to talk about their dead child: "You can't because you don't know how to speak," she retorts (75), and she expands this negation to include all men: "I don't know rightly whether any man can" (40). She interprets his casual conversation about that birch fence as a sign that he cannot truly care about the baby's death. Ironically, Amy uses speech to avoid speech, a pattern that is self-defeating for her and that puts her husband in a double-bind: if he does not speak with her, they will remain isolated, but if he tries to speak she shoots him down, ensuring that their isolation will continue. One wonders if the husband's words "are nearly always an offense" not because of what he's saying, or how, but because he is the one speaking to her—through neither his fault nor her own, necessarily, speaking with him is just too painful for her.

Still, his demand to know what is happening does provoke a conversation in which both the husband and the wife reveal that they are using different bases for their modes of grieving. The husband believes that if they love each other, they can work through anything. He wonders why she is taking her "mother-loss of a first child / So inconsolably—in the face of love. / You'd think his memory might be satisfied" (67–69). She immediately interprets this as "sneering" (70), but he probably intends just the opposite feeling. Earlier he has promised to try to stay away from sore topics in conversation, if she'll let him know what to avoid, but he is not truly happy about it, saying, "I don't like such things 'twixt those that love" (56). The reason is that he sees love as requiring complete openness, and he offers this definition of a good relationship: "Two that don't love can't live together without them [compromises] / But two that do can't live together with them" (57–58).

But while he is asking her to "Let me into your grief," she is dealing with a much deeper fear of isolation and death—one that finally denies any use in talking. Just after saying, "You *couldn't* care," she switches suddenly into a speech on the futility of human relationships in the face of death:

> "The nearest friends can go
> With anyone to death, comes so far short
> They might as well not try to go at all.
> No, from the time when one is sick to death
> One is alone, and he dies more alone.
> Friends make pretense of following to the grave,

But before one is in it, their minds are turned
And making the best of their way back to life
And living people, and things they understand.
But the world's evil. I won't have grief so
If I can change it. Oh, I won't, I won't!" (101–11)

Here she is caught in a double-bind of her own: after describing the futility of human companionship, she asserts her will (ironically, "I won't!") to deny superficial attitudes toward death and grief—which, of course, ensures that she will experience the isolation and loneliness that so horrify her. This is what makes her inconsolable. Readers get a glimpse of Amy's fears early in the poem, when the husband asks what she is looking at and "her face changed from terrified to dull" as she shifts her terrified gaze from the infant's grave to look dully at her husband. She is dealing with an existential crisis so threatening that it affects her facial expressions.

Unfortunately, the husband does exactly what she says people do in the face of death and isolation. After her longer speech, he does not respond to the horrible fear that she has just revealed, but instead he condescendingly comments on the effect of speaking that fear: "There, you have said it all and you feel better. / .... / The heart's gone out of it" (112–14). But she snaps back, "*You*—oh, you think the talk is all. I must go—" (116). And with that, each reverts to her or his initial form of grief: she is poised to flee, to avoid talking, while he threatens to use force to keep her in the house.

The tragedy is that both husband and wife desperately want to end their isolation, but that they offer the opposite of what the other one needs: he wants openness and companionship, but she denies his right to speak; he wants to talk, while she does not trust what she sees as idle speech. And they prove each other right. The husband does not fully understand what his wife is dealing with, and so he really cannot assuage her grief in conversation—especially when he cannot talk without the self-centered threat of force. But in threatening to flee, and refusing to let him speak, she perhaps denies him—and herself—the chance to share the burden of loss. While it may not be possible for anyone truly to understand another's grief, Amy removes even the chance that her husband's companionship might help.

This marriage is foundering; this brief conversation demonstrates each of what Gottman identifies as the four most damaging patterns in marriages: criticism, contempt, defensiveness, and stonewalling (27–34). The wife (whose name ironically comes from the same root as *amorous* and the French word *amour*, "love") reveals these patterns in especially clear form, as she criticizes the husband and tries to stonewall his initial attempts to open the discussion, treating his later entreaties with contempt. But although less explicitly, he is also defensive and indirectly critical of her lack of openness, and the threats of violence create a barrier to discussion. Still, there may be a glimmer of hope for this couple. Despite each person's apparent intention to carry out his or her threat, at the end of the poem Amy is still in the house with her husband, and he has not resorted to force, remaining in his seat on the stairs. They are still together, but just barely, and what happens in the next few minutes could determine their future as a couple. Frost drops the curtain on this domestic drama at its point of greatest tension, leaving readers to ponder the couple's situation—will they find a way to get back together, or will this "home" be buried?

Having to Be Taken In: "The Death of the Hired Man"

In "The Death of the Hired Man" readers see another childless couple who also experience the death of a member of their household—in this case Silas, the hired hand. The way they talk about Silas makes him seem like a child because it appears that Silas was not fully capable of taking care of himself. But the situation has some key differences from that in "Home Burial" because the child is, in fact, an old man literally on his dying day. This couple's relationship is in much better shape than the man and woman grieving their infant son—Mary and Warren are on easy, secure terms with each other. The situation is calmer, too—there is not an obvious, immediate crisis because neither they nor readers learn about Silas's death until the end of the poem. The couple's conversation focuses more on how to approach a particular problem, perhaps vexing but not insurmountable. Finally, as they talk, their conversation gradually reveals that several layers of family are involved here.

The most obvious family situation is Mary and Warren's marriage, and readers get a sense of their relationship early on when Mary runs quietly to greet Warren at the door: she pushes him back outside, saying, "Silas is back" (Frost 5). Her push is gentle, and he allows himself to be pushed: she is confident that he will go along with her, and he assumes she has a good reason for not letting him enter immediately. She further commands him to "Be kind," then "drew him down / To sit beside her on the wooden steps" (7, 9–10). These interactions are small and easily overlooked, but their quiet intimacy and mutual respect imply a lot about the strength of their marriage (Gottman 79–80); Frost's characterization here is subtle and effective.

As in any good marriage, the couple has perspectives that are different, but that complement each other. Mary and Warren hold different opinions, but they understand and respect each other's views. Mary gently chides Warren, to soften his truculent, contradictory, response: "When was I anything but kind to him? / But I'll not have the fellow back" (Frost 11–12). Warren is used to making such bluff statements, it seems, and Mary is used to countering them successfully with quieter but still direct responses. Even though their debate can be lively, this way of discussing the world and making decisions works for them.

Of course, Warren has not yet seen Silas, while Mary has watched how Silas "lay / And rolled his old head on that sharp-edged chair-back," unable to keep his eyes open (154–55). She tells Warren, "he has come home to die" (114), later adding, "You'll be surprised at him—how much he's broken. / His working days are done; I'm sure of it" (159–60). Warren can make bluff and cynical statements because he has not yet seen Silas face-to-face; but Mary cannot ignore the pathos right in front of her, seeing the frail man indirectly pleading for help.

But even in her compassionate reaction, Mary reveals that neither she nor Warren have ever given Silas much respect. Here is where the second family-type relationship appears. On one hand the spouses talk about Silas as if he were a child in his understanding of the world, needing kindly but firm supervision. On the other hand, they see their responsibility to Silas as limited because he is a grown man. Warren's initial response, "I'll not have him back," is based on a warning that Silas could choose to hear or ignore: "I told him so last haying. . . . / If he left then, I said, that ended it" (13–14). Silas had the option to do as he wished, but he also had to suffer the consequences. Still, Warren's ultimatum is couched in a sense of superiority that makes it similar to the choices many parents give their teenage children—knowing that the teenagers likely do not have the maturity or resources to take responsibility for themselves. But Warren's ultimatum has a sharper edge: "What good is he? Who else will harbor him / At his age for the little he can do?" (15–16). Silas gets less respect than teenagers because he is declining rather than growing. There is even some exasperation at how the wayward child-man will act: "What help he is there's no depending on. / Off he goes always when I need him most" (17–18).

The parallels between Silas and a teenager continue: Silas's wish "to earn a little pay, / Enough at least to buy tobacco with" (20–21), sounds like a teenager asking for more allowance, but Warren the parent responds, "I can't afford to pay / Any fixed wages, though I wish I could" (22–23). Like a teenager, Silas must be satisfied with being housed and fed. But unlike a teen, Silas has contracted to work as a field hand for room and board, and if he sometimes needs to ask for spending money, it is because Warren is not paying cash. Because Warren refuses to pay cash—though Silas actually said "he ought to earn a little pay" (19)— Silas must beg or borrow.

This does not sit well with Silas, who does have the free agency of a grown man. Warren recognizes this, but cynically: "You can be certain,

/ When he begins like that, there's someone at him / Trying to coax him off with pocket money— / In haying time, when any help is scarce" (26–29). But in his cynicism, Warren overlooks what other farmers value: he complains when Silas leaves for higher wages as if it were a personal betrayal. Even though Warren himself is not giving Silas any cash, he expects a kind of familial loyalty—he is irritated when Silas acts like a grown, self-determining man.

Mary, for her part, also seems to denigrate Silas, calling him "worthless" (152) and saying, "Of course he's nothing to us, any more / Than was the hound that came a stranger to us" (119–20). But Mary still recognizes the pride Silas has as a self-respecting man. Warren asks why Silas does not get help from his own brother, who lives nearby and is apparently well-off, but Mary knows:

> "I can tell you,
> Silas is what he is—we wouldn't mind him—
> But just the kind that kinsfolk can't abide.
> He never did a thing so very bad.
> He don't know why he isn't quite as good
> As anybody. Worthless though he is,
> He won't be made ashamed to please his brother." (147–52)

In this passage readers see a third family relationship: Silas is the hapless, bumbling child who never succeeded like his brother did, and has apparently been judged for his seeming failure. But because Silas still values himself as a person, and rightly so, he sees the relationship with his blood brother as apparently weaker than the ties he has with Warren and Mary. They may not respect him fully, but they respect him more than the brother seems to.

As Mary and Warren reminisce, however, yet another sort of family relationship appears—though only as something Silas desired, but could not have. Mary recounts how Silas argued constantly with a college student named Harold Wilson, who worked for a summer on the farm. Silas was aggravated by the young man, but he could not let go of their relationship—Mary remembers it because the confused and aged Silas in the present has been mumbling about it half-consciously. It appears that Silas wanted to play something like a fatherly role with the student, but "Harold's young college boy's assurance piqued him" (76). Harold looked down on Silas's skills for "witching" water—Silas "could find water with a hazel prong" (85)—and for his part Silas could not understand why Harold might actually want to study Latin. But still, Silas says "you'll have to get him back. / He says they two will make a team for work: / Between them they will lay this farm as smooth!" (64–66). Silas wants to show the boy that there is wisdom outside college books.

Warren acknowledges that Silas was an expert on "how to build a load of hay" (90):

> "He bundles every forkful in its place,
> And tags and numbers it for future reference,
> So he can find and easily dislodge it
> In the unloading. Silas does that well." (92–95)

While Warren's tone is humorously condescending here, he follows that description with an intriguing statement: "You never see him standing on the hay / He's trying to lift, straining to lift himself" (97–98). Silas—at least in this regard—is never self-defeating, and he knows how to direct his effort with the best results. But in the most poignant lines of the poem, Mary continues: Silas "thinks if he could teach [Harold] that, he'd be / Some good perhaps to someone in the world" (99–100)—otherwise, Silas has "nothing to look backward to with pride, / And nothing to look forward to with hope" (103–04). Silas desperately wants a mentoring, fatherly relationship with Harold in part because he has never had a fully respected role in any other family he has ever had. Silas, too, is missing a child.

The question of what to do with Silas now prompts Warren and Mary to think about the meaning of "home." In fact, Mary assumes that as a couple they are in fact Silas's home: "he has come home to die," she says, but Warren "mocked gently" the notion of "home" (114, 116). Warren knows the term is not fully accurate because Silas is an employee rather than their blood relation, and he had chosen to leave. But Warren also knows that their relationship with Silas is more than economic—as a farmhand Silas was a member of their household; he has come to them now for "harbor" because, even though he left earlier, their long relationship has been both personal and economic.

Still, when Warren gives one of the most famous definitions of home, it is based on obligation rather than gracious hospitality: "Home is the place where, when you have to go there, / They have to take you in" (122–23). Mary responds less legalistically, saying, "I should have thought it / Something you somehow haven't to deserve" (124–25). But as John Hollander notes, "these definitions [are] profoundly complementary. . . . ultimately paraphrases of the same notion" (32): people take care of others because they care for them as human beings. Even though Warren does not seem to admit that he feels an obligation, he is only protesting mildly. He knows that help from Silas's brother is not really an option, and he knows that, despite his declaration not to take Silas back, they really are not going to throw the man out.

Through all this Warren has been talking about Silas without actually seeing the man—neither literally nor metaphorically. Mary finally tells him, "Go, look, see for yourself" (Frost 162), and when he returns ("too soon, it seemed to her" (172)), Warren is no longer talking tough. In fact, he says nothing, but "slipped to her side, caught up her hand and waited" (173). The poem ends with taciturn acknowledgment: "'Warren?' she questioned. / 'Dead,' was all he answered" (174–75). For all their debate earlier, now they must take responsibility. Even in death, Silas depends upon their family-like relationship, and they must recognize his worth as a person that they cared about. Warren has seen the absent "child" face to face, and cannot deny that Silas belongs with them.

The ending of the poem might seem anticlimactic—after all, Mary and Warren do not actually have to live with Silas in their home at all. The poem's dramatic structure is cleaner this way—but it also is not done. In their discussion, Warren and Mary have brought out a number of views about how to treat their fellow man, and now they have to live with those revealed thoughts: because Silas is dead, they cannot find out exactly what would have happened next; they cannot test their ideas about home or their feelings for him in his newly returned reality. Rather, now they must wonder—how would we have responded?

Conclusion

"Home Burial" and "The Death of the Hired Man" present quite different scenarios in which Frost as poet brings the question of loss before readers. Readers know almost nothing about the dead child in "Home Burial"; outside gender, the son has neither personality nor identity, so he is doubly absent—physically gone and individually blank. The grieving parents are reacting to their loss as an abstract concept, as the death of a child rather than the death of their own unique son.

By using a blank, generic identity for the child, the poem shifts attention away from the child to the parents: how they take the loss, and how they relate to each other in its wake. If the child's personality is left open, he can be identified with almost anyone. This might make it easier for the mother to identify with him in her terror about death, and might also allow the husband to see the son as perhaps just the first of several children, rather than taking the loss of this particular child "inconsolably." And Robert Frost himself might unconsciously identify with the boy, as Frost indirectly examines what his own loss might have meant to his parents. In "Home Burial," Frost explores the loss of a child for what it means to the parents.

"The Death of the Hired Man" shows the varied depths and intricate relationships that are lost when any human being dies. By setting up multiple family structures, Frost can examine several different ways in which people can "lose" a child; but by putting Silas in a childlike relationship to Mary and Warren, Frost brings all those losses home so that parents must react. While they are not Silas's biological parents, Mary and Warren stand in for any two parents who have not valued their child correctly—as Frost's own parents, especially his father, did not value him. And so as Mary and Warren recognize what Silas has meant to them, so can Frost re-create what he himself meant—or should have meant—as a family member in his own damaged childhood.

Each of these poems, then, provides Robert Frost with a way to re-coup emotionally what was absent from his own rough childhood in San Francisco. He explores for his own sake, and he shows to readers, what is lost when a childhood is destroyed, whether by natural death or in an abusive relationship. In a sense, Robert Frost the battered child is trying to go home. But "Home Burial" and "The Death of the Hired Man"—the two poems that are virtually his only portrayals of children in a family situation—only value a child in his death. There is some solace in seeing what the two couples have lost when their children are gone, and how much the loss affects them, indirectly showing the value of the child. But in the way that Frost plotted out each poem, the child, from the very beginning, is already and always will be absent—his childhood is gone.

Notes

1. The second most well known poem that features a child is "Out, Out—," but the boy who has his hand cut off in that poem plays a largely passive role, and the poem ends with the seemingly callous conclusion that other people, "since they / Were not the one dead, turned to their affairs" (line 34)—(please note that all poems cited here refer to texts in *Frost: Collected Poems, Prose & Plays*, ed. Richard Poirier and Mark Richardson). While the children's playhouse in "Directive" suggests the experience of someone who has tripped over children's toys many times, there are no children present but rather a reference to innocence lost: "Weep for what little things could make them glad" (44). "Storm Fear" outlines a family—"I count our strength, / Two and a child" (9–10)—but otherwise ignores the child.

   A few lesser-known poems do contain realistic portrayals of parent-child relationships. "The Exposed Nest" both explores and demonstrates the vulnerability of young creatures. "The Bonfire" discusses the fear of war with children. The speaker in "Not of School Age" has a minimal roadside encounter with a very young boy whom he does not know. The minor poem that perhaps has the clearest relationship between parent and child is "A Girl's Garden," but like "Birches" the speaker is a grown woman narrating childhood experiences from memory. On a humorous note, Frost drops his own children's names into "Maple" as hypothetical examples of common names for children!

Finally, although Frost titled his first collection of poetry *A Boy's Will*, so that the whole collection is supposed to represent a boy's or youth's maturation, that overarching theme is rather stilted and clumsily handled; further, the individual poems themselves really are not about children.

Works Cited

Chronology. *Robert Frost: Collected Poems, Prose, and Plays*. Ed. Richard Poirier and Mark Richardson. New York: Lib. of Amer., 1995. 929–55.

Francis, Lesley Lee. "Robert Frost and the Child: 'Mother Goose' and 'The Imagination Thing.'" *Massachusetts Review* 45.2 (2004): 256–68.

Frost, Robert. *Robert Frost: Collected Poems, Prose, and Plays*. Ed. Richard Poirier and Mark Richardson. New York: Lib. of Amer., 1995.

Gottman, John R., and Nan Silver. *The Seven Principles for Making Marriage Work*. New York: Crown 1999.

Hollander, John. "It All Depends." *Social Research* 58.1 (1991): 31–49.

Parini, Jay. *Robert Frost: A Life*. New York: Holt, 1999.

Richardson, Mark. "Parables of Vocation: Frost and Pound in the Villages of (Gingrich's?) America." *Essays in Literature* 23.1 (1996): 99+.

Sheehy, Donald G. "The Poet as Neurotic: The Official Biography of Robert Frost." *American Literature* Vol. 58.3 (1986). 393–410.

Thompson, Lawrance. *Robert Frost: The Early Years, 1874-1915*. New York: Holt, 1966.

Toth, Sheree L., Erin L. Pickreign, and Julie A. Gravener. "Child Abuse and Neglect." *Encyclopedia of Human Relationships*. Ed. Harry T. Reis and Susan K. Sprecher. Thousand Oaks: Sage, 2009.

Woititz, Janet Geringer. *Adult Children of Alcoholics*. Pompano Beach: HCI, 1990.

Family in Dante's *The Divine Comedy*_____

Nicla Riverso

Dante was an attentive observer and interpreter of the feelings and beliefs of his society. He created realistic depictions of contemporary society by putting into play his ethical and moral values in order to express the emotions, anxieties, ambiguities, and ambitions of his age. *The Divine Comedy* (written between 1308 and 1321) is an exemplary work with which to demonstrate how Dante used his literary production to depict the morality, ethics, and mores of the fourteenth century. Here, I will examine the way in which Dante describes the attitudes of his age with respect to family dynamics by focusing on the value placed on conjugal love, affection for children, and relationships with ancestors, all of which he saw as hugely important.

Dante's *Divine Comedy* introduces a number of different kinds of relationships between husband and wife: stories of eternal love, forgotten love, violence in love, and adultery. What I will point out is that each story represents a particular domestic situation that took place in a very specific social and political environment. The urban society of Dante's era was changing quickly; the feudal aristocracy and old nobility were increasingly obscured by the expansion of the emerging wealthy urban class, who originated a new social order. Even though social, political, and economic changes were happening very quickly during the fourteenth century, life inside the fourteenth-century domestic sphere remained tied to old custom and traditions. Even as towns were adopting a bourgeois way of life, women were still expected to be completely dependent on their husbands and to swear to lifetime fidelity and obedience to them (Kleinschmidt 136–40). Women were judged on the basis of their relationships with their husbands and on their devotion to their families. They could be depicted either as the sinful Eve or the modest and pure Virgin Mary (Pereira 9).

Dante's *Divine Comedy*—which is divided into parts: *Inferno*, *Purgatory*, and *Paradise*—offers insights into the relationships between husbands and wives, their private lives, their marital unions, and the circumstances that brought them to either respect and love, or despise and detest one another. One of Dante's prime examples of conjugal felicity is found in the episode in which Dante meets Forese Donati, who praises his wife Nella for her prayers that allowed him to pass quickly through Purgatory. Nella is a representation of a perfect wife: a virtuous woman who devotes herself to prayer in order to improve the condition of her dead husband. Forese speaks of his wife with kindness, deep love and respect:

> All the more dear and pleasing to the Lord
> is my sweet widow who greatly loved,
> the more she is unique in doing good. (Musa 3:227)[1]

Forese points out the way in which his wife is different from other women of her time; unlike them, she is distinguished for her virtues. Nella is an exemplary wife in that she continues to love her husband even after his death. She stands out as unique in a world where customs and manners have become increasingly corrupted and perverted; her modesty, purity, and sobriety contrast with the behavior of "Ladies of Florence who, bold faced, / now walk our city streets as they parade their bosom to the tits." (Musa 3:229)

Marcia (Marzia), the wife of Cato of Utica the Youngest, is another exemplary wife whose conjugal love should be remembered and revered.[2] Marcia accepted her husband's decision to cede her to Quintus Hortensius, a Roman orator and a close friend of Cato. As Hortensius did not have any heirs from his marriage to his former wife, he asked Cato to allow him to take Marcia as his own wife in order that she would bear him children. After Hortensius's death, Marcia begged to be allowed to become Cato's wife once again. Dante tells us that even while in Limbo, Marcia was still so grateful to Cato for taking her as his wife again that, even though they were separated by death, she continued to love him and to pray for his soul. In conversation with Cato, Virgil affirms Marcia's love for Cato:

> of your dear Marcia, still praying for your soul,
> O blessed heart, to hold her as your own. (Musa 3:7)

Cato remembers Marcia's attachment and devotion and declares that he desired to please her while they were both still alive. Cato tells Dante:

> Marcia was so enchanting to my eyes
> That while I was alive
> There was no wish of hers I would not grant. (Musa 3:7)

Even though lending and borrowing wives or daughters was not considered illicit among the Romans (and in fact was a normal practice in the case that a friend needed help producing an heir that would guarantee the family's succession), Marcia's story must have seemed to Dante a particularly vivid sacrifice on the altar of her love. We find that Dante also mentions Marcia in his *Inferno,* along with Lucretia, Julia, and Cornelia, all exemplars of female civic virtue and honesty. According to Dante, Marcia is worthy of being counted among the greatest women of antiquity.

But not all wives are like Nella and Marcia, and Dante points out other marital relationships that develop in a very different way. When Dante meets Buonoconte da Montefeltro, for example, he finds the Ghibelline warrior experiencing enormous grief and shame because his wife Giovanna, his daughter Manentessa, and his brother Federico had forgotten him.[3] Because none of his family prayed for his soul, Buonoconte was forced to stay in Ante Purgatory forever:

> No one, not even Giovanna, cares for me,
> and so I walk ashamed among these souls. (Musa 3:47)

In Purgatory and Ante Purgatory the dead profit by the prayers of the living. The bond between the dead and the living is vital because the prayers of the living can help reduce the amount of time that the soul would have to spend in Purgatory. As such, people who continue to care deeply for their dead family members show their true love for them through their prayers—which also offer them comfort for their loss and greater healing from their grief. In contrast, those who neglect the dead show insensitivity as well as a lack of respect, esteem, and love for those who have passed to eternal life. It is therefore a very bitter pill for those such as Buonoconte da Montefeltro to swallow when they find that they are not loved by their families after their deaths, and worse, when they learn that they were probably never loved during their lifetimes. It is also very hard for them to accept that they will never be able to leave Ante Purgatory because of this. Nino de' Visconti experienced exactly this grief upon finding that his wife, Beatrice d'Este, had completely forgotten him and, after his death, had removed her widow's white bands and married Galeazzo Visconti. When he meets Dante in Purgatory, Nino implores him to remind his daughter Giovanna to pray for him:

> When you have crossed the enormous gulf once more,
> tell my Giovanna she should plead for me,
> for prayers from guiltless hearts are listened to.
> I think her mother has stopped loving me,
> for she has put aside those bands of white
> which she, poor soul, will soon be longing for. (Musa 3:77)

Nino de' Visconti is embittered because he feels betrayed by his wife not only in love, but in politics. During Dante's era, women were encouraged to remain chaste and faithful to their husbands even after they had died.[4] Beatrice, in contrast, married another man—and worse, she married into another branch of the Visconti. She had been the daughter of Obizzo II d'Este and had belonged to a family with solid Guelph traditions. She betrayed her first Guelph husband and her family by marrying the Ghibellines Galeazzo Visconti of Milan. Dante recalls Nino's marriage story to point out the fickleness, infidelity, inconstancy, and frailty of female love. Nino's words express his sad acknowledgment that his wife was the sort for whom, if a man was out of sight, he was also out of mind:

> From her it is not difficult to learn
> how long love's flame burns in a woman's heart,
> if sight and touch do not rekindle it. (Musa 3:77)

Dante's condemnation of Beatrice is harsh and pitiless, revealing his own rigorous morality and his disappointment in the new mores developing during his age.

Dante loses no opportunity for accusing Florentine women of vanity and a lack of morality. Through the character of Forense Donati, Dante expresses his judgment on the kind of Florentine women who, according to him, had become even worse than the lascivious women who lived in the wild mountainous region of Sardinia called Barbagia: "For the Barbagia of Sardinia counts among its women many far more chaste" (Musa 3:229).

Even though widows were not encouraged to remarry, their families would often arrange a second marriage if the widow was still young (as in the case of Beatrice). In these situations, the widows' families were glad to have a second chance at finding a husband who could offer benefits and advantages not just to the widow, but to her entire family. It is important to remember that during this era, aristocratic families often used marital unions to create alliances that were political and economic—and that it was not easy for the women to oppose their family's desires and pressure (Klapisch-Zuber, "Cruel Mother" 126). In Beatrice's case, and granting that in her marriage to Nino de' Visconti she had only produced a daughter, and granting as well that her father was dead, Beatrice's brother, Azzo VIII, obliged her to remarry, hoping that she would produce a male heir (Parker 136–40). Piccarda Donati's story, described by Dante in his *Paradise,* is another example of the vulnerability of women to the arrogance and power of the men in their families. Piccarda was forced by her brother Corso to leave the monastery of Santa Chiara at Monticelli where she was a nun and marry Rossellino della Tosa in order to secure a politically powerful alliance for the Donati family. Dante's decision to place Piccarda in the Heaven of the Moon—or in other words in the lowest sphere, dominated by the darkness "Blest within the lowest sphere" (Musa 5:25)—can be read as his disappointment that she did not resist her brother's will and hence failed to remain chaste. Even though Piccarda was a victim of a political arrangement, as in the case of Beatrice d'Este, Dante is pointing out the weakness of women who failed to remain chaste and faithful without also considering the social customs and political realities of his time.

In the *Comedy,* Dante largely represents women as descendants of Eve in that they are portrayed as leading men to sin. When Dante meets Iacopo Rusticucci among the sodomites in the seventh circle of Hell, for example, this man, once an honorable political leader, introduces himself by saying:

> I was Jacopo Rusticucci, and it is certain that
> my beast-like wife first drove me to my sin. (Musa 1:149)

Rusticucci blames his sin on his wife's obnoxious nature just as Adam blames his eating the apple from the Tree of Knowledge on Eve. Dante's use of the term "fiera moglie," implies that the recalcitrance and beastliness of Rusticucci's wife drove him to commit the sin of sodomy. Dante does not provide any other information about Rusticucci's wife, leaving the reader intrigued and curious about the badly matched marriage that turned Rusticucci perverse.

In his commentary on the *Comedy* Giovanni Boccaccio recalls Rusticucci's sad destiny, brought about by Rusticucci's wife's ferocity as follows:

Some say that he had married a woman so reluctant and perverse and so devoted to the kind of new customs and manners that we often see now, that it was impossible to do anything with her and that his life was unbearable with her; for this reason Mr. Jacob moved away from her and took to the misery of this vice. (3:217; author translation)

Furthermore, after his discussion of Rusticucci and his relationship with his wife, Boccaccio dwells on the dangerousness of certain women and on the damage that they can bring to their husbands. Boccaccio recommends that men not be hasty in getting married; on the contrary, he suggests that they should come to marriage with much caution (3:217). It is evident that this feeling was shared by many men in the fourteenth century, as according to both Dante and Boccaccio, there was a breed of women who were responsible for making their husband's lives miserable—particularly women who chose to ignore older and more traditional customs.

Among the numerous relationships between husbands and wives described in Dante's *Comedy,* there is no shortage of stories that have a violent epilogue. One of these is the story of Francesca da Rimini, who committed adultery with her husband's brother, Paolo Malatesta, and who then died a violent death. Even though Dante condemned the two lovers, placing them in the second circle of Hell reserved for the souls of the lustful or carnal sinners, he describes the story of their adultery in such a graceful way that readers can clearly see the poet's sympathy for Francesca. Even in Hell, Francesca remains a well-born gentlewoman who behaves and speaks in such a courtly manner as to move Dante to compassion and pity: "The torment that you suffer / brings painful tears of pity to my eyes" (Musa 1:49), so much so that when the canto ends, the poet, overcome by sadness, weeps and then faints "And fell to Hell's floor as a body, dead, falls" (Musa 1:51). Dante, who judged Beatrice d'Este so severely for remarrying rather than remaining chaste and faithful to her husband after his death, is moved to pity for Francesca; he describes her as angelic, even though he thought her sin very regrettable.[5] Moreover, Dante appears to want to soften his readers' hearts with respect to the adulterous story by placing it in a romantic context. Dante dwells at length on the scene wherein the lovers take pleasure in reading together about Lancelot and Guinevere's love. Even though Francesca's and Paolo's story ends in tragedy when Francesca's husband kills them both, the narrative of their love develops as a romance following the formula of traditional courtly love.[6]

Dante's familiarity with the story probably made him sympathetic toward Francesca. Giovanni Boccaccio has a similar point of view, describing Francesca as an innocent girl who was deceived by her father, Guido da Polenta, into marrying the ugly, old, and deformed Gianciotto Malatesta instead of his handsome younger brother Paolo, with whom she was in love. It is also possible that Dante pitied Francesca because he esteemed and was grateful to Guido Novello da Polenta, Francesca's nephew, who offered Dante shelter in his home in Ravenna when late in life, he was banished from Florence.

Francesca's story offers a social context in which to examine yet another testimony to the limited opportunity and lack of freedom that women had in marriage during the Middle Ages. Because marriage was typically a political alliance between two families, marrying for love was a very rare occurrence, particularly within the upper classes. Women such as Beatrice d'Este and Francesca were expected to obey their fathers (or, absent a father, other male family members) and in most cases, as in Francesca's story, the arranged marriage would be between a young girl and a much older man who would not have met before the wedding (Duby 7–8).

Pia dei Tolomei was another victim of an arranged marriage. The Tolomei family was one of the richest and oldest members of the nobility of Siena. Pia was given in marriage to Nello dei Pannocchieschi, a powerful lord of the Sienese Maremma. After their marriage, however, Nello charged his wife with infidelity, imprisoned her in the Castel di Pietra, and then murdered her by throwing her from a window. Shortly thereafter, he married Margherita Aldobrandeschi who was likely his lover already. Pia's speech is described by Dante as gentle, elegant, and gracious—entirely worthy of a noblewoman. Pia's composure in her speech and manner is astounding: even thought she was violently and unjustly murdered, she avoids all personal accusations and shows no desire to revenge herself on her husband, nor does she demonstrate any hatred toward him.[7] Notwithstanding any of this, however, her family forgot her. Thus the only favor that Pia asks of Dante is to pray for her in order to accelerate her ascent to Heaven:

> Oh, please, when you are in the world again,
> and are quite rested from your journey here, [. . .]
> oh, please remember me! I am called Pia. (Musa 3:51)

But Dante's representation of family is expressed not only by the relationships between wives and husbands that he describes, but also those between parents and their children. The affection that he describes parents having for their children is so strong that it lasts even beyond death. Manfredi introduces himself to Dante in Purgatory, and immediately asks Dante to tell his daughter that—even though he was slain in Benevento by Charles of Anjou and that, since he had been excommunicated, he was not allowed a Christian burial—he was saved from eternal destruction by his faith. Manfredi feels honored by his daughter and proudly points out that she gave birth to two sons who became the kings of Sicily and Aragon:

> When you are with the living once again,
> go to my lovely child, mother of kings
> who honor Sicily and Aragon;
> whatever may be rumored, tell her the truth. (Musa 3:29)

These verses show Manfredi's affection and love for his daughter Costanza, as well as his anxiety that she know about his condition. As such, he begs Dante to make him happy by telling her about his fate.

Another father who refers to his daughter with loving and benevolent words is Nino de' Visconti. When Dante met him in Purgatory, Nino asked Dante to remind his daughter Giovanna to pray for him. He recalls her as innocent and pure—in contrast to her mother, whose name Nino refuses to mention because he feels so insulted by her remarriage. Even though Giovanna was only nine years old when he died, her father nonetheless hopes that his beloved daughter's innocent and gentle prayers can be heard in Heaven and will help him to purge his soul.

The love of a father toward his child is again represented through the character of Cavalcante dei Cavalcanti who, when he sees Dante in Hell, rises up from his fiery tomb and asks why his son Guido, a famous poet and Dante's close friend, was not with Dante. Cavalcante knows that his son was equal to Dante in genius and therefore had hoped and expected to see them together. Dante describes his meeting with Cavalcante dei Cavalcanti as follows:

> He looked around as though he hoped to see
> if someone else, perhaps, had come with me
> and, when his expectation was deceived,
> he started weeping: "If it be great genius
> that carries you along through this blind jail,
> where is my son? Why is he not with you?" (Musa 1:93)

Cavalcante's love and the affection for his son is clear, but so is his ambition and pride as he worries that the boy has not been adequately acknowledged for his brilliance. His concern is the anxiety of a father who is afraid that his child has been denied the artistic fame that he deserves. Moreover, Cavalcante's attachment to his son is demonstrated by his interest in merely getting news of Guido from Dante and finding out about his son's fate. Dante's use of the past tense when he is talking about Guido and his failure to quickly respond to Cavalcante, however, causes a misunderstanding; after hearing Dante speak, Cavalcante falls back inside his tomb in despair thinking that his son has already died:

Instantly, he sprang to his full height and cried,
"What did you say? He had? Is he not living?
The day's sweet light no longer strikes his eyes?"
And when he heard my slight delay of silence
in answering his question, he collapsed
into his tomb, not to be seen again. (Musa 1:95)

Cavalcante's reaction to Dante demonstrates the deep grief that can be felt by a father, here, who wrongly believed that his son had died young. Even though Cavalcante was a damned soul subject to infernal torture, his pain increased when he heard about his son's fate.

In the *Comedy*, a moving and tragic story that sees a father and his children and grandchildren as protagonists is the narration of Ugolino della Gherardesca.[8] In 1288, Archbishop Ruggieri betrayed and imprisoned Ugolino, along with Ugolino's sons Gaddo and Uguiccione, as well as Ugolino's grandsons Anselmo and Nino (nicknamed Brigata). After they had been imprisoned for nine months the tower was locked up and the men were left to starve to death. Dante describes Ugolino as a father suffering terrible grief and numb from the pain of being incapable of helping his children:

I heard my children sobbing in their sleep; you
see they, too, were there, asking for bread.[...]
Then from below I heard them driving nails
into the dreadful tower's door; with that,
I started in silence at my flesh and blood.
I did not weep, I turned to stone inside; they
wept, and my little Anselmuccio spoke: "What is
it, father? Why do you look that way?" (Musa 1:319)

Ugolino is speechless and his heart turns to stone because he is powerless to give his children what they are asking for.[9] He foresees their tragic fate and cannot help them.[10] When the sun allows some light into the prison, Ugolino sees that his sons' expressions mirror his own feelings of hopelessness and fear for the future; he feels anguish at the sight of his suffering children and bites his own hands. His children interpret this gesture as sign of hunger and, demonstrating their great love for their father, offer to sacrifice themselves as food for him:

> A meager ray of sunlight found its way
> into our painful cell, and I could see
> myself reflected four times in their faces;
> I bit my hands in anguish. And my children,
> who thought that hunger made me bite my hands
> were quick to draw up closer to me, saying
> "O father, you would make us suffer less,
> If you would feed on us: you were the one
> who gave us this sad flesh; you take it from us." (Musa
> 1:319, 321)

Much as he loves them, and even though he is unable to help his children in any practical sense, Ugolino nonetheless puts no effort into offering them spiritual or emotional consolation.[11] He reacts to his inability to change the fate of his sons and grandsons by withdrawing into absolute silence. He cannot find a single word to bring them any relief:

> I calmed myself to make them less unhappy.
> That day we sat in silence, and the next day.
> The fourth day came, and it was on that day
> that my Gaddo fell prostrate before my feet,
> crying: "Why don't you help me? Why, my father?" (Musa
> 1:321)

Ugolino's deep torment is based on his belief that his innocent male progeny are paying for his mistakes with their lives.

With Ugolino's story, Dante depicts a family tragedy wherein Ugolino witnesses, powerless, the death of his male heirs and therefore the destruction of his descendants and his lineage. He watches as his children die of starvation, one by one. His grief is deep and desperate and nothing can assuage it. His grief and pain are transformed into a desire for revenge and in *Inferno* he is described as brutally, harshly, and cruelly gnawing the skull of his enemy, Archbishop Ruggieri, as if he were a beast.[12]

Dante also describes parents who are not only joyful to reunite with their children in the afterlife, but whose love for their children increases after their various deaths because of the pain of separation that death imposes. In *Paradise*, Dante represents maternal pride through the figure of Saint Anne, the mother of the Virgin Mary, who sits directly across from Saint Peter, next to whom sits Mary. Saint Anne is the only soul in the Celestial Rose who is not looking up at God; instead, her gaze is fixed delightedly and fully upon her daughter:

> Across from Peter, see there, Anna sits,
> so happy to be looking at her daughter,
> she does not move an eye singing Hosanna (Musa 5:321)

Similarly, in canto 15 of the *Paradise*, Dante recalls the episode wherein Aeneas visits his father in the underworld, as narrated by Virgil in his *Aeneid*. Dante describes the scene as the pious ghost of old Anchises joyously greeting his son Aeneas upon perceiving him in Elysium. Anchises displays a passionate affection and love for his son and welcomes him warmly, referring to him as part of his blood: "Cast from the hand the sword, thou blood of mine" (*Aeneid* 835):

> With like affection did Anchises' shade
> rush forth, if we may trust our greatest Muse,
> when in Elysium he beheld his son. (Musa 5:143)

Dante introduces this episode of Aeneas meeting his father in Hades in order to compare it to his own encounter with his great-great-grandfather Cacciaguida. Cacciaguida is depicted as a paternal figure who welcomes his progeny with the same happiness and affection shown by Anchises when he sees his own son. When Cacciaguida meets Dante, he joyfully exclaims:

> "O blood of mine, O grace of God.
> To whom, as to thee was heaven's gate ever twice opened?"
> (Musa 5:145)

Cacciaguida again underlines the blood relationship with his descendent when he addresses Dante, saying:

> "Branch of my tree, the mere expectancy
> of whose arrival here gave me delight." (Musa 5:147)

Cacciaguida, who describes himself as the root of the family tree of which Dante represents the present leaf, offers a detailed history of Dante's ancestors, emphasizing the noble origin of their lineage.[13] Moreover, as Anchises did with Aeneas, Cacciaguida reveals to Dante the future events of Dante's life, as a father who wishes to prepare his child to face both the pleasant and the unpleasant facets of life.

Through Cacciaguida, Dante depicts images of early Florence where women exemplarily fulfilled their duties as wives and mothers—spinning their own fabric, caring for their children, singing them songs, and telling them stories about the origin of their town:

> One watching tenderly above the cradle,
> soothing her infant in that idiom
> which all new parents love to use at first;
> another, working at her spinning-wheel

surrounded by her children, would tell tales
about the Trojans, Rome, and Fiesole. (Musa 5:149)

These images are a product of Dante's ideal of family life, wherein marriage is centered on procreation and female virtue, and wherein virtue is based on domestic work; in other words, a world in which women preferred to spend time at home with their children rather than desiring a public life. In introducing this description of early Florence through Cacciaguida's narrative, Dante aims to enhance the appeal of his ideal of a sober and simple life in order to criticize the libertine customs of the women of his age, as well as their desire to live luxuriously and profligately:

Florence, enclosed within her ancient walls
from which she still hears terce and nones ring out,
once lived in peace, a pure and temperate town:
no necklace or tiara did she wear,
no lavish gowns or fancy belts that were
more striking than the woman they adorned. (Musa 5:149)

In Cacciaguida's narrative, Dante furthermore points out that, in the past, dowries did not impoverish the brides' fathers both because girls married when they were older and because the value of what they were expected to bring into marriage was not so high. This reflects and describes the fact that, during Dante's era, dowries had become a burden for the bride's family. A wife was expected to bring a large amount of money, as well as goods and property, to her husband upon marriage. Dante clearly disapproves of this "matrimonial market," based on the exchange of what were, apparently, material goods, and feels nostalgic for the time when everything was simpler and more sober, particularly with respect to dowries:

In those days fathers had no cause to fear
a daughter's birth: the marriageable age
was not too low, the dowry not too high. (Musa 5:149)

In *The Divine Comedy*, Dante illustrates aspects taken from the society of his era. His literary production is an important means of affording readers the possibility of understanding the social, ethical, cultural, moral, economic, political, and civic situations of fourteenth-century life in Italy. His descriptions of family dynamics, relationships, and interactions take an important place in *The Divine Comedy* and offer a variety of situations wherein family bonds have different values, valences, and meanings. Dante depicts both breakable and unbreakable relationships based on love, on support and friendship, and on indifference and hostility. But Dante was not impartial; his poems also invite readers to understand his personality, as well as his political, ethical, and moral thinking. His writing reveals his difficulty in accepting the transformations in his era, as well as the new customs and paradigms, particularly those having to do with women's changing roles with respect to their families and their public lives.

Notes

1. All translations of Dante's *Divine Comedy* are from Mark Musa in *Dante Alighieri's Divine Comedy*.
2. The story of Marcia is told by Plutarco in *Cato Minor* 25, 4–9, and in Lucan's *Pharsalia*, II, 326ff. On the topic of marriage exchange among the Romans see Susan Treggiari, Peter Garnsey, and Eva Cantarella.
3. Buonconte di Montefeltro, son of Dante's friend, Guido di Montefeltro, who fell in the battle of Campaldino (June 11, 1289). He was wounded in the neck and his body was never found.
4. See Christiane Klapisch-Zuber.
5. On the description of Francesca, see Marianne Shapiro.
6. See Renato Poggioli.
7. On Pia's description by Dante, see Thomas Goddard Bergin, Diana Glenn, and Marianne Shapiro.

---

8. On the popularity of Ugolino's story in literature and figurative art, see Frances A. Yates.

9. On the "drama of paternity" in Ugolino, see Francesco De Sanctis.

10. On Dante's sympathy for Ugolino's character and his story, see Robert Hollander.

11. On Ugolino's inability to help his children spiritually, see John Freccero.

12. On the bestiality expressed by Ugolino's behavior, see Donna L. Yowell; on Ugolino's grief as a source of rage, anger, and revenge, see Vittorio Russo.

13. On Dante and "the nobility of blood" and blood-pride, see Roberto Bizzocchi.

Works Cited

Bergin, Thomas G. *A Diversity of Dante*. New Brunswick: Rutgers UP, 1969.

Bizzocchi, Roberto. "La nobiltà di Dante: Cultura nobiliare, memoria storica e genealogia fra Medio Evo e Rinascimento." *I Tatti Studies: Essays in the Renaissance* 4 (1991): 201–15.

Boccaccio, Giovanni. *Il commento alla Divina Commedia e gli altri scritti intorno a Dante*. Ed. Domenico Guerri. 3 vols. Bari: Laterza, 1918.

Cantarella, Eva. "Famiglia romana e demografia sociale." *Iura* 43 (1992): 99–111.

Dante Alighieri. *Dante Alighieri's Divine Comedy*. Trans. Mark Musa. 6 vols. Bloomington: Indiana UP, 2000.

———. *La Divina Commedia; Inferno, Purgatorio, Paradiso*. Eds. Umberto Bosco and Giovanni Reggio. 3 vols. Firenze: Le Monnier, 1988.

De Sanctis, Francesco. "L'Ugolino di Dante." *Opere*. Torino: Einaudi, 1967. 681–704.

Duby, Georges. *Love and Marriage in the Middle Ages*. Chicago: U of Chicago P, 1994.

Freccero, John. "Bestial Sign and Bread for Angel." *Dante: The Poetics of Conversion*. Cambridge: Harvard UP, 1986. 152–66.

Garnsey, Peter, and Richard Saller. *The Roman Empire: Economy, Society, and Culture*. Berkeley: U of California P, 1987.

Glenn, Diana. *Dante's Reforming Mission and Women in the Comedy*. Leicester: Troubador, 2008.

Hollander, Robert. "Inferno XXXIII, 37–74: Ugolino's Importunity." *Speculum* 59. 3 (1984): 549–55.

Klapisch-Zuber, Christiane. "The 'Cruel Mother': Maternity, Widowhood, and Dowry in Florence in the Fourteenth and Fifteenth Centuries." *Women, Family, and Ritual in Renaissance Italy*. Chicago: U of Chicago P, 1985. 117–31.

———. "Women and the Family." Trans. Lydia G. Cochrane. *Medieval Callings*. Ed. Jacques Le Goff. Chicago: U of Chicago P, 1990. 285–311.

Kleinschmidt, Harald. *Understanding the Middle Ages: The Transformation of Ideas and Attitudes in the Medieval World*. Rochester: Boydell, 2000.

Lucan. *Pharsalia*. Trans. Jane Wilson Joyce. Ithaca: Cornell UP, 1993.

Parker, Deborah. "Ideology and Cultural Practice: The Case of Dante's Treatment of Beatrice d'Este." *Dante Studies, with the Annual Report of the Dante Society* 111 (1993): 131–47.

Pereira, Michela. *Né Eva né Maria: Condizione femminile e imagine della donna nel Medioevo.* Bologna: Zanichelli, 1981.

Plutarch. *Plutarchi Vitae parallelae: Phocion et Cato Minor.* Lipsiae: Teubner, 1931.

Poggioli, Renato. "Tragedy or Romance? A Reading of the Paolo and Francesca Episode in Dante's Inferno." *PMLA* 72. 3 (1957): 313–58.

Russo, Vittorio. "Il dolore del conte Ugolino." *Sussidi di esegesi dantesca.* Naples: Liguori, 1966. 147–81.

Shapiro, Marianne. *Woman, Earthly and Divine, in the Comedy of Dante.* Lexington: UP of Kentucky, 1975.

Treggiari, Susan. *Roman Marriage: iusti coniuges iusti coniuges from the Time of Cicero to the Time of Ulpia.* New York: Oxford UP, 1991.

Virgil. *The Aeneid.* Ed. Robert Fitzgerald. New York: Random, 1983.

Yates, Frances A. "Transformations of Dante's Ugolino." *Journal of the Warburg and Courtauld Institutes* 14.1–2 (1951): 92–117.

Yowell, Donna L. "Ugolino's 'bestial segno': The De 'vulgari eloquentia' in Inferno XXXII–XXXIII." *Dante Studies, with the Annual Report of the Dante Society* 104 (1986): 121–43.

Tradition and Family in Modern British Poetry _____

Brian Edwards and John V. Knapp

How modern poets engage families has undergone a dramatic shift since the 1950s, principally because more women have found their voices. Even a cursory glance at the history of British literature will spotlight the paucity, until very recently, of canonized poetry by women. As a result, family has been determined largely by men, and frequently by men acting with the authority of both church and crown. The rigid codification of class made career choices for single women limited to becoming a nun or a governess, which was as high up the social ladder as a young woman of intelligence and average birth could aspire in the nineteenth century. And while working-class women, of course, made the everyday business of England hum, "there was no formal system of education for girls outside convent walls until the late sixteenth century" (Robinson 14). Those well born and with liberal parents (or, a liberal father at least) could enjoy a private education, a point that Virginia Woolf reiterates in *A Room of One's Own* (1928). Woolf's lecture outlines why women needed a place of their own and an annual income in order to write. For every successful nineteenth-century writer—Jane Austen, Christina Rossetti, George Eliot (or Mary Anne Evans, who used a male pseudonym in order to be taken seriously as a writer)—there are thousands more who never had a chance.

Beyond the limiting of female voices, however, is the larger concern of how twentieth-century women are portrayed in literature—as mothers, sisters, daughters, wives—and by whom. In 1907, the Abbey Theatre, Ireland's newly founded national theater, staged a performance of John Millington Synge's *The Playboy of the Western World* (1907) that caused a riot. The reason is largely that Synge's mocking of hero worship (the mock hero is a son who has supposedly violently slain his father; he is discovered by a clever young woman) rang true, and it was a truth many Dubliners were not willing to confront. James Joyce shows his audience the same face in *Ulysses* (1922), as does Sean O'Casey in his trilogy of Dublin plays, including *The Plough and the Stars* (1926), which had a similar effect on an Abbey Theatre audience two decades after Synge.

Despite their unmasking of the domestic violence so prevalent in Irish folklore and among the poor, and so prevalent in Irish culture and stereotypical in literature and film, O'Casey and Joyce were still men describing women's roles. Much of the latter half of the twentieth century has been an attempt by literary women to take control of the narrative that defines them. Thus, this essay includes two poems by women that address the traditional view of women and families. Poet Stevie Smith attacks the domestic violence that was so much a part of life for women in the working classes in England and Ireland and so common in D. H. Lawrence's early novels—*Sons and Lovers* (1913) and *The Rainbow* (1915). Smith traces the source of domestic violence to religious beliefs that blame women for original sin. Eavan Boland takes a similar approach in the poem "Miss Eire"; she examines the stigmatism of independent women, pregnant or already raising children, and concludes that native Irish Gaelic has always limited female choices. Sometimes, however, world-changing events, World War II and the struggles for Irish independence, for instance, allow single women to take greater control of their lives by redefining themselves—an effect that can only be achieved in the language of the English colonizer.

Seamus Heaney, Boland's contemporary and countryman, provides the male equivalent of redefining oneself in a changing Irish culture. His choice is one that involves family history and his place in that Irish legacy. It also hints at another option that reflects the civil unrest that had once again struck Ireland. When faced with this family history, Heaney does what will one day win him the Nobel Prize in Literature: he writes a poem—in this case, "Digging." Philip Larkin, a bachelor and a librarian, will give voice to the tension many white males felt as the British Empire ended after World War II, resulting in an influx of former colonials and the rise of independent women. Laurence Lerner includes the following in his commentary on Larkin's poems from the

1950s: "For all his youthful contempt for respectability and hard work, he never lived on his wits, hated Bohemianism, and depended on (and valued) the regular routine and respectability he so enjoyed mocking" (Lerner 16–17).

Bachelorhood is a view of family, and in England one could be a respectable bachelor. It has very often caused a different reaction in America, but for his own particular reason Lerner points to Larkin's callous description that blamed his mother's "monstrous whining monologues" at mealtime (qtd. in Lerner 2), though Lerner quickly adds that Larkin was devoted to his mother in her widowhood. This does not make a particular point about Larkin's view of women, only his view of marriage and family. With no emotional security in his own family, perhaps Larkin avoided it in adult life. "Maiden Name" explores this discomfort with marriage. Larkin's poem, just as each of the previous three, represents a different perspective on family and family psychology, just as each illustrates how traditions and history influence the choices we must make.

J. H. Dettmar and Jennifer Wicke include in their biographical notes to Stevie Smith the following detail: "The public appeal of her poetry was somewhat harmful to its reputation, especially at a time of such poetic ferment in Britain—Yeats, Auden, Spender, Thomas, and others were creating the most innovative, deeply serious and sophisticated poetry of the century" (2914). It is also a masculine tradition of dominance that Smith, née Florence Margaret Smith, renders as a cruelty perpetrated and maintained through organized religion. But Smith's work is more unusual still in that this spoken word poet includes drawings that illuminate her themes. The drawing for "How Cruel Is the Story of Eve" has a single ballerina dressed only in a tutu in the plié position. It suggests a submissive posture (a curtsey), but juxtaposed against the spoken words of "Oh what cruelty, / In history what misery" that challenge basic assumptions of a tradition that accepts male dominance as the presumed natural order. The opening stanza declares the opposite of what readers have been taught: not that Eve sinned and created human misery, but that she has been blamed for it. Such framing allows men to define marriage relations, while treating women as possessions, "to barter," "buy," and "rule" because God has "said it" and hence ordained it (12–17).

Of course, this view of women as possessions also exists in the Bible. It is reinforced in British epics such as Milton's *Paradise Lost*. What Smith suggests is that the natural relations between humans do not conform to the description above. To her speaker, the reason for male dominance reflects the role of dominance men have adopted, which makes women "lower." Consequently, women must become practiced at deception—"[grow] cunning" (28)—in order to induce men to supply them with food and shelter, and to "kill enemies" (31). Moreover, if men did not feel "superior," then they would punish women and their "tender children" (32–35).

Family issues such as these raised by Smith were jarring at the time; they speak openly of violence against women and blame chauvinism for it, a bias she traces to its source—the creation and subsequent role of women and the fall. Elements in the Bible offer plenty of reinforcement, including the following from Timothy I:

> 11) Let the woman learn in silence. 12) But I suffer not a woman to teach, nor to usurp authority over the man, but to be in silence. 13) For Adam was first formed, then Eve. 14) And Adam was not deceived, but the woman being deceived was in the transgression. 15) Notwithstanding she shall be saved in childbearing, if they continue in faith and charity and holiness with sobriety. (1 Tim. 11–15)

Psychological studies support Smith's view of violence transfer. As reported by David Almeida, Elaine Wethington, and Amy L. Chandler, fathers are more likely than mothers to transfer unresolved conflict in the parental dyad to parent-child dyads: in other words, they tend to misplace anger from spouses to children. Hence, in response to critics who argue that the story of Eve is only a legend or a story, the speaker retorts: If so, then what purpose does the "legend" serve except to "blame to women most" and then punish them for it. As the speaker reminds us, this "legend" tinctures "all human thought" but is not part of the other animal kingdom; such organization (legend) cannot be "found among animals," for instance (40–46).

Male-female relations have traditionally positioned women as either help-meets to their husbands; or, as Milton's poet-prophet insists in the opening of *Paradise Lost*, the source of "all our woe" (1.3); or both at once, as Milton does in book 9. Milton's poem does "color all human thought" concerning God and the station of women. His Adam rhapsodizes about Eve before he finally submits, but he reminds her that it was she who transgressed, and in book 10 he condemns her in language that Smith denounces: "Out of my sight, thou Serpent, that name best /Befits thee with him leagu'd, thy self as false /And hateful; nothing wants, but that thy shape, / Like his, and colour Serpentine may shew" (10, 867–70), which First Timothy reinforces. The irony in Smith turns on the fact that the speaker knows that nature is involved in making humans attractive to one another (it is our "animal" nature, of which she earlier speaks), and it is what males have exploited since.

It is this success, fueled in part by the traditional myth, which is both oppressor and oppressed, and which is at the very core of Ellen Dissanayake's argument about the adaptive function of art. The human species survived and evolved because it developed sophisticated ways of making meaning in comprehending the world (through language or ritual, for example), but prior to that because natural selection engineered humans with highly sophisticated circuitry for both communal living and the love and nurturing they require from one another. People are preconditioned to respond to emotion and display emotion as early as birth (before it could possibly be learned); the speech patterns that mothers use with infants in baby talk, sometimes called motherese, are often the same sound patterns found in poetics. The metrical cadence of speech has evolved into complex forms of art, but complex forms derived from basic human instinct (Dissanayake 40–50).

With an irony so subtle one might initially miss it, Smith concludes "How Cruel Is the Story of Eve" by expressing the dichotomy of an unfortunate relationship between nature and myth. After acknowledging that men and women are the products of nature, she continues, adding that human life would have become extinct "if men and women had not loved each other / Naturally, naturally" (53–54).

The pun on *naturally*—as an expression used to agree with something obvious, and because it is part of the natural, animal existence that relies on human instinct, thus nature—provides a transition for the speaker to draw conclusions about the nature of life and myth. In essence, the speaker muses that even ignoring "mythology" men and women would have died without "it" and that all would be "emptiness" and "silence" now (55–59) One must pause at the meaning here. Initially, it might appear that Smith supports mythology because without it humans would have perished. Close inspection suggests that the "it" humans would have died from is exactly what Dissanayake illustrates in her first chapter, a chapter in which she traces the roots of human emotion and subsequently art from the special emotional pair-bond between mother and child. Of course, children come from liaisons between parents, and without love and affection, life as we know it would have gone extinct, as have nearly ninety percent of all species. Love, aggression, and conformity are what typify the human species—poetry, music, and dance are means used to magnify and communicate those feelings. As evolutionary biologist Olivia Judson says of highly social creatures such as humans: "the ability to adjust our behavior to fit a given social environment is one of our main characteristics, yet it's so instinctive we don't even notice it, let alone consider it worthy of remark" (154). Smith does examine the implications for human conformity:

> Oh dread nature, for your purpose,
> To have made them love so. (60–61)

Smith suggests that domestic violence (and violence that is so much a condition of modernism) does not result from natural order because humans are engineered for social contact that extends to larger kin groups, but which includes the trap that just as instinctively humans can exclude with violence that leads to abuse—one suggested reason why more than a few stepparents tend to be aggressive toward stepchildren. Thus the violence of which she speaks must have a cultural human element that acts in opposition to human instinct, and indeed it does: legend, myth, tradition.

Eavan Boland also examines stereotypical roles, but in Irish culture. "Miss Eire" traces aberrant male-female relations as rooted in a Gaelic heritage that is fast becoming extinct—the extinction of world languages is a major concern in the twenty-first century because it generally signals the end of the accompanying culture. She also suggests that the rugged Irish man of the land of whom Heaney writes is a tradition and legend of cloaked domestic violence. As Jody Allen Randolph suggests, "Boland was interested in disrupting the image of women and the family, essential to the iconography of nationalism" (3). In essence, Boland attempts to defrock the duality of womanhood represented in Irish lore, and in the resulting emancipation free her and other women from the domestic violence embedded there. Thus, the speaker exclaims that she "won't go back" to a country "displaced" into a language of "old dactyls" and "oaths made" by candlelight (1–6). Although the focus is on poetics and language (a dactyl is a poetic foot containing one accented syllable followed by two short ones, like "Higgeldy-Piggeldy"), which she counters with the guttural sounds at the end of the poem, the imagery focuses on the rural domesticity of traditional Ireland in the second stanza: Ireland is home to "the small farm" and "scalded memory" where "the words . . . make a rhythm of the crime" (7–13).

Gaelic, then, presents time only as "time past. / A palsy of regrets" (14–15); for the speaker that means the language traps her in the roles reserved for women, to submit without a voice to violence that is made a legend in the poetry, in a language that has been displaced (by English), as has the speaker, who will end up in England. In essence, Ireland for women is too often expressed in literature and music that masks domestic violence and blames the victim. These "roots are brutal" (17), the speaker contends, because her behavior is circumscribed by those who control language, thus behavior. Going back to the old language, in other words, means going back to the old ways, and the old ways mean domestic violence and riots. In the newly adapted language, though, she can fashion a new family system for women and children that breaks free of traditional family roles and the mythic silencing with which Gaelic poets have oppressed them.

The poem continues by wrenching away from a hostile past whose "songs . . . bandage up the history" (12–13) that have become sedimented into a family system that normalizes aberration; Irish literature and lore is filled with superstition and terror aimed at women and children, characterized by W. B. Yeats in his 1886 poem, "The Stolen Child," that depicts a child being lured away by evil fairies. Moreover, independence in women in her culture through a man's eyes (and the church, embodied in the priest), brands the woman as "a sloven's mix" of "silk" and a "dove-strut" down by the British "garrison" (18–22). From the male's perspective there is only one reason an Irish "girl" (the one in the "gansy" coat) would spend time around the British garrison. She "who practices / the quick frictions, / the rictus of delight" (23–25) is clearly the whore (the other half being the Madonna—the virgin) in the traditional Irish dichotomy of womanhood. Ironically, the poem itself hinges on the speaker's ability now to express the female view of the victimhood foisted on them by males and encoded in the literary language men have kept to themselves. When Seamus Heaney and others edited the first inclusive Gaelic/Irish Anthology, Boland roundly criticized them for the lack of women selected; it is symbolically rendered when the setting shifts to England.

The young woman stands on the dockyards with her new child—a bastard perhaps, but not illegitimate—in her new language and with her new independence after the war. Her new language is free of the constraints that the cultural iconography imbedded in Gaelic reserves for women and children: the "brutal roots" of a parochial, rural life. The speaker clutches "her half-dead baby" where the wind mixes "the immigrant guttural" and the "vowels of homesickness" (32–38), and understands that English is like "a scar" that "heals" in time into "a possible imitation" of the mother tongue (40–44). One cannot necessarily remove the heavy, brutal roots of behavior in another language, but it is difficult to describe the "scalded memory" without "the animal tallows of the candle," or to reclaim the silenced voice of centuries that have been the subject of Irish poets and the impetus for the rousting ways of Irish men raised on the shoulders of priests, whose own misogyny is barely cloistered.

Although it might be tempting to read a more pessimistic message into these lines—the "scar" that is a "possible imitation" might seem to suggest that the new language might be like the old—the speaker insists that we focus on the guttural sounds. These rough throaty sounds must seem burdensome to a tongue laden with soft Gaelic vowels. But guttural sounds pervade German and English (the former being the partial root of the latter), and though they might seem daunting, they represent an opportunity to redefine her role as a poet, a woman, and a mother. After all, a half-dead baby is also a half-alive baby, so that if nursed properly back to health it will recover. Boland uses the scar metaphor as the successful nurturing of baby back to health and subsequently the poet's tongue to patch up with a scar, which heals into a facsimile of the former life and would-be poet now liberated on the dock. Optimistically, then, as the poem illustrates, English has become more than a "fine" scar. Boland herself led a privileged life. Her father was an ambassador to England and the United States; she is a noted scholar and a brilliant poet whose work is just now really beginning to receive the recognition it deserves. Her poetry suggests that, for women and families, the Irish culture and subsequently its language have always limited their ability to be heard.

For Seamus Heaney, as for so many young Irishmen in the 1960s, traditional family meant the tug of the land that Boland suggests is part of their Gaelic heritage. Heaney describes this dilemma in the poem "Digging." From the very outset the pun in the title will become the central metaphor for making meaning in the poem. The central metaphor of digging is meant both in its literal iteration—to cut into the earth with a spade to extract its nourishment (potatoes)—and in its figurative sense—to research, to search for clues, to look deeply for meaning. Why the speaker feels compelled at this point in his life seems clear when the metaphor is traced through to the poem's conclusion, which the poem's first image invokes:

> Between my finger and my thumb
> The squat pen rests, snug as a gun. (1–2)

Under most circumstances the idea of the pen and the gun would not necessarily suggest political upheaval; guns have a variety of uses, but in Ireland in 1966 for a twenty-one-year-old fresh from university, the image has particular meaning. If Heaney chooses political radicalism (hinted at in the allusion to the popular axiom—the pen is mightier than the sword), then the method of choice at that time would have been terrorism. The Irish Republican Army (IRA) has been listed as a terrorist group because it has terrorized civilians as political action. It is difficult for many Americans to envision, but there are today countries in the Middle East where a young man is faced with a similar choice. Suicide bombers often come from these recruits. What is unique in Heaney's poem, however, is how he approaches his heritage. In fact, he seems to be examining his family—the male breadwinners in his family that is—as he takes stock of himself by comparison; it is a poem of initiation from childhood to adulthood. Hence the poem begins with the dilemma the speaker faces—fighting (physical action) or writing (intellectual pursuit) in stanza 1—then shifts to what is outside the window and that which will create the feeling (in this case strike the right chord of feeling, nostalgia without sentimentality, genuine admiration, and love) in stanza 2 as the speaker describes "a clean rasping sound" beneath the room where he sits as his father's "spade" cuts the "gravelly ground," "digging" (3–5).

There are two dynamics at work here that characterize Heaney specifically and Irish poetry generally. Heaney uses sound for movement, and the movement allows readers to participate with the speaker. Picture the poet at a desk in his room on the second floor of his family cottage. He composes as we watch. We listen to the scratch of his pen as he gestures toward the window; perhaps he turns at the sound he then describes, and the sounds he conveys with onomatopoeia that reproduces the sound he hears to create movement as we too listen to the shovel grinding against the gravel (which is what a shovel on gravel does sound like). The second dynamic is that the sound becomes a rhythm that redirects attention from the gun and its dilemma to the more personal one the young poet, the man of letters, faces: how does he square his calling with a family of farmers, a family that boasts the best at what they do? Hence the speaker looks down till his father's "straining rump" in the "flowerbeds" comes up "twenty years away" to another time when he dug "through potato drills" (5–9) that the speaker will then describe through the perspective of a child.

In the second stanza, Heaney's speaker juxtaposes his father in the present, digging in the garden, with the one of his youth who dug up potatoes for a living, and it is his father's "craft" that the boy admires. We know this because of the description that follows in the next stanza, and which begins with a reminder of what is at stake for the speaker, when he begins with "the coarse boot" on the shovel that is "levered firmly" just inside the knee. In short, the spade is like a part of the father; thus tool and farmer are one. The stanza continues and readers sense the growing admiration in the child who comes through the adult speaker describing his father's precision in slicing "to scatter new potatoes and "loving their cool hardness" (13–14).

At this point Heaney has reached a transitional moment in his search for purpose. Is it enough that the father was a good farmer and provider? Is this truly his heritage, and if he chooses it must he abandon the other life he might lead? We sense the transition in the short, two-line stanza that is pure sentiment. "By God, the old man could handle a spade. / Just like his old man" (15–16). What strikes the reader here is the revelation in the speaker's voice. He admires the father today even as he remembers him then. As he remembers him then, he also remembers his grandfather, who in the next stanza "cut more turf in a day / Than any man on Toner's Bog" (17–18). Is it the boast of a small boy to his companions? For the speaker the legend of his grandfather comports with his own memory of the man. "Once I carried him milk" (19), though the fact that it was "once" could speak to either that it only happened once or that once is emblematic for any number of other times it might have happened at that time in the speaker's life, the moment becomes indelible to the child because it is rooted in family pride. The fact that the bottle is "corked sloppily with paper" (20) provides yet another pun for how one digs. It is on paper that the speaker mines his past and produces these sentiments. In turn, these sentiments conjure the imagery that conveys those feelings then and now to the speaker and then to us, even though what is described simply relates the physical activities of grandfather, who "straightened up / To drink it then" went right back to work "nicking and slicing neatly" as he continued digging (20–24).

The speaker's father is associated with potatoes and a garden, with providing for the family. The speaker's grandfather is associated with the family heritage of being the best turf digger, a hard worker and provider who contrasts with the icons that Boland criticizes in "Miss Eire." To the speaker, who remembers the day he brings grandfather a drink, the grandfather is digging, not in the sense that he merely labors, but that he illustrates what that digging means—being the best of who you are. In the penultimate stanza, the speaker pools the images of father and grandfather into a single sensation that is emblematic of each of them and what they release in his mind. The "potato mould" and the "soggy peat" "through living roots" (25–28) are the binds that tie him to his family.

The young man has come to that moment when his next choice must be manhood; there is nowhere left to go and he cannot be what the men in his family have been. In the final stanza, he repeats the central image in the first, but with a profound difference that directs the meaning from outside to within. As in the first, the pen rests in his hand, but rather than "snug as a gun" the speaker now declares that he has found a new meaning for his life—he can maintain his family's heritage, its history, without resorting to the violence that strikes terror in friends and neighbors as easily as the British colonizers. In the final line, the axiom that has gone missing in the family sentiment is now as snug as the spade against his father's knee: the pen is both mightier than the sword and can dig deeper than the sharpest shovel. What he owes to his lineage is not their talent with a spade, but their devotion to a skill that the boy admires and the man imitates.

Whether or not Philip Larkin is a misogynist or simply reveling in male independence, his poem "Maiden Name" makes it clear why women poets such as Smith and Boland demand a chance to define their own familial roles as woman, professional, or spouse. His poem begins with an act: "Marrying left your maiden name disused" (1). It is not unused, or misused; her "maiden name" has become disused, or no longer in use or used for its original purpose—an idea that will be returned to at the end of the poem. What Larkin does now is to draw attention to the contrasts that are striking either by their absence or amplification. The speaker taunts that the maiden name's "five light sounds" do not "mean" the young woman's "face," "voice," or her myriad "variants of grace" (2–3); in short, her former name can no longer be associated with the young woman he knows. In the concluding lines of the stanza, however, Larkin introduces one of the paradoxes for which he is famous, a paradox that has led some scholars to re-examine Larkin's treatment of his subject and audience. Gillian

Steinberg claims that "Larkin's tendency towards sympathy with the poem's characters . . . extends to an even deeper and more consistent sympathy for or understanding of the reader and the reader's expectations" (122). The question left is sympathy for whom: the speaker of the poem, the single woman of his memory, or the married woman he contrasts?

Larkin next introduces language by virtue of the law and the linguistic logic that results. The speaker resumes by acknowledging that the former young woman he knew has been "thankfully confused" legally "with someone else" (i.e., her husband's wife), so she "cannot be semantically" identified with "that young beauty" now contained within the maiden name, or in Larkin's verse: "It was of her that these two words were used" (4–8). Such language seems innocuous enough until we examine some of the words and what they imply. The adjective "thankfully" when addressing the now married woman who is confused with the former beauty implies that the unmarried "girl" differs from the married "woman." In other words, she has been transformed from the former beauty into the wife. At this point, however, when coupled with "by law" and "semantically," the redefining of the person by language is the same as the substitution of physical relations. The young woman will now be defined by association with her husband, and because of the marriage she can never be seen as primarily or only that beauty again.

The second stanza develops this metaphor of transmogrification, as the maiden name is "a phrase applicable to no one" (8). The maiden name is "lying just where [she] left it" the day she married, and the abandoned maiden name now remains only in "old lists" and "programmes, a school prize or two" and her puppy love letters tied with "tartan ribbon" (9–11); only these items now symbolize to that "young beauty" what the maiden name reflects. In short, the maiden name merely represents the whole life before marriage. What it is, of course, is "scentless, weightless, strengthless," and "untruthful." Typically, although the language points to denotation, the measurements are not tangible. Lacking weight, strength, and truth does not correspond to flesh. "Try whispering it slowly" (12–13) suggests that if she is just the memories and memorabilia of the girl who collected that self, then that self is no longer a living organism after marriage. The implication is that the name is merely a reference to what is past; it is not a flesh and blood past, either. It has meaning as it relates to the items described in the stanza, but not as a representation of the newly married woman. For the speaker at least, a maiden name is one that can only be someone who no longer exists; it is the only description of the phrase that the speaker can infer.

Larkin concludes the second stanza by equivocating: "No, it means you. Or since you're past and gone" (14). This final line of the second stanza does not complete the thought. It continues into the beginning of the third stanza with the main clause: "It means what we feel about you then" (15). Not only does the name have no intrinsic value any longer, but it can only be supported on any level of meaning by the ways in which those who knew her pre-marriage retain that previous association with her. In other words, she cannot be separate and the same, only separate. The speaker continues with three abstract lines that refer to the young woman's qualities now lost forever in the flesh. He calls her "beautiful," "near," and "young," and "so vivid" that she could still be there, "unfingermarked again" (16–18). To be "fingermarked" means one must be either transparent or reflective, like the plastic that might cover a scrapbook of her papered past. It also implies a physical touch that contrasts the abstract language he uses to describe her in that papered past.

If, however, there was any doubt about that opening image about marriage, Larkin seals it in the final lines with the same kind of taunt with which he begins it. The maiden name is now the "old name" and what it "shelters" is the "faithfulness" of those who will keep the memory "vivid," but the price to the married woman will be a steep one "of losing shape and meaning less" in lockstep with her "depreciating luggage laden" (19–21). What the speaker signals is that he at least cannot hold both views of one woman. The young woman is either the one whom he fondly recalls, whose beauty and grace were flawless, or the one now whose value and worth is symbolized in the family "baggage" with which she is laden. Not only is she baggage, but she is also "laden" with her own "luggage"—the stores of experience acquired through growing up. To the speaker, though, the maiden is no longer associated with the luggage she carries but with the baggage (wife) she has become and the self she cast aside, the "maiden name" that no longer points to a maiden. It also suggests Larkin's rather chauvinistic view that women cannot be married without becoming property, or "luggage."

Clearly, Larkin has a bachelor's jaded view of marriage, perhaps the result of his early family experience and emblematic of his choice to remain a bachelor. Unfortunately, one drawback of such bachelorhood is a problematic understanding of women. This can be said because middle-class men in early twentieth-century English society often led lives of near total isolation from girls during their developmental years. The tone of Larkin's poem suggests an adolescent boy who has an idle crush on his older neighbor, and ends with the backhanded compliments of ridicule and scorn.

The Victorian certainty of family permanence as the microcosm of an empire that boasted "the sun never sets on the British empire," and which informed the period, would be put to the test during World War II and would end abruptly after the war ended. The separate spheres that divided Victorian society into the male world and the female world, which for women was dominated by duty to family and church, would end in an international conflict that saw the death or maiming of nearly an entire generation of young men. It would also signal an end to the conservative pastoral tradition that informed both society and poetry.

Eavan Boland and Stevie Smith show readers that whoever controls the narrative (religion, myth) controls how society is organized. As women writing to free families from the rigid control of the church and men, they exemplify Great Britain in flux. The same can be said of

Philip Larkin, whose definition of the family role a wife plays—versus the single young woman she once was—reflects the very writing against tradition in which Smith and Boland engage. Although it might not seem so, Seamus Heaney also wrestles with family and heritage in a shifting social world as he tries to fit his intellectual work into the labor and heritage of his father and grandfather. The voices presented here vary dramatically, but their individual social conditions, and the life choices they themselves make, contribute to their understanding of the changing family dynamic in Great Britain after the decline of empire.

Works Cited

Almeida, David M., Elaine Wethington, and Amy L. Chandler. "Daily Transmission of Tensions between Marital Dyads and Parent-Child Dyads." *Journal of Marriage and the Family* 61.1 (1999): 49–61.

Boland, Eavan. "Miss Eire." *Collected Poems*. Manchester: Carcanet, 1995. 102–03.

Dettmar, Kevin J. H., and Jennifer Wicke, eds. *The Longman Anthology of British Literature: The Twentieth Century.* 3rd ed. Vol. 2C. New York: Pearson, 2006.

Dissanayake, Ellen. *Art and Intimacy: How the Arts Began.* Seattle: U of Washington P, 2000.

Eliot, T. S. *Selected Prose of T. S. Eliot.* Ed. Frank Kermode. New York: Harcourt, 1975.

Fussell, Paul. *The Great War and Modern Memory.* 1975. New York: Oxford UP, 2000.

Heaney, Seamus. "Digging." *Selected Poems: 1966–1987.* New York: Noonday, 1990. 3–4.

Jameson, Fredric. *A Singular Modernity.* London: Verso, 2002.

Judson, Olivia. "The Selfless Gene." *The Atlantic.* Oct. 2007. Rpt. in *The Best American Science and Nature Writing.* Ed. Jerome Groopman. Boston: Houghton, 2008. 143–54.

Larkin, Philip. "Maiden Name." *Collected Poems.* Ed. Anthony Thwaite. New York: Farrar, 2004. 53.

Lerner, Laurence. *Philip Larkin.* 2nd ed. Devon: Northcote, 2005.

Milton, John. *Complete Poems and Major Prose.* Ed. Merritt Y. Hughes. New York: Macmillan, 1957.

Mithen, Steven. *After the Ice: A Global Human History, 20,000–5000 B.C.* 2003. Cambridge: Harvard UP, 2006.

Randolph, Jody Allen, ed. *Eavan Boland: A Sourcebook.* Manchester: Carcanet, 2007.

Robinson, Jane. *Bluestocking: The Remarkable Story of the First Women to Fight for an Education*. London: Penguin, 2009.

Smith, Stevie. "How Cruel Is the Story of Eve." *New Collected Poems of Stevie Smith*. New York: New Directions, 1988. 118–19.

Steinberg, Gillian. *Philip Larkin and His Audiences*. London: Palgrave, 2010.

Wollstonecraft, Mary. *Vindication of the Rights of Women (1792)*. London: Penguin, 1985.

Domestic Forces in Leo Tolstoy's *Anna Karenina* ____

Brett Cooke

Family is central to *Anna Karenina* (1873 to 1877). One need look no further than its famous first line: "All happy families are alike; each unhappy family is unhappy in its own way" (1).[1] Leo Tolstoy's novel illustrates this maxim by narrating the rise and fall of several couples. He provides readers with a numerous but limited range of potential pairs for comparison: Anna and Karenin, Anna and Vronsky, Vronsky and Kitty, Kitty and Levin, and Dolly and Stiva, yielding a rich trove of relative assessments.

A moment's consideration, however, suffices to call Tolstoy's dictum into question. Perhaps Anna's new home with Vronsky is ultimately cold as was hers with Karenin, but were the Scherbatskys, Kitty and Dolly's natal family, truly that similar to the Levins, except in their perceived happiness? How much similarity suffices? At what point? (Families are dynamic systems.) Are the Olbonskys, with their six children and philandering father, happy or unhappy? What if both? Are there relative degrees of happiness or unhappiness? (Of course, there are.) And does this statement apply to millions of families worldwide, with their different structures and traditions? Is there only one formula for family happiness? What, then, is the secret Tolstoy never explicitly reveals?

Ultimately, it does not matter. Tolstoy manages to grasp our attention and keep it over hundreds of pages because family fortunes are important to most of us. Evolutionary criticism predicts we will be interested in matters which have been crucial to our success, in this case reproduction. Few do not care about romantic love, the much-desired cement of the domestic social contract. This is usually valorized as marriage; we happily read about it in innumerable stories. We never tire of evaluating the health of families and would prefer it if we could love our parents and they us, much as we hope to share the same with our offspring and siblings. We acutely sense when things are going right, more so when they are not. Although significant variations persist, the nuclear family of children and collaborating adults who raise them is a human universal in all cultures, given the obvious advantages of spontaneous, indeed pleasurable, domestic cooperation. All viable societies are organized to establish dependable means of raising children. This includes Russia of the 1870s when Tolstoy wrote *Anna Karenina*. Assuring this support explains why conservative societies at that time were reluctant to permit unhappy couples to divorce and why custody of children continues to be a vexing matter. All of these issues are at the heart of *Anna Karenina*, as they are in many classics.

Evaluating different family experiences is essential to reading this novel. Tolstoy uses Dolly Oblonskaya as a veritable external examiner. Well before the central scandal begins, Dolly senses the problematic nature of the Karenin household: "there was something false in the whole shape of their family life" (66). Later she visits Anna and Vronsky's estate and discerns a similar artificiality, so much so that she hastens her departure; Dolly's judgment clearly presages Anna's catastrophe. Sadly, the title character finds that she cannot manage to build a happy family. Meanwhile, Dolly virtually moves in with her sister Kitty at the Levin estate, obviously finding a stable domicile there for her children. For their part, the Oblonsky brood proves to be discerning themselves, happy to play with Levin, but after the ball they no longer approach Anna—apparently sensing a negative change in their aunt, even before she acknowledges her infatuation with Vronsky (97). Home building involves establishing affective bonds among family members. Tolstoy develops a symmetrical pattern contrasting two families: while Anna forgets her son and admits that she cannot love her daughter, the last event in the novel is Levin's recognition of love for his and Kitty's baby boy. As one family undergoes dissolution, another is growing and, indeed, thriving.

Preference for marriage, the core subject of the novel, is not to be taken for granted. The novel was written partly as a rebuttal to recent attacks on the nuclear family and marriage with the aim of liberating people, especially women, from domestic roles and replacing their family values with allegiance to a wider society. Nikolai Chernyshevsky's novel, *What Is to Be Done?* (1862), advocates open marriage, wherein both parties would be free to have lovers and be free of any obligations for mutual exclusivity (Pevear ix). Divorce offers a means of correcting mistakes in pairing and as a source of relief for partners subjected to various forms of conjugal abuse. Tolstoy used his novel to consider the options of a woman in a loveless home. That the Karenin household is respectful, wealthy, and socially prominent shows how Tolstoy focused his study of families on the one missing ingredient: romantic love.

Fathers are expected invest in their biological offspring. A positive model is set by Levin's brother-in-law Arseny Lvov, who compromises his career to provide an education for his sons (682). This example of self-sacrifice poses a contrast to Stiva Oblonsky, who undermines his children's prospects by neglecting his family's finances as he chases other women. Although Stiva is eventually able to gain a better-paying job, Dolly is repeatedly forced to sell off her land. This invalidates his repeated assertion that his womanizing harms no one. Raising physically and socially viable children usually requires the long-term support of not just the mother, but, indeed, other family members as well. When Dolly worries about her family's future, Kitty and Levin come to their rescue by inviting them to spend summers at their estate. Levin persuades Kitty to yield her inheritance to her sister. They are, after all, seeing to the needs of their nephews and nieces.

This concern begins with the title: our heroine bears the feminine variant of her husband's surname, Karenina. Symbolically she is more a member of his family than he is hers. Such male-favored asymmetry is characteristic of patriarchy, the dominant family culture throughout nineteenth-century Europe and economically developed societies elsewhere. Anthropologists explain this bias as a means of encouraging paternal investment in children by assuring husbands regarding the paternity of their offspring. Their children share their surnames, as if the men possess them. This is true for daughters only until their marriage, whereupon, per common practice, they adopt the name of their husbands—very much as if ownership had passed from one man to the other. Indeed, this transfer is symbolically enacted in wedding rituals when the father "gives away" the bride to her groom.[2] Knowing that Stiva Oblonsky is Anna's brother, no Russian reader needs to be told that Anna's maiden name was Oblonskaya; this appellation was automatic as it was later with the adoption of her married name. This tradition of surnames is a prop to patriarchy and consequent male domination of women.

Maintenance of paternal surnames is meaningful only if children bear the names of their biological fathers, especially for sons who are then able to pass them on to their progeny. In other words, patriarchal surnames convey male bloodlines. Note how the conservative Levin proudly asserts, "I consider myself an aristocrat [. . .] who can point to three or four *honest* generations in their families' past" (172; emphasis added). He questions Vronsky's legitimacy, wondering about his mother, "God knows who she didn't have liaisons with . . ." (172). Surnames are an immediate impetus to sexual fidelity, especially that of the mother, as the foundation of a happy family.[3] Vronsky bemoans the fact that, per Russian law, any son he and Anna might have would bear her husband's surname (627). Furthermore, their children legally would be bastards, with no rights of inheritance, and subject to social discrimination as such.[4] Further, illegitimate children cannot inherit their parents' noble titles, obviously another prop to patriarchal sexism and the enforcement of female conjugal fidelity. Until her marriage Anna was Princess Oblonskaya, much as Vronsky was a count. Their daughter, however, cannot share his title, an important distinction in European society of his time, since they are not married. This may hold little meaning for twenty-first-century Americans, but Count Tolstoy was interested in aristocrats, despite his repeated assertion of democratic values.

Russian culture, however, exerts a second degree of marking, one unique in Europe and that, as Liza Knapp claims, also "reinforces patrimony" (14). As their middle name Russians automatically bear patronyms, a variant of their father's first name. It never changes. When readers learn that Stiva's middle name is Arkadievich, they also then know that his sister Anna's is Arkadievna and that their father must have been Arkady Oblonsky. This system implies no information about their mother—or mothers. Other forms of calculation are entailed. If Konstantin Dmitrievich Levin's half brother is Sergei Ivanovich Koznyshev, it is obvious they shared a mother, not a father. Russians do not have to be told that his full brother, Nikolai, is also Dmitrievich Levin. Clearly they are the products of their mother's second marriage.

Tolstoy uses first names in an unusual manner. Normally authors differentiate their characters with distinctive names. But *Anna Karenina* includes five Annas, two Sergeis, and two Alexeis—a state of affairs confusing to readers. It is uncommon, though entirely possible, for sons to share their father's first name. This would create a rather uncreative doubling, as in Ivan Ivanovich, something avoided in *Anna Karenina*. Alexei Karenin's son is Sergei and Levin's is Dmitry (probably in honor of the boy's paternal grandfather). If maintained down the male line, it would be difficult to distinguish one Ivan Ivanovich from another within a family. Russians do not use name suffixes such as *junior* or *senior*, but appear to prefer for each person to have his own combination of names. Furthermore, differentiation is only possible among paternal siblings by means of the first name, as with Konstantin Levin and Nikolai, while there is nothing to link them to their stepbrother. Tolstoy usually refers to his male hero by his surname, and Nikolai by first name. However, both Anna's husband and her lover are Alexei, an entirely possible coincidence, but also a source of confusion for her, especially when she later dreams that she is married to *both*. In a certain sense, she is. Insofar as personal names are thought to denote something unique to the individual, this lack of distinction suggests something common to both. Mercifully, Tolstoy usually refers to them by their last names. This doubling creates a resonance clear only to Russians in that one cannot use the patronym to determine whether Anna's daughter is the offspring of Vronsky or Karenin. In either case she would be Alexeevna. Yet worse, Russian society did not recognize Vronsky as her biological father; instead, the child's legal surname becomes Karenina, a consequence that only further contributes to their tangled affairs. This is somewhat resolved when Karenin legally adopts the girl after Anna's suicide.

Names also buttress another distinction, that of close intimate acquaintances from all others. In one form or another this dividing line exists in most languages, albeit at diverse points of relation in different societies.[5] Modern English dropped the distinction between *thou* and *you*; the former somewhat persists in our basis of address in first names, especially with affective forms such as Kitty or Dolly in this novel. But in Russian the second person singular form is usually accompanied by nicknames, without the patronym. Anna refers to her son Sergei as Seryozha. English translations of the novel also blind some readers to Tolstoy's unusual use of English nicknames—Dolly instead of Dasha for Darya, Kitty instead of Katya for Ekaterina, and Betsy instead of Liza for Elizaveta (Tverskaya); additionally, Annie is used for her daughter and, indeed, Stiva (Steve) instead of Styopa for Stepan. That Anna never is referred to as Anya or Annie by anyone seems strange.[6] Furthermore, she addresses her husband stiffly by formal first name and patronym—Alexei Alexandrovich—even when speaking in the familiar voice (*ty*). And he replies like the bureaucrat he is:

> I want to warn you [. . .] that by indiscretion and light-mindedness you may give society occasion to talk about you. Your much too animated conversation tonight with Count Vronsky [. . .] attracted attention. (146)

There is little wonder that their marriage seems so cold—and eventually fails.

We should consider that we are reading a novel principally about a woman, characteristically strange for a time in which women were still regarded and treated as the inferior gender and denied many rights shared by men. This raises the question as to why a woman should justify so much attention, a question pertinent to novels of adultery like *Madame Bovary* (1856), *Effi Briest* (1894 to 1895), and *The Portrait of a Lady* (1880 to 1881). Concern for paternal certainty is the rationale for the double standard which calls for significantly greater constraint of women than men. In most societies, including Russia, men were relatively free to violate their marital promises without social or legal sanction. This contrast is made distinctly clear when Anna attends the opera—and her mere appearance ignites a scandal. A woman in the next box openly refuses to sit in her presence and leaves in fury, calling much hostile attention to be cast on Anna. All this is witnessed by her lover Vronsky, sitting quite unnoticed in the audience. He is able to participate in society unhindered, while she is ostracized.

Anna Karenina frankly observes the unequal status of women, something one character traces to the biased manner in which both law and public opinion punishes adultery (391). Once Anna makes an open break with her husband, Russian society closes off her range of action to the point that she can have neither friends nor any sort of occupation. Meanwhile, her brother Stiva only suffers Dolly's threat to leave and divorce him, a punishment she quickly realizes will more directly lead to her ruin and that of their children. Like many other betrayed wives, she decides to maintain the family, even though Stiva soon returns to his philandering ways and continues to neglect his dependents. One might argue, however, that unfaithful husbands risk their lives, but this is likely only if they have an affair with another man's wife. Guests at the Oblonskys discuss Vasya Pryachnikov, who challenged his wife's lover to a duel and shot him dead, "like a real man!" (391–2). Of course, as Karenin notes, this requires that the faithful husband risk his own life for "a criminal wife" (280). In essence, infidelity is treated as a property offense by one man against another.[7] A woman, as Dolly learns, has little recourse.

At the time, women's behavior was intensely guarded by their male relatives, if not also by society at large. This can be traced to some of the essential facts of reproductive biology. It would be a rare mother who was not certain who her children are. On the other hand, fathers cannot be so assured. Due to internal conception and the lack of estrus, a limited period of the year—i.e., heat—when females of other species conceive, men cannot be certain as to who are their biological offspring. If genes influence behavior, those that promote their own reproduction are more likely to persist than those that do not. It then follows that most men do not want to be duped into supporting another man's child. One of the common and most feared sanctions was being labeled as a cuckold—the husband of an unfaithful wife. In any time and place, deceived husbands greatly outnumber deceived wives, yet there is no term for the latter (Cooke 115). It is as if they do not matter. Men, on the other hand, fear stigmatization due to their wives' infidelity. When he learns of the affair, Karenin demands that Anna keep it secret, that she observe social propriety. But he soon sees that his political career is beginning to slip.

In this novel true paternal uncertainty seems unlikely. Yet there are two cases of male jealousy blown out of proportion. When Karenin discovers Anna's betrayal, he suspects that their eight-year-old son is not his own. No reason, other than her present behavior, is given to think that Anna might have been unfaithful years ago. Levin has every reason to be happy in his marriage to the eminently faithful Kitty, whose face radiates "innocent truthfulness" (450). Nevertheless, he continues to brood over how she once preferred Vronsky to him. Levin has trouble controlling thoughts of her infidelity, although her demure behavior gives him no basis for suspicion. When their guest Vasya Veselovsky persists in flirting with her, Levin rudely expels him from their estate.

With the availability of paternity testing in the twenty-first century the possibility of paternal deception is remote, but it was not so in the past. People had to take whatever measures were available to increase husbands' confidence in their paternity. As a result, women's dress, their hair, and especially their relationships were closely scrutinized. They were not allowed to freely associate with men—not without some sort of chaperones—nor even with adulterous women, lest it might seem they become infected. Although an unfaithful wife herself, Betsy Tverskaya fears to be seen with Anna once her friend begins to live openly with Vronsky.

Until the development of modern means of genetic testing, fertility clinics, and sperm banks, marriage was society's best means of shaping future generations. Marital traditions can be viewed as methods of assuring the building of healthy families through solid, indeed, faithful, conjugal bonds. Matchmaking, engagement, and weddings are thus important rituals in all societies, including Russia. Much of the Russian Orthodox wedding ritual is described at length in the novel, a passage which must be very familiar to Russian readers (451–57). It notably includes instructions for spouses to be faithful to one another.

The novel begins at a crucial juncture in Russian social history—a time when the Russian tradition of the matchmaker was declining. Such is how Kitty's parents got married. An intermediary suggested a match; the pair then had a chance to meet one another. The *svata*, in this case Kitty's grandaunt, conveyed their impressions and, since neither vetoed the match, they agreed to marry with their parents' blessings (44). Despite their disagreements regarding Kitty, the Shcherbatskys are a very happy couple. But this method does not always work for the best, for this is how Anna was guided, also by an aunt, to marry Karenin.

At the beginning of the novel, Kitty's mother muses about other methods of courtship and marriage coming into Russia. One, presumably French, but also found in many non-European societies, called "for the parents to decide the children's fate" (44). Although it "was not accepted, and was even condemned," by most, it had its proponents; Betsy Tverskaya says that the "only happy marriages I know are arranged ones" (44, 137). The reason for its unpopularity is probably the bride and groom having little say in one of the most fateful decisions in their lives. Forcible misalliances serve as the negative pole of many narratives. Obviously, modern populations increasingly believe it helps if some romantic love is involved in the formation of families.

Nevertheless, parents typically expect to exert a guiding influence. The Shcherbatskys are waiting for Vronsky to seek his mother's blessing before proposing marriage to Kitty. For his part, Vronsky defies his mother's disapproval of his open affair with Anna. Meanwhile, Princess Shcherbatsky is troubled by the supposedly English practice whereby "girls of Kitty's age formed some sort of groups, attended some sort of courses, freely associated with men, drove around by themselves." She is upset to see that "many no longer curtsied, and, worse still, they were all firmly convinced that choosing a husband was their own and not their parents' business" (44). Clearly she is discomfited at this loosening of parental control and consequent liberal behavior. Parents carry a great investment in a daughter's prospects; her children will be their grandchildren. Readers are told that "the old prince, like all fathers, was especially scrupulous about the honour and purity of his daughters; he was unreasonably jealous over them" (44). When Vronsky spurns Kitty, the prince exclaims, "There are and always have been laws against such young devils!" (122). He talks of challenging Vronsky to a duel, but he takes no action. Evidently times had changed. Trying to discern how one's daughter might be dependably married imparts great interest to this and other classic novels.

In *Anna Karenina* women are treated as their parents', then their husband's, capital. Kitty complains to Dolly about her father, that "it seems to me all he thinks is that I've got to get married. Mama takes me to a ball: it seems to me she only takes me in order to get me married quickly and be rid of me. [. . .] The so-called suitors I can't even look at. It seems as if they're taking my measurements" (126). Balls constitute a limited form of assortative mating, where men are welcome to approach and invite women to dance. Kitty at first enjoys considerable popularity, evidently regarded in her first social season as attractive. At the ball she expects Vronsky to make a commitment to her. She refuses many partners for what she thinks will be the decisive *mazurka* at the end of the evening. Instead, he dances with Anna.

Another common practice was for families to hold regular open houses. The Shcherbatskys hold theirs on Thursdays, the Karenins on Mondays; no invitation is necessary (32,106). As with balls, Tolstoy does not have to specify that only guests of sufficient social rank will be admitted, which effectively screens eligible bachelors. Care has to be exercised in the surveillance of daughters. Once lost, their reputations can only be regained with difficulty. In order to protect their marketability as brides, eligible women had to carefully control their comportment. As Dolly reminds Levin, a woman of their class cannot make a romantic initiative without risking her all-important and hard to regain reputation for sexual purity. Indeed, she must not allow any bachelor to court her for too long without "declaring his intentions." Otherwise people will believe she favors him and thereby scare off other possible suitors. Karenin was pressured into marrying Anna; her aunt "insinuated" that "he had already compromised the girl and that he was honor-bound to propose" (507). Kitty damages her reputation by giving the impression that she loves Vronsky; she then has difficulty attracting a suitor and, at age eighteen, already fears becoming an old maid (397). Note how long it takes Levin to renew his courtship, despite several hints that Kitty is now receptive to his offer.

A major feature of the mating process, prominent in *Anna Karenina*, is the evaluation of potential spouses according to their families. Here, too, past behavior is viewed as the best indication of future fidelity. Siblings are judged by family associations. The happiness of the Shcherbatskys after more than thirty years of marriage suggests the promise of fidelity from each of their three daughters. Kitty's behavior is impeccable. Lvov's devotion as a father allows us to infer the same for Nataly. Despite Stiva's betrayal of his family, Dolly continues to love him. Meanwhile, Stiva is an inveterate womanizer. The novel begins in crisis when Dolly discovers his affair with the family's governess. This proves to be predictive of Anna's violation of her marriage vows.

Vronsky seems to be the veritable image of what women desire in prospective husbands; he is rich, handsome, popular, educated, and enormously talented. In effect, he gives promise of becoming a generous provider. He offers to turn his inheritance over to his brother and is quick to give 200 roubles to the family of the worker killed at the train station. Indeed, this charitable action catches Anna's eye; she wonders if he did it for her sake, even though they had just met (65, 73). What is there not to like about him? Kitty's mother believes that Vronsky satisfies all of her desires for a husband for her daughter: "Very rich, intelligent, well-born, a brilliant military-courtly career, and a charming man. One could wish for nothing better" (44).

But then there is Vronsky's family background. Kitty and her family do not know that he has little intention of starting a family. It is noted that "Vronsky had never known family life. His mother in her youth had been a brilliant society woman who, during her marriage and especially after it, had had many love affairs, known to all the world. He barely remembered his father and had been brought up in the Corps of Pages" (56). In other words, Vronsky experienced no respect for marriage in his family-of-origin, but more likely learned, even if obliquely, a penchant for womanizing. This is seemingly confirmed when we learn that his married brother keeps a mistress. Tolstoy never tells us, but surely Anna knows his background. Does this knowledge contribute to her suspicion of his fidelity, that, seemingly without any particular cause, she is unable to trust him, especially when she has no other recourse?

Worse, Vronsky's family background, or rather lack of one, presages his failure to build a happy family of his own with Anna. Early in the novel we are informed that, while courting—and compromising

Kitty—"marriage had never presented itself as a possibility to him. He not only did not like family life, but pictured the family, and especially a husband […] as something alien, hostile, and, above all, ridiculous" (57). What a loving family life might have given him is a capacity for empathy and spontaneous cooperation. In that same passage Tolstoy tells readers that he is unable to imagine Kitty's predicament, that she might be expecting an offer from him. There thus is little surprise that his later efforts to forge domestic bonds are so unconvincing. Karenin refuses to yield custody of Seryozha to Anna partly for fear of how their son will be raised.

Levin, on the other hand, gives every indication of being trustworthy. Clearly his family background is very influential. As the youngest son he inherited the family home. Presumably this Russian tradition ensured care for aging parents, even though his died long ago. Levin is attached to the estate as a shrine to them: "It was the world in which his father and mother had lived and died. They had lived a life which for Levin seemed the ideal of all perfection and which he dreamed of renewing with his wife, with his family" (95). The only problem at the time was that he did not have a wife, having just suffered Kitty's rejection. But he renews his suit with success. At the end of the novel Levin witnesses Kitty breastfeeding and bathing their infant son. Having been part of a family, he wants a family. On the other hand, Karenin was not only an orphan, but he lost his only brother. Perhaps there is no surprise that he has few friends.

According to Frank J. Sulloway's concept of adaptative radiation, siblings from the same family grow up differently and seek different family niches to avoid direct competition with one another. They also are sensitive, especially the younger, to "adverse comparisions" (cited in John V. Knapp 17–18). This seems to hold for Levin's family. He does not like being compared to either his half-brother Sergei, a renowned intellectual, or his full brother Nikolai, who has had a motley career. Levin, for his part, is every bit the responsible estate proprietor, in effect the reverse image of the dissolute, nihilist Nikolai. Perhaps inevitable for the youngest son, he does not enjoy Sergei's respect, but he fulfills his responsibility in handling their common assets and he cares for Nikolai on his deathbed. Although Nikolai has a common-law marriage of sorts with Masha, their family background seems to have a lingering influence on Sergei, who remains faithful to the memory of his dead fiancé, Marie.[8] Meanwhile, the domestic bliss of Kitty's parents accounts for Levin's love. He was infatuated with each of their daughters in turn, only Dolly and Nataly found other husbands first. Evidently Levin is in love with the entire family and, thanks to Kitty, is finally able to marry into it.

Another perspective apparent to Russians is that, through Levin, the author was reliving how his own family shaped his personality. Levin is based on Lev, the Russian original for the writer's formal name, Leo. Tolstoy inherited Yasnaya Polyana as the youngest son. The novel reflects his closeness to his three full brothers and sister, two of whom died young, like Nikolai. He eldest brother, also a Sergei, had a common-law wife, again like Nikolai. Tolstoy used his novel to consider how his family came into being and influenced his life. Like Levin, he is much influenced by the image of a mother who died when he was a toddler: "[He] barely remembered his mother. His notion of her was a sacred memory, and his future wife would have to be, in his imagination, the repetition of that lovely, sacred ideal of a woman which his mother was for him" (95). Clearly this infantile fantasy has a formative effect on him: "He was not only unable to picture to himself the love of a woman without marriage, but he first pictured the family to himself and only then the woman who would give him that family [. . .] for Levin [marriage] was the chief concern of life, on which all happiness depended" (95). This influence overwhelms his earlier promiscuity: like many Russian gentlemen of his time, including Vronsky, Levin had many affairs with peasant women and prostitutes. Like Tolstoy, Levin gives his young bride his diaries to read on the eve of their wedding. In both cases, their love survived this unnecessary crisis.

Tolstoy uses his own experience to suggest how happy families are created. He married one of the three Behrs girls. Interestingly, the Shcherbatsky sisters follow Russian tradition by marrying in the order of their age. Tolstoy ran into some initial objections when he did not propose to the eldest, Liza, but rather, the second, Sonya. Scholars have long wondered whether it was the youngest, Tanya, whom he most loved. The description of how Levin is late to his own wedding for lack of a pressed shirt re-creates Tolstoy's own experience. Both real and fictional marriages were the result of long acquaintance and significant spiritual harmony.[9] And then there is the curious manner in which both pairs finally got engaged; Kitty and Sonya Behrs had to decipher proposals in the form of word puzzles. This virtually required them to read their future husbands' minds. This suggests psychological cohesion, a high degree of metacommunication, essential for spontaneous and empathetic cooperation in a family (John V. Knapp 19). Notably, this level of communication is entirely missing in Anna and Karenin's marriage, where they rarely imagine what the other is thinking.

This biographical evidence indicates that Tolstoy used his novel to carry on an open-ended investigation of family systems, in this case his own. As we should hope with any course of productive thought, there are surprises. Against all expectation, including what was said earlier about paternal certainty, Karenin develops an affective bond with Anna and Vronsky's illegitimate daughter. Indeed, when Anna almost dies from childbirth, he steps in and sees to the infant's care. Could it be that this proximity breeds bonding, regardless of the fact that Karenin is not genetically related? Indeed, Annie is the physical representation of Anna's betrayal. True, Karenin later questions his affection for Annie, but, nevertheless he fights for custody of his son and eventually for her as well. Meanwhile, Seryozha is disoriented by his mother's affair, unsure how to regard Vronsky, and develops antipathy toward his own father. Was he sensing a shift in his paternal support, or is this due to his sense of betrayal when he is falsely informed that his mother is dead? Here, as elsewhere, Tolstoy senses additional domestic forces at hand.

The most important surprise involves the heroine herself. Scholars have long noted how the novel began with Tolstoy's curiosity regarding the suicide of his neighbor, Anna Pirogova, who threw herself under a train. He first drafted her as unattractive, apparently as part of a lesson on the wages of (female) sin (Turner 19). But clearly her image developed in an unexpected direction as the author thought about her and what forces drove her to her dire act. The Anna who first steps off a train near the beginning of the novel with her dark eyelashes and vibrant smile is regarded as one of the most beautiful women in literature. She attracts special attention because she is filled with so much promise and so much danger, both to herself and to her society. Dolly, viewed by Gary Saul Morson as the "moral compass" of the novel, envies Anna's freedom and refuses to reproach her (607–08; Morson 180). She understands that Anna could not have done otherwise. Clearly Tolstoy, an acknowledged conservative in domestic affairs, was using his novel to consider alternative means of constructing happy families.

Notes

1. All references to the novel are by page number of the Pevear and Volokhonsky translation.
2. In the traditional Russian wedding the groom ritually purchases the bride.
3. Liza Knapp points out that there was contemporary objection to this patriarchal practice. The drafts of the novel refer to Emile de Girardin's suggestion that "many of the problems caused in family life because of adultery could be eliminated if women were granted more sexual freedom and if children always took their mother's name" (Liza Knapp 19).
4. Tolstoy was well aware of how his closest friend, the great poet Afanasy Fet, strived for decades to be recognized by his natural father's surname, Shenshin.
5. Anna Berman notes that Russian is usually precise in defining in-law relationships, containing as many as three times as many terms as English. Her 2009 paper shows that Tolstoy's novel contains an unusually dense network of "lateral kinship ties," whereby siblings, in-laws, etc., depend on each other for help.

6. Liza Knapp cites this as an indication of Anna's "isolation" (Liza Knapp 15).
7. Cf. Schwarz, 276–79.
8. This yields yet another doubling of first names, since both are Maria.
9. However, this was much tested in the decades that followed *Anna Karenina* when Tolstoy and his wife staged a protracted, intense, and very public battle over the institutions of marriage and the nuclear family. This drama is nicely encapsulated in the film *The Last Station* (2009) based on Jay Parini's novel of the same title.

Works Cited

Berman, Anna. "A Breach in the Kinship Network: Rethinking Family in *Anna Karenina.*" American Association for the Advancement of Slavic Studies. Boston. 2009.

Cooke, Brett. "Pushkin and the *Femme Fatale*: Jealousy in *Cygan.*" *California Slavic Studies.* Ed. Henrik Birnbaum. Vol. 14. Berkeley: U of California P, 1992. 99–126.

Knapp, John V. "Family Systems Therapy and Literary Study: An Introduction." *Reading the Family Dance: Family Systems Therapy and Literary Study.* Ed. John V. Knapp and Kenneth Womack. Newark: U of Delaware P, 2003.13–26.

Knapp, Lisa. "The Names." *Approaches to Teaching Tolstoy's* Anna Karenina. Ed. Liza Knapp and Amy Mandelker. New York: MLA, 2003. 8–23.

Morson, Gary Saul. Anna Karenina *in Our Time: Seeing More Wisely.* New Haven: Yale UP, 2007.

Pevear, Richard. Introduction. *Anna Karenina.* By Leo Tolstoy. Trans. Richard Pevear and Larissa Volokhonsky. New York: Penguin, 2000, vii–xvi.

Schwarz, Joan I. "Eighteenth Century Law and *Clarissa.*" *The Clarissa Project.* Ed. Carol Houlahan Flynn and Edward Copeland. Vol. 9. New York: AMS, 1999. 269–308.

Tolstoy, Leo. *Anna Karenina.* Trans. Richard Pevear and Larissa Volokhonsky. New York: Penguin, 2000.

Turner, C. J. G. *A* Karenina *Companion.* Waterloo: Wilfrid Laurier UP, 1993.

Marrying the Right Relatives: Family Ties in Jane Austen's *Pride and Prejudice*_____

Massimiliano Morini

Pride and Prejudice, Marriage and Money

While most—if not all—nineteenth-century novels can be said to describe family life in one way or another, very few novelists have explored this area of human experience with as much consistency or thoroughness as Jane Austen. All of Austen's mature books focus on the description of a limited number of nuclei—the "3 or 4 Families in a Country Village" she advised her niece Anna to work on in her own novel (*Selected Letters* 176)—and end with the creation of more nuclei uniting some of the members of the original families. Between that typical beginning and that inevitable end, the spectacle of courtship unfolds under the eyes of parents and relatives: the young people meet when the families call on their neighbors, and also at balls and on other social occasions; they fall in love, form open or secret engagements, and sometimes they elope whether they are engaged or not—thus facing social disgrace. It comes as no surprise, then, that these novels are unsavory for those who like adventure and excitement: even romantic love is a comparatively tame topic in Austen (the elopements always take place out of narrative focus), and all the characters' energy is spent within the context of the family, and with the purpose of forming a new one.

Pride and Prejudice (1813), arguably the most popular of Austen's novels, perfectly fits the above description. At the beginning, readers meet Mr. and Mrs. Bennet and their five unmarried daughters—Jane, Elizabeth, Mary, Kitty, and Lydia. The Bennets move in a very narrow circle of country acquaintances, the foremost of which are Sir William Lucas and his family. Very soon, however, their lives are enlivened by the appearance of Mr. Bingley, a young eligible bachelor, who brings along his sisters and his somber friend Mr. Darcy. In the opening scene of the novel, Austen describes Mrs. Bennet's excitement at the news of Mr. Bingley's coming to stay in the neighborhood:

> Why, my dear, you must know, Mrs. Long says that Netherfield is taken by a young man of large fortune from the north of England; that he came down on Monday in a chaise and four to see the place, and was so much delighted with it that he agreed with Mr. Morris immediately; that he is to take possession before Michaelmas, and some of his servants are to be in the house by the end of next week. (1)

Mrs. Bennet's one purpose in life, as this very first exchange with her husband makes clear, is marrying off her progeny—and readers may be inclined to laugh at her, as witty Mr. Bennet (inwardly) does, for being so sure that this "young man of large fortune," with servants and "a chaise and four" (a closed carriage drawn by four horses), will inevitably want one of their daughters. But as it turns out, the good-natured Mr. Bingley will actually end up marrying the Bennets' good-natured eldest daughter, Jane—this being one of the four weddings that are celebrated in the course of the narrative. The other three marriages completing the final familial reconfiguration will unite dumb Mr. Collins with plain Charlotte Lucas, rakish Mr. Wickham with silly Lydia Bennet (the youngest of the Bennet hatch—a mere fifteen years old!), and, most importantly, Mr. Darcy with Elizabeth Bennet.

The difficult, bickering courtship between Elizabeth and Darcy is, quite obviously, the central event of the whole novel, for both structural and thematic reasons. On the structural plane, Elizabeth is the protagonist and the narrator's reflector—she is almost always at center stage, and readers get to see, hear, and judge people and events through her eyes, ears, and mind (Morini 44–48). While thematically, *Pride and Prejudice* can be said to be about Elizabeth and Darcy's prejudices and their personal and family pride, they have to be overcome before the two of them are able to recognize and appreciate each other. It is also important to note that the provisional title of an earlier draft of the novel was *First Impressions*—and again, it is Elizabeth and Darcy who will eventually grow past their first impressions of each other and learn to love each other's true selves.

All the same, even though the transformation of this love-hate relationship into one of mutual love and affection is told with such ability that it has gripped the attention of generations of readers, it would be simpleminded to read *Pride and Prejudice* as a mere tale of romantic love. Love is there, one feels and supposes (though the narrator typically takes over and briefly summarizes the action, such as when Darcy's final proposal is accepted by Elizabeth), but it is by no means the single driving force of the narrative. Love, in fact—like pride, like prejudice—is only understandable in the social and financial context in which it takes place: for just as Mrs. Bennet's excitement at the appearance of a rich tenant for Netherfield is motivated by practical, rather than sentimental, considerations, the initial disparities between Darcy and Elizabeth are social as much as personal. Darcy, after all, is the half-aristocratic owner of the great estate of Pemberley, while Elizabeth is only going to receive a meager one thousand pounds at her mother's death.

Thus, while social and financial matters are not in themselves sufficient to explain why a character pairs off with another (looks, intelligence, and sympathy have to be considered as well), no marriage, no engagement, and, indeed, no form of personal interaction is understandable in Austen's fictional world without reference to social hierarchy and family fortunes. The following sections, therefore, will look respectively at familial and social relations in this social and financial light, as well as at Elizabeth's consciousness of the rifts between her own family and Darcy at the moment in which her feelings for him begin to change.

All Families Are Equal—but Some Families Are More Equal Than Others

The description of Austen's novels as pivoting on "3 or 4 Families in a Country Village" is at once accurate and misleading, in that it creates the image of a peaceful rural community in which all parties are on an equal footing, and quiet uneventful evenings are spent playing cards or listening to the young people at the piano. Actually, though that kind of description superficially fits all of the novels (*Pride and Prejudice* being no exception, though in this case the country families inhabit at least three different places), several qualifications are needed to make it reflect the social realities that Austen's fiction describes. First, one needs to remember that though three or four families may form a sort of community for the space of the narrative, these are rarely, if ever, equal in social and financial terms—and this inequality tends to influence their respective codes of behavior and the way they relate to each other. Second, it is important to bear in mind that in the world that Austen describes, family ties were much stronger than they normally are in today's Western societies, so that each individual move had to be gauged in terms of its reverberations on a wider circle. Conversely, one must also note that though social and financial status may determine familial and individual behavior, there is always some room for individual development—in other words, no two families are the same in "Austenland" (cf. Morini 79), even when their situation in life is the same. By the same token, no two characters in the same family or in similarly situated families react analogously to analogous events (to prove this point, one need only look at the difference between Elizabeth and Lydia Bennet).

It is exactly at this intersection between social determinism and individual choice that it is profitable to read *Pride and Prejudice*. The social class which inhabits Austen's novels—that is, the non-working rural gentry and its working associates (or "pseudo-gentry"; cf. Spring) like parsons and lawyers—can once again project a false sense of social immobility, due to its dependency on landed wealth and its fairly traditional lifestyle. Actually, as Raymond Williams has demonstrated in *The Country and the City* (108–19), if the richer families were able to live on their private land-related income (the Darcys-de Bourghs in *Pride and Prejudice*), those whose estates were smaller (the Bennets) continuously ran the risk of being swallowed up by the working middle classes (the Bingleys, and, in a much smaller and more precarious way, the Lucases), who used their trade-acquired money to buy or rent estates which would allow them to supersede "older" families. In this paradoxical situation, in which flux was almost the rule yet acquiring one's wealth by trade was a social minus, marriage was the main instrument of upward mobility—especially for the daughters and younger sons of landed families, since the estate normally changed hands through primogeniture (it was handed down to the eldest male heir). At the same time, though, as certain social historians have noted, middle-class parents started to grant their children unprecedented liberties in the course of the eighteenth century—particularly, though not only, in the choice of a mating companion. In other words, by the time Austen started writing it was customary for the children to choose their own spouses, provided that their choice was more or less in keeping with the social and financial position of the family (Perry 28–29).

As hinted at above, at least three different layers of the rural gentry are represented in *Pride and Prejudice* and each of these layers corresponds to a different degree of relative individual liberty. Theoretically, the rich and aristocratic Darcy-de Bourgh family can form alliances in all directions—and yet in this kind of kin group there is a marked tendency toward endogamic (within-family) marriage because matrimonial alliances between relatives keep the family property undivided. This is seen in Lady Catherine de Bourgh's insistence that Darcy and his cousin, her own daughter, were "destined" for each other from infancy (271), as well as in her advice to Mr. Collins regarding marriage to one of the Bennet girls, Collins' distant cousins on the father's side (cf. Corbett 32–33). The Bingleys, coming as they do from a commercial family who bought its way into the gentry, have an interest in marrying recognized members of the latter—and in point of fact, the very class-conscious Bingley sisters are equally intent on "catching" Darcy and on promoting their brother's marriage with Darcy's sister, Georgiana. Finally, the Bennets represent the lowest rung of the ladder in the society Austen depicts: Mr. Bennet is "a gentleman" (he has an estate and no profession), but his wife is an attorney's daughter (20); their income is so slight that their daughters must count on a favorable marriage as the only way of remaining in their father's class.

The Bennets, however, are not merely defined by their social and financial plight: other families in the Austen canon are in similar situations (the Dashwoods in *Sense and Sensibility* [1811], or the Watsons in the eponymous unfinished novel), but it is only the Bennets who have fascinated generations of readers with their mixture of contrasting characters engaging in witty, entertaining conversation. The main reason for this is the original mismatch between the two parents: Mr. Bennet married the former Miss Gardiner in his enthusiasm for "youth and beauty, and that appearance of good humour," but soon after the wedding, her "weak understanding and illiberal mind, had [. . .] put an end to all real affection for her" (180). As a consequence of his domestic unhappiness, Mr. Bennet appears to be more interested in his books and his tranquility than in the welfare or correct behavior of his family. Left to their own resources, unguided by an indifferent father, most members of the Bennet household commit blunders and improprieties which are duly noted by their neighbors. All the sisters, for instance, are "out" at once, whereas one would normally expect only two or three of them to be available on the marriage market at a time. Lydia and Kitty are constantly, and scandalously, stalking the officers of the Hertfordshire militia, and most of the family—including its patriarch—indulge in comments which are often perceived as tactless or vulgar. As those haughty arbiters of manners, Lady Catherine de Bourgh and Mr. Darcy sum it up for Elizabeth:

All! What, all five out at once? Very odd! —And you only the second. — The younger ones out before the elder are married! (128)

The situation of your mother's family, though objectionable, was nothing in comparison of that total want of propriety so frequently, so almost uniformly betrayed by [your mother], by your three younger sisters, and occasionally even by your father. (152)

In a family founded by so oppositional a couple, it is perhaps inevitable that the offspring will tend to follow one model or the other, while a more balanced role and character blend will be relatively rare. In the distribution of available models it is clear enough that Kitty and Lydia, with their exclusive and vocal interest in clothes and men, are rather faithful replicas of Mrs. Bennet (whose favorite is Lydia because "she is so good-humoured"; 2). Elizabeth, on the other hand, clever, witty, and self-willed as she is, takes after her father and is her father's pet (2). And if Mary is a sort of empty parody of Mr. Bennet's intellectual interests and bookishness (she is also the only plain one of the five sisters), Jane, the eldest, is the one member of the family who seems to blend both available models—the easy temper of the maternal side being counterbalanced in her case by a capability for quiet ratiocination, which she may well have learned from her father.

Jane's rational meekness makes her ideally suited for survival in the patriarchal world described by Austen: she will attract dominant men by being pretty and modest and, unlike her mother, Lydia, and Kitty, will not disgust them by being stupid. It is Elizabeth, however, with her wit and intellectual independence, that has attracted generation after generation of Austen readers and critics. Many twentieth-century critics, in particular, have seen her as the embodiment of a romantic or quasi-revolutionary individualism which, in setting itself against the conventions of the established order, prefigures the modern triumph of personal attributes and private endeavor over familial ties and social connections (for a summary of these individualistic readings, see Butler 197–203). But if it is true that Elizabeth, relatively powerless though she is, consistently refuses to be taken for granted in her relations with power—and if it is this consistent refusal, as well as her mixture of "sweetness and archness" (38), that attracts haughty Darcy despite his prudential reservations—it is also evident that she is a product of her class and family environment, and she shows her full awareness of this at every major crisis in the plot.

Elizabeth's great moments as an individualist, of course, are the two occasions on which she refuses an offer of marriage—first from the insipid and sycophantic Mr. Collins, and then from a not-yet-humbled Mr. Darcy. In both cases, her interlocutors use the language of social convenience to underline the fact that their proposals, rather than they themselves, cannot reasonably be expected to face a denial. Mr. Collins tells her that in his position as the rightful inheritor of Mr. Bennet's estate, he has thought it right to "choose a wife from among his daughters," and he assures Elizabeth that "no ungenerous reproach" for her relative poverty "shall ever pass my lips when we are married" (81–82). Darcy informs her of his ardent love virtually in the same breath as he lists all the reasons for not marrying her, including her "inferiority" and the "degradation" of allying himself to the Bennets; given the difference in their respective conditions, he never entertains a single doubt as to the acceptance of his offer. Elizabeth, for her part, disabuses both suitors in the language of individual inclination. She tells Mr. Collins that their marriage would be a source of personal unhappiness for both, saying "You could not make *me* happy, and I am convinced that I am the last woman in the world who could make *you* so" (82). She begs him to allow her to judge for herself and to pay her the compliment of believing what she says: "Do not consider me now as an elegant female intending to plague you, but as a rational creature speaking the truth from her heart" (83). In the case of Darcy, she assures him that whatever antipathy she may feel for reasons connected with her family—namely, for his efforts in separating Jane from Bingley—her refusal is, again, ultimately based on personal reasons alone:

From the very beginning, from the first moment I may almost say, of my acquaintance with you, your manners impressing me with the fullest belief of your arrogance, your conceit, and your selfish disdain of the feelings of others, were such as to form that ground-work of disapprobation, on which succeeding events have built so immoveable a dislike; and I had not known you a month before I felt that you were the last man in the world whom I could ever be prevailed on to marry (148).

In both instances, Elizabeth is very well aware of the material advantages a match with Collins or Darcy would bring to herself and her family, but she still chooses to act on the basis of individual preference. On the other hand, even in these extreme acts of rebellion against what might be expected of her (her mother threatens that she "will never see her again"; 85), she shows herself to be a product of her family and class. When the first rejection takes place, and Mrs. Bennet is incredulous and enraged, Elizabeth finds support in her equally individualist father, who upholds individual choice in sentimental matters and would not wish to see her married to a simpleton. He tells his daughter, "An unhappy alternative is before you, Elizabeth. From this day you must be a stranger to one of your parents. Your mother will never see you again if you do *not* marry Mr. Collins, and I will never see you again if you *do*" (85). And when Elizabeth turns down Darcy's much more advantageous offer, she also does so—whatever her protestations to the contrary—out of family-related ill-will, her present suitor having been "the means of ruining, perhaps for ever, the happiness of a most beloved sister" (146). Also, as soon as Darcy leaves her room, she realizes with awe the strength of affection which must have led such a great man to propose such an unequal match (148–49); this shows that, though she does not wish to attach herself to someone she does not love, she knows full well the social value of matrimony.

In other words, Elizabeth's freedom of movement, while it may be greater than her sisters' or her mother's, is still defined and confined within the limits of her family unit and the class to which she belongs, even though Lydia, Kitty, and Mrs. Bennet allow themselves greater liberty in social conversation, or in mixing with men in improper ways. This confinement becomes apparent at times of crisis, when her family is threatened or she herself is accused of improper behavior by her social betters. When Lady Catherine tries to bully Elizabeth into keeping away from Darcy, for instance, Elizabeth tells her haughty interlocutor that if her nephew is a gentleman, she is "a gentleman's daughter" herself (272). When Mr. Bennet decides to allow Lydia to go to Brighton after the officers—a social blunder that will result into her elopement with fortune-seeking Wickham—Elizabeth tries to dissuade him on the grounds that such permissiveness would cast a black shadow on *all* the family, saying, "If you were aware [. . .] of the very great disadvantage to us all, which must arise from the public notice of Lydia's unguarded and imprudent manner [. . .] I am sure you would judge differently in the affair" (176). Most importantly, when the actual elopement takes place, Elizabeth immediately shows her full awareness of the dreadful consequences that Lydia's behavior is going to visit on her sisters. While Jane is thankful for the neighbors' interest in their misfortune, Elizabeth knows better than that, and does not entertain a single doubt on the functioning of her society:

> "[Lady Lucas] had better have stayed at home," cried Elizabeth, "perhaps she *meant* well, but, under such a misfortune as this, one cannot see too little of one's neighbours. Assistance is impossible; condolence, insufferable. Let them triumph over us at a distance, and be satisfied." (222)

It is by analyzing the Lydia-Wickham crisis, and by understanding the way in which it is solved, that one can fully understand the interaction between individual and family ties in *Pride and Prejudice*, as well as the size of the extended kin group that can be said to share in a family's joy or pain. When the elopement is discovered, and it soon becomes clear that the couple is not going to Scotland to be married, it is Mr. Gardiner, Mrs. Bennet's brother, who first starts chasing them in London and who reports on his progress in letters addressed to his "dear Brother" (229). Mr. Gardiner's involvement in this thorny business is not simply a measure of his kindness, nor is "brother" a misprint for brother-in-law. In Austen's real and fictional world, the family ties acquired by marriage were considered to be every bit as strong and binding as those between people of the same blood (cf. Corbett 39). Therefore, the main reason why Mr. Gardiner helps the Bennets is that the disgrace would be a blemish not only on his "brother's" family, but also on his own. Conversely, as soon as a rumor of Lydia's false step reaches beyond the borders of Longbourn, Mr. Collins writes to offer his condolences; the manner of his address ("My dear Sir") and his somewhat gloating certainty that nobody "will connect themselves with such a family" (225) make it clear that, while close enough for him to wish to distance himself from their disgrace, the Bennets are not so close to him that he cannot simply give them up.

Even more interesting, in terms of the interaction between individual and familial forces, is the relatively happy solution of the Lydia-Wickham affair, which comes about thanks to Darcy's good offices and ready finances. Again, it is not only solicitude for a friend (Elizabeth) which leads Darcy to offer money to Wickham so as to induce him to marry. In part, he feels responsible for Wickham—family ties again: Wickham was his father's protégé—and Darcy wants to endear himself to Elizabeth. But his real motive is that he intends to marry Elizabeth—an unequal connection enough, but one which would become downright impossible if Elizabeth's sister became a lost woman. In marrying Elizabeth Bennet, he would become a brother to all the other Bennet sisters, and that is only possible if the four of them can be seen as socially respectable. Therefore, he buys Elizabeth's sister's marriage, and the irony is that when he himself marries Elizabeth, and Jane marries Bingley, the overall value of the whole Bennet family is greatly enhanced, so that the two remaining sisters, by acquiring rich and influential brothers, will now stand a far greater chance of marrying well. Even Lydia and Wickham will be able to hope for some social advancement or, at the very least, financial assistance. Before Darcy's final proposal to Elizabeth, the Bennets' neighbors register the change in the family's fortunes, and the narrator remarks on the little distance between "luck" and "misfortune":

> The Bennets were speedily pronounced to be the luckiest family in the world, though only a few weeks before, when Lydia had first run away, they had been generally proved to be marked out for misfortune. (267)

Conclusion: Elevating One's Family Through Marriage

Immediately after her first rejection of Darcy, Elizabeth starts changing her mind about him, feeling that maybe her pride misled her into judging *his* pride too harshly. The first stage in this psychological about-turn is brought about by Darcy's letter, in which he relates the particulars of his father's and his own dealings with the volatile Wickham; but, arguably, the moment when Elizabeth's shame is turned into something like admiration and love is when she visits Darcy's ancestral estate of Pemberley with her uncle and aunt. It is at Pemberley that Elizabeth first notices those aspects of Darcy's pride that, far from being morally reprehensible, are connected with family traditions and a landlord's responsibilities toward his tenants. The orderly state of Darcy's estate, the love his servants bear him, all serve to reinforce Elizabeth's sense that she was misguided by her first impressions—as does Darcy's own behavior, which, after what went on between them, is remarkably humbler.

Again, though, it would be simplistic to view Elizabeth's new fascination in purely personal terms; and again, considerations about the social position of her family, and what would happen if the Bennets were to ally themselves with the Darcys, are never too far from her mind as she admires the house and grounds. In this sense, the description of the estate that readers get as soon as the trio of tourists come to Pemberley is a revelation:

They gradually ascended for half a mile, and then found themselves at the top of a considerable eminence, where the wood ceased, and the eye was instantly caught by Pemberley House, situated on the opposite side of a valley, into which the road with some abruptness wound. It was a large, handsome, stone building, standing well on rising ground, and backed by a ridge of high woody hills; and in front, a stream of some natural importance was swelled into greater, but without any artificial appearance. Its banks were neither formal, nor falsely adorned. Elizabeth was delighted. She had never seen a place for which nature had done more, or where natural beauty had been so little counteracted by an awkward taste. They were all of them warm in their admiration; and at that moment she felt, that to be mistress of Pemberley might be something! (184)

On the face of it, this is a mere factual description of the general appearance of the place; but of course no description is innocent, as those who study style know well; even an apparently neutral stretch of prose will inevitably carry the signs of a worldview in the terms in which it is couched (Fowler 132). In this case, one has to remember that Pemberley is seen through Elizabeth's eyes, and therefore the terms used by Austen in this narrative passage convey her protagonist's instinctive reaction to her surroundings. Pemberley, as various critics have pointed out, is certainly seen by Elizabeth as an example of natural architecture and land planning—as "a mean between the extremes of the improver's art and uncultivated nature" (Duckworth 123). But it is also worth noting that many of the nouns and adjectives in the passage have to do with such geometric qualities as height and size: "from a considerable eminence", the trio of beholders see a "large" house on "rising ground"; in front, "a stream of some natural importance is swelled into greater." Everything is high, important, and imposing and it is no wonder if by the end of the passage Elizabeth feels that to be mistress of this place would have been "something." The connection of this terminology with the idea of nobility, and with

Darcy's exalted position in society, is not explicit, but it is bound to glide into any reader's mind.

Even here, however, Elizabeth is not merely under the spell of wealth and position—she is also continuously, even if automatically, calculating her own social position with respect to Darcy's, and is ever mindful of the consequences that her being "mistress of Pemberley" would have on her family. When she realizes that "something like re-gret" is creeping up on her, she fights the feeling by reminding herself that had she accepted Darcy, "my uncle and aunt would have been lost to me: I should not have been allowed to invite them" (186); and soon afterward, when Darcy actually introduces himself to the Gardiners, she finds it "consoling, that he should know she had some relations for whom there was no need to blush" (193). Once again, with all her wit and independence of judgment, Elizabeth is as fettered to her family as anybody else in Austen's fiction—and certainly more than the likes of Lydia, who act independently because they are too young and self-centered to imagine the consequences of their actions.

In the twenty-first century, and in most contemporary Western fic-tion, the individual is at one and the same time a product of family and a free agent in a potentially limitless world; and, in such a world, whenever a person or a character forms a new family, he or she will obtain a degree of independence from their family-of-origin that would have been unthinkable in Austen's society. In *Pride and Prejudice*, as in all the novels of the Austen canon, each individual marries into a family, rather than out of it; and even individualism can only be under-stood as each person's individual voyage through the circumstances of his life with a full baggage of familial connections and obligations.

Works Cited

Austen, Jane. *Pride and Prejudice*. Oxford: Oxford UP, 2004.

Austen, Jane. *Selected Letters*. Ed. Vivien Jones. Oxford: Oxford UP, 2004.

Butler, Marilyn. *Jane Austen and the War of Ideas*. Oxford: Clarendon, 1975.

Corbett, Mary Jean. *Family Likeness: Sex, Marriage and Incest from Jane Austen to Virginia Woolf*. Ithaca: Cornell UP, 2008.

Duckworth, Alistair M. *The Improvement of the Estate: A Study of Jane Austen's Novels*. Baltimore: Johns Hopkins, 1971.

Fowler, Roger. *Linguistic Criticism*. Oxford: Oxford UP, 1986.

Morini, Massimiliano. *Jane Austen's Narrative Techniques: A Stylistic and Pragmatic Analysis*. Farnham: Ashgate, 2009.

Perry, Ruth. *Novel Relations: The Transformation of Kinship in English Literature and Culture 1748–1818*. Cambridge: Cambridge UP, 2004.

Spring, David. "Interpreters of Jane Austen's Social World: Literary Critics and Historians." *Jane Austen: New Perspectives*. Ed. Janet Todd. New York: Holmes, 1983. 53–72.

Williams, Raymond. *The Country and the City*. London: Chatto, 1973.

"A Whole Family of Hurstons": Black and White Kinship in Zora Neale Hurston's Family Narrative___

Tim A. Ryan

Zora Neale Hurston told the story of her family twice in print. Her first novel, *Jonah's Gourd Vine* (1934), presents the tale of John Pearson, an energetic and eloquent Baptist preacher who achieves great success in his community, but who goes into a painful decline after the death of Lucy, his long-suffering, yet tirelessly supportive wife. Published eight years after this novel, Hurston's autobiography, *Dust Tracks on a Road* (1942), reveals just how much *Jonah*'s narrative owes to the author's actual family history. The opening chapters of *Dust Tracks* relate how the real-life John Hurston—just like his fictional counterpart—married Lucy Potts against her parents' wishes and started a family with her in the all-black town of Eatonville, Florida, where John soon became a prominent churchman. The autobiography goes on to describe how, after her mother's untimely death, the young Zora Hurston became a virtual orphan as a result of her father's neglect—just like the Pearsons' daughter, Isis, in *Jonah*.[1]

The fact that Hurston drew upon personal experience in writing her first novel as well as her autobiography is not especially surprising or unusual. What *is* peculiar is that the apparently factual version of events is no more reliable than the overtly fictional one. Robert Hemenway does well to remind readers that *Jonah's Gourd Vine* is "an autobiographical novel, not a document for understanding Hurston's private life. . . . the reader should be wary of accepting Hurston's fictional characters as autobiographical admissions" (189). He might reasonably say the same thing about *Dust Tracks*. Certainly, numerous scholars have commented upon the profound unreliability of Hurston's autobiography. Kathleen Hassall, for example, notes that *Dust Tracks* blatantly "reinvents facts, withholds information, [and] blurs the distinction between history and fiction" (161). Paola Boi similarly concludes that the author's autobiography is "undoubtedly much closer to a work of fiction than to a reliable self-portrait" (191). In other words, *Dust Tracks on a Road* is no less novelistic than *Jonah's Gourd Vine* in its imaginative dramatization of the author's family life, and the character of Zora in the autobiography is no less an artistic creation than John in the work of fiction.

If some readers might be frustrated by the fact that neither book provides a true account of Hurston's family history, then there are compensations for the literary scholar. That the author produced two distinct versions of the same basic story is incredibly helpful as far as interpretive analysis is concerned. The parallels and the distinctions between the two books reveal a great deal about Hurston's use of the family as a symbol in her works. Furthermore, the author's depiction of family relations in *Dust Tracks* helps to illuminate the nature of John's triumphs, ordeals, and failures in *Jonah's Gourd Vine*.

A recurring issue in Hurston's writing is the challenge of being black in a white-dominated and racially-divided society. Hurston was fiercely proud of her African American heritage and was fascinated by the unique and enriching qualities of black rural culture in the American South and the Caribbean. Her deep love of African American folk-culture is clearly reflected in her anthropological studies, *Mules and Men* (1935) and *Tell My Horse* (1938), as well as in such works of fiction as *Their Eyes Were Watching God* (1937) and *Jonah's Gourd Vine*. Simultaneously, however, Hurston was an ambitious individual who wanted to establish herself as a prominent author in mainstream American culture. This goal required her to engage actively with the white-controlled publishing industry and demanded that she be recognized by a predominantly white reading public. In short, Hurston sought access to the rewards and resources which, at that time, only elite white society could offer, while also staying true to her rural black roots. As a result, like many of her fictional characters, Hurston was an eternal wanderer, caught between her cultural origins and the prospect of broader horizons—which is to say, caught between black and white America.[2]

The difficulty of negotiating between black and white worlds is frequently dramatized in Hurston's fiction in terms of family, specifically in terms of children's relationships with their parents or with parent-substitutes. In both *Jonah* and *Dust Tracks*, the troublesome confluence of black and white races in American life has resulted not in a single multicultural family, but in stark divisions between separate black and white family groupings. While slaveholders in the nineteenth century often talked hypocritically about my "family, black and white" (Genovese 73), Hurston's writings deal with the fact that people of color in the modern United States must struggle to find meaningful ways of coming to terms with being both American and African American—which is to say, being a member of this nation's white *and* black families. Hurston's controversial depiction of her relationships with white parent figures in *Dust Tracks on a Road* sheds light on the specific source of John's frustration and failure in *Jonah's Gourd Vine*.

Since its publication in 1942, readers have tended to characterize Hurston's autobiography as an unfortunate embarrassment, largely because of its evasive treatment of racial issues. Harold Preece, for example, dismissed the book as "the tragedy of a gifted mind, eaten up by egocentrism [and] fed on the patronizing admiration of the dominant white world" (qtd. in Miles 65). More recently, scholars have sought to redeem the book's reputation by arguing that it only appears to pander to white readers and to sidestep the issue of racism. Critics now argue that, in *Dust Tracks*, Hurston uses sly insinuation and subtle irony to draw attention to racial inequality and critique complacent white society.[3]

Neither of these contrasting viewpoints of *Dust Tracks* is entirely satisfactory. It is naive to suggest, as the early reviewers did, that the book reveals Hurston to be nothing more than a shameless sycophant who was prepared to say whatever was necessary in order to appease white editors and sell books. Such a characterization entirely neglects the extent to which Hurston's work consistently celebrates the beauty and complexity of black culture, and it ignores her overt criticism of racism as a virulent disease in American life.[4] Present-day scholars, however, may be in danger of going to the opposite extreme by overstating Hurston's credentials as a warrior for racial justice. If Hurston is indeed often "putting on whitey" in the pages of *Dust Tracks*—seeming to say what white editors and readers want to hear while satirically implying the opposite—this notion does not explain every single element of the text. It also does not account for the well-established fact that Hurston actually did possess some fairly reactionary attitudes, which she was not shy about voicing in later years, such as her notorious statement in opposition to school desegregation in the 1950s (Hemenway 336).

Both views of Hurston—the author as racial revolutionary and as conciliatory ally of whites—have some basis in truth. Throughout her life and career, Hurston fought valiantly against a society that was inclined to deny her individuality and dismiss her culture purely on the grounds of race. Simultaneously, however, she understood that, in order to have a meaningful career as a writer, she must flatter social elites and connect with white readers, whatever compromises were required. *Dust Tracks on a Road* is a vivid representation of these conflicting impulses in Hurston's life and work, and the author's autobiography specifically dramatizes these tensions in terms of parent-child relationships.

In *Dust Tracks*, Zora constantly redefines and re-creates her family in order to suit her individual needs. First neglected by her father and then left motherless by Lucy's early death, Zora develops alternative parent figures—what sociologists call alloparents[5]—to aid in her education, her development as an individual, and her success in the world. What is striking is that so many of these parent substitutes are white. When Zora is a child, her alternative parents include a white man who assists at her birth and becomes a spiritual godfather, and two northern women. As an adult, she continues such relationships, including those with Mrs. R. Osgood Mason, a wealthy patron whom she never fails to call "Godmother," and the renowned anthropologist Franz Boas—to whom she refers as "Papa Franz" and who, in turn, is happy to acknowledge, "Of course, Zora is my daughter" (178).

The critical tendency is to assume that these relationships between black "child" and white "parents" in the autobiography are entirely oppressive, patronizing, and implicitly (if not always explicitly) racist. It has become common for scholars to assert that Zora only submits to her white benefactors as a matter of "economic survival" (Kam 84). Critics usually define the success of *Dust Tracks* based upon the extent to which they believe Hurston, the narrator—if not necessarily Zora, the protagonist—is able to critique and rise above the power of her arrogant white mentors.[6]

This primary focus upon the tyrannical nature of the interactions between Zora and her pseudoparents in *Dust Tracks* often leads critics to underemphasize the other side of Hurston's depiction of these relationships. While the white godfathers and godmothers in *Dust Tracks* are undeniably self-important, condescending, and even, at times, downright racist, Zora is still able to develop relationships with them that are, in many respects, affectionate and mutually rewarding. If Hurston often wears a mask of compliance while laughing at her white sponsors behind their backs, Zora also seems to genuinely like and respect them and to cherish their interest in her. On one hand, Hurston reports that her white godmother could be "merciless" (185). On occasions, Mason would accuse her protégée of "dissipating your powers in things that have no real meaning," and would cut off Zora's protestations with a curt admonition: "Keep silent. Does a child in the womb speak?" (184).[7] On the other hand, Hurston claims to share "a psychic bond" with Mason, and acknowledges that "Godmother could be as tender as mother-love" (183, 185). Clearly, not all of the author's declarations of love and esteem for her white patrons are ironic and, for their part, these patrons play as significant a role in Zora's life as any of her black mother-figures—from Lucy Hurston herself to Big Sweet, the powerful matriarch who takes Zora under her wing in the violent "jook" joints of Polk County during the author's first anthropological research expedition.

Hurston's autobiography, then, redefines and extends the notion of family.[8] The relationships between Zora and her white godfathers and godmothers in *Dust Tracks* are as complex, multifaceted, and changeable as any relationship that involves an unequal power balance—including a parent-child relationship. Zora's exchanges with her white benefactors involve both love and oppression, both reverence and rebellion. The author's genius and triumph in *Dust Tracks* is to construct her relationships with her white quasi-parents as genuinely meaningful ones, while simultaneously satirizing the racial power differentials upon which these interactions are based. There is no better illustration of the complicated nature of the relationships between Zora and her white alloparents than her involvement with her white godfather early in the book.

It becomes evident at the outset of *Dust Tracks* that John Hurston is an emotionally absent father as far as Zora, his second daughter, is concerned. In fact, he "threatened to cut his throat when he got the news" of her birth. "It seems that one daughter was all he figured he could stand," Hurston explains. "I don't think he ever got over the trick he felt I played on him by getting born a girl" (35). Furthermore, while Zora's mother encourages all her children to aim high—to "jump at de sun"—John Hurston is much less uplifting. In his opinion, "it did not do for Negroes to have too much spirit. He was always threatening to break mine or kill me in the attempt. . . . He predicted dire things for me. The white folks were not going to stand for it. I was going to be hung before I got grown. Somebody was going to blow me down for my sassy tongue" (29).

For Zora, however, the solution is simple: she replaces her indifferent and dispiriting biological father with a more loving and inspiring substitute. Significantly, she does not hesitate to recruit a white man for this role—the very kind of person that her actual father says will not accept her. This man is the opposite of John Hurston in every respect: white, rather than black; encouraging instead of discouraging; intimate instead of dismissive; warmly profane instead of coldly pious. Whether this person existed in real life or is simply another imaginative addition by the author, the fact remains that, in the absence of a functional biological father, Hurston provides a compensatory substitute in the pages of *Dust Tracks*. This white man—unnamed in the text but usually referred to as Zora's "godfather"—is symbolic of Hurston's acknowledgment of the necessity for connecting with the white world as well as black culture.

From the very first, this white godfather, despite his race, has a more elemental connection to Zora than her biological father. According to the narrative, Lucy Hurston was alone when she gave birth to Zora. Since John Hurston was out of town and the local midwife failed to appear in good time, Lucy was obliged to depend upon a passerby to cut the umbilical cord and sponge off the baby (37). In short, this unnamed white man performed the roles of both father and midwife, shepherding Zora's entry into the world.

As Zora begins to grow up, the white godfather acts as her first teacher and provides her with a sense of connectedness. While Zora feels cut off from her unimaginative community and unreceptive adults, "the robust grey-haired white man who had helped get me into the world" remains the "one person who pleased me always" (48). Her unofficial white godfather takes her on fishing trips, gives her peanut bars, applauds her free spirit, and instructs her candidly in the values of life— which is to say that he acts toward her exactly as a devoted and loving father might (49–51). His most important principles are: "People with guts don't lie . . . . Don't you never let nobody spit on you or kick you [and] . . . . learn right now, not to let your head start more than your behind can stand. Measure out the amount of fighting you can do, and then do it" (49–50). In other words, the white man teaches Zora to always tell the truth, to resist any kind of abuse, and to choose her battles wisely.[9]

Young Zora takes these lessons on board, but, given the man's racial attitudes, she also has to adapt them radically in order for them to be useful. For all his kindness and despite the fact that he is the most influential and inspiring figure in Zora's life besides her biological mother, it is evident that the godfather unthinkingly accepts the racist orthodoxies of his culture. As a consequence of this fact, he provides Zora with a valuable first lesson—if not necessarily a salutary one—in how to interact with white people who are part of a system built upon racial discrimination and racist assumptions, regardless of their personal generosity or their genuine human concern for a black girl's welfare.

Hurston's narration underlines the limitations of the white man's paternalism by emphasizing his willingness to use obscenely racist language while seeking to educate young Zora. When advising his goddaughter to always be honest, the white man says bluntly, "don't be a nigger . . . Niggers lie and lie!" (49). This is a shocking moment in the text—and is made even more shocking by the African American author's repeated attempts to excuse such overt racism. Hurston first explains in a footnote, "the word Nigger used in this sense does not mean race. It means a weak, contemptible person of any race" (49). Barely two pages later, Hurston reiterates this flimsy excuse, but this time in the text itself, and in slightly different terms: "I knew without being told that he was not talking about my race when he advised me not to be a nigger. He was talking about class rather than race" (51).

The fact that Hurston apologizes for her white godfather's language not once, but twice, should tip readers off to the fact that her real purpose is not to neutralize the impact of such casual racism but, in fact, to amplify it. To borrow a line from Shakespeare, "the lady doth protest too much," and the African American narrator's rationalization of the godfather's offensive words is evidently absurdly ironic. Regardless of whatever other connotations the word may carry in the godfather's mind, when a white man in the segregated South uses the word "nigger" in conversation with a young black girl, there is no ambiguity whatsoever about what it primarily means.[10] No astute reader can doubt for a moment how profoundly degrading the godfather's language is to the young girl. This scene presents a painful paradox that has been all too common in American society, especially in the years before the Civil Rights era: white people could have great affection and concern for individual men and women of color, even though they were indoctrinated into thinking of them generally as mere "niggers."

What the white godfather is actually telling young Zora here is that he believes her racial identity will be an obstacle to her success in life—and it is therefore her responsibility to leave her African American origins as far behind as possible. The white godfather considers Zora a kind of spiritual daughter and loves her because he clearly believes that she transcends the negative qualities that he identifies with being black. His solution for her is "don't be a nigger"—and to adopt those qualities he associates with whiteness instead. Like Zora's biological mother, he wants his goddaughter to "jump at de sun," but he implies that, in order to do so, Zora will need to conform absolutely to the values and expectations of white culture. This is a harsh lesson, if, sadly, a realistic one. As Zora discovers throughout the book, her success in life is very much dependent upon her acceptance by whites—whether professors at college, publishers, or readers.

Zora absorbs what is useful about this advice, but the important point is that the author cleverly satirizes the racist assumptions upon which it is based. Godfather's three fundamental principles are that you must never lie, must never allow anyone to abuse you, and must pick only those fights that you can win. However, when the white godfather uses the word "nigger" in front of Zora, he *is* abusing her, even as he counsels, "never let nobody spit on you or kick you" (50). Although he says it is better to kill someone and go to jail than to accept an insult without retaliating (50), it should be self-evident that "nigger" is such a frequent epithet in the South at this time that, were Zora or any other black person to fight back every time a white person used that term, the violence would be unending. In other words, this is a battle that neither Zora nor the black community at large can reasonably win. Zora's problem is that if she follows godfather's command that she "measure out the amount of fighting you can do" (49), then she must ignore the rule about not accepting abuse—because she cannot reasonably fight him or the entire white South. There is only one solution to this quandary: the authorial voice steps in to tell us that "nigger" is not actually a racial term and, therefore, Zora has not been insulted and does not need to retaliate. This is an elegant joke on the author's part—and one that she plays upon the readers as well by vehemently denying that "nigger" is a racist epithet for a person of color, even when they should know better.

Like the author, young Zora ingeniously adapts the self-contradictory advice given by her godfather. If she cannot accept abuse without fighting back or take on the white South and win, even when it is inevitable that people will insult her by calling her a "nigger," then she must find a loophole. Fortunately, the white godfather provides one: he does not specifically say "Don't lie"; what he actually says is "don't be a nigger . . . Niggers lie and lie . . . . So don't let me hear of you lying" (49). While Zora does not respond directly to these proclamations, her brilliant solution is apparent in her behavior throughout the rest of the book. One way Zora ensures that her godfather never hears about her lying is to lie so well that nobody will ever accuse her of not telling the truth. What the white father actually tells her, without realizing it, is that, as a person of color, it is crucial that she develop an aptitude for lying since she will not be able to reap the benefits of being mentored by whites if she cannot prevent herself from honestly expressing what she thinks of their racial attitudes. In subsequent chapters, Hurston describes how Zora develops a remarkable facility for imaginative lying—which is to say, becoming a storyteller, a profession at which she will excel (79–91). Acknowledging how the imaginary world of her childhood often seemed more vivid than the real one, she even confesses that "my phantasies were still fighting against the facts" (91).

In order to enjoy a relationship with the white father who loves her, yet who also considers her a "nigger," Zora must exercise her considerable imaginative faculties to the utmost. She develops a way to accept his paternal companionship and encouragement, while also rejecting and subverting his failure to respect her as a person of color. Through subtle literary strategies, Hurston rakes the godfather over the coals for his racism, but can still honestly declare of him, "There went a man!"

(53). Zora uses similar strategies in her later interactions with white parent figures, such as Godmother Mason and Papa Franz Boas. While the young Zora is often obliged to conform to their demands and expectations, the adult Hurston uses sly satire to critique and dismantle their sense of white superiority. She loves them and benefits from their paternalism—but she also rebels against them.

It is not only in her interactions with white mentors that Hurston reinvents the nature of family. Throughout *Dust Tracks*, Zora creatively negotiates between multiple parent-figures and the often-contradictory advice that they provide. John Hurston warns her not to be "sassy" with whites, whereas Lucy tells her not to be a "mealy-mouthed rag doll" (29). Her mother tells her to be ambitious and "jump at de sun," but her father asserts "you ain't white," which, the author explains in a footnote, means "Don't be so ambitious. You are a Negro and they are not meant to have but so much" (46). One female relative is outraged at Zora's imaginative storytelling, which she considers "lying," whereas her mother understands that this is "just playing" (80). Her father and grandmother suggest she should never be open with whites, but her white godfather counsels her to always tell the truth. Her parents instill her with pride in her blackness, whereas her white godfather talks of "niggers." The advantage of having multiple parent figures and so many forms of advice is that Zora has the freedom to pick and choose—not only what advice she will take on board, but who will be her significant parental figure at any given moment. Her pious black father is neglectful, but her profane white father is to some extent a source of inspiration. The white female sponsors at school provide only material rewards while the biological black mother provides spiritual encouragement. Her black family provides a crucial sense of belonging and a cultural tradition, but the white adults in her life can grant access to broader horizons. Zora desires more options and possibilities than a single family can provide, so she creates multiple parents for herself, and she responds to each and every one of them in complex ways.

Some critics remain uncomfortable with Hurston's embrace of the white world in *Dust Tracks*, and some are skeptical about how empowering her disguised critique of that world is. Judith Robey, for example, concludes that Hurston's "method of outsmarting without offending her white audience is not, however, one that empowers the speaker" (n.p.). It is useful, therefore, to consider what Zora is able to reap from her membership in white family groups in *Dust Tracks* in contrast to John Pearson in *Jonah's Gourd Vine*. In fact, John's inability to define himself adequately in relation to any family, black or white, is the essential cause of his downfall in the book. While his failures as a father and husband are evident and much-discussed by critics,[11] equally significant is the fact that he is unable to forge any meaningful relationship with the white world, specifically his biological white father, Alf Pearson.[12] In the light of Zora's interactions with her white godfather in *Dust Tracks*, John's passive and unfulfilled relationship with his actual white father in *Jonah* is striking. Unable to engage consciously with his white family and ancestry, John's horizons rapidly close inwards.

Whiteness is continually associated with progress, opportunity, and mobility in *Jonah's Gourd Vine*. The book begins with John watching some white people out of the window of the Crittenden family's modest shack, curious about "whar dey gwine" (2). While John is confined to the cotton patch or the cabin, whites have freedom of movement and their travels are a source of fascination. Furthermore, when John leaves home and crosses over the creek into Notasulga, he associates social advancement with whiteness—such as schools where black children "learn how to read and write like white folks" (13).

In such a world, John's mixed-race identity and light skin are a distinct advantage. He is a "yaller god" and "uh lump uh gold" (3, 2), according to Ned Crittenden, John's resentful stepfather. Ned remembers that during slavery, "Ole Marsa always kep' de yaller niggers in de house and give 'em uh job totin' silver dishes and goblets tuh de table. Us black niggers is de ones s'posed tuh ketch de wind and de weather" (4). Slavery had been abolished in America for more than a decade at the time that the narrative opens, but the legacy of the institution insures that light-skinned African Americans continue to carry higher status in society.

To his credit, John is not much concerned with his mixed-race identity or his light skin. As one of his many lovers observes, "you ain't color-struck lak uh whole heap uh bright-skin people" (52). Indeed, John seems more amused by his skin color than anything else: when he inadvertently startles a group of laborers at a camp one night, he merely thinks it is funny that "Y'all thought Ah wuz white" (59). Throughout the novel, John firmly identifies himself as a man of color, and he is attracted to the all-black town of Eatonville as a place where "uh man kin be somethin' . . . 'thout folks tramplin' all over yuh"—by which he clearly means *white* folks (107).

Admirable though John's race loyalty and apparent indifference toward his light skin are, his alienation from his white heritage is ultimately a profound disadvantage. While both Amy, his mother, and the Reverend Cozy assert that "wese uh mingled people" (9, 159), John is unable to imagine any meaningful connection between himself and the white world, despite his mixed parentage. When his ambitious wife, Lucy, suggests that they should buy their own home, John's simple excuse for not doing so is "wese colored folks" (109), which is reminiscent of John Hurston's "you ain't white" in *Dust Tracks* (46). Certainly, John and Lucy Pearson share something significant in common with John and Lucy Hurston. As the author writes in *Dust Tracks*, "my mother was the one to dare all. My father was satisfied" (235).

While John begins the novel as an ambitious and curious man, he ultimately finds himself treading water. Early in the narrative, he is determined to explore the world across the creek, to ride a train, to get an education, and to join an all-black community. His skills as a preacher ultimately make him the most prestigious man in Eatonville. Simultaneously, however, he is dogged by an absence of coherent purpose and a crippling lack of agency. The black community considers him less a self-made man than the product of Lucy's clear-eyed vision, ambition, and encouragement. "Anybody could put hisself on de ladder wid her in de house," one observer notes (110). John cannot even claim credit for his skills as a preacher. He acknowledges that "dat ain't me talkin', dat's de voice uh God speakin' thru me" (122). At one point, he even complains that "uh man can't utilize himself"—and it is certainly true in his case: he cannot seem to find a goal or meaning in life (128). Furthermore, John repeatedly throws everything away—and finally destroys himself—because of his relentless sexual promiscuity. While John attributes his womanizing to "de brute-beast in me" (88), his compulsive philandering seems more like a symptom of frustration, a channeling of unfulfilled dreams into sexual conquest.

Where John specifically differs from Hurston is in his inability or refusal to acknowledge his white ancestry. This failure to engage with his white family is one of the central sources of his eternal frustration. Where Zora, in *Dust Tracks*, constructs a local white man as her spiritual father, it is evident that John's literal father is the prosperous white planter Alf Pearson. Significantly, however, John seems not to recognize this man as a parent, even though he takes his last name. For his part, Alf clearly realizes that John is his offspring and treats him with a great deal of favoritism, but he holds back from openly acknowledging him as a son. Unlike Zora, who is able to imagine an array of white people as parent-figures, and who is able to elicit from them the recognition that she is their daughter, John remains a disconnected and powerless orphan as far as his white family and white society are concerned.

Since neither John nor Alf acknowledge their connection to one another, their relationship is doomed from the outset. Alf gives John multiple opportunities and benefits: he sends him to school, gives him clothes, employs him as a foreman, and comes to John's aid when his philandering lands him in serious trouble. As long as Alf fails to acknowledge his patrimony, and as long as John remains oblivious to it, however, theirs cannot be a functional father-son relationship. Instead, it more closely resembles the association between a paternal master and a pampered slave. Indeed, upon first seeing John, Alf declares that he "would have brought five thousand dollars on the block in slavery time" (17). John remains imprisoned by Alf's view of him: despite all the advantages he enjoys, he cannot make himself independently wealthy, like the prominent black Potts family in the novel, and he continues to live in the quarters on the plantation, just as slaves did a generation before. Where Zora can subvert the white father's label of "nigger," in *Dust Tracks*, John is shackled by the label "house-nigger" in *Jonah*. Zora's advantage is that she is genuinely able to think of the white godfather as a spiritual parent, whereas, for John, his actual father will never be anything other than "Mist' Alf" or "suh" (85, 99). John just does not have the imagination to construct Alf as a father-figure, let alone recognize him as his actual father.

John's ancestry remains a mystery to him. During a dance at the plantation, the narrator tells of slaves who maintained their culture despite being kidnapped from their home: "I, who am borne away to become an orphan, carry my parents with me" (30). At this point in the story, both John's black mother and white father are present, but, un-like the slaves of former times, John does "not carry them with him" because, as Ned later comments, he "don't even know his pappy" (44). Unable to know himself, John is incapable of understanding his mo-tives or controlling his behavior. As Alf says of John's misdemeanors, "I'm not going to ask you why you've done these things partly because I already know, and partly because I don't believe you do" (99).

Ultimately, John must flee the plantation precisely because he can-not identify his white father—and because Alf will not acknowledge his black son. When John beats up Lucy's brother for stealing their marriage bed, the white population turns against John and he is pursued by vengeful night riders. This is a profound irony: white vigilantes aim-ing to lynch the son of the local white planter for the crime of beating an affluent black man. John's problem is that he has taken his status as a favorite too far without the advantage of being acknowledged as a true heir. The patrollers would never dare act against a man known as Alf Pearson's son, even if it was a public secret, but they will not hesitate to lynch an uppity "house-nigger." Alf will give John sufficient money to escape safely, but more than that he will not do, and John will not ask. Alf is unwilling and John is incapable of turning his mixed-race status into any kind of substantial and lasting advantage.

Throughout his life, John continues to mistrust the white population and refuses to engage with it. As a proud black man in a racist society, this is admirable—but his pride is also self-defeating and detrimental to his well-being. For example, when Hattie, John's second wife, files for divorce, John refuses to defend himself in the courtroom or to call witnesses. He explains: "Ah didn't want de white folks tuh hear 'bout nothin' lak dat. Dey knows too much 'bout us as it is, but dey some things dey ain't tuh know . . . . Dey thinks wese all ignorant as it is" (169). This is a principled stand, but it also leaves John vulnerable and powerless. John soon learns, furthermore, that the black community is really not all that different from the white community:

> He saw that though it was over at the courthouse the judge and jury had moved to the street corners, the church, the houses. He was on trial everywhere, and unlike the courthouse he didn't have a chance to speak in his own behalf. (184)

The black township, then, is as eager to humiliate John for his peccadilloes and to make him the object of gossip as the white courtroom—with the only difference being that the African American community allows the accused no opportunity to defend himself.

While Zora, in *Dust Tracks*, is able to negotiate between her black and white families, John, in *Jonah*, is merely stranded between them. He is an ambitious and gifted man who cannot ultimately "utilize" himself (128). He may cross the creek and become mayor of Eatonville, but he cannot visualize anything grander, such as participating in the African American Great Migration to the northern states in which so many of his congregation participate. To move to New York or Chicago would almost certainly mean engaging with the larger white-dominated world, which is something that John, despite his parentage, refuses to do.

Early in the novel, John develops a fascination with trains—vivid symbols of American progress and social mobility. Upon first seeing and hearing a locomotive, John expresses his determination to understand the meaning of its noisy engine. He is convinced that the train "say something but Ah ain't heered it 'nough tuh tell what it say yit. . . . Ahm comin' heah plenty mo' times and den Ah tell yuh whut it say" (16). John never fulfills this aim. His isolation from his parentage and from white society means that he must be excluded from the promises of white, modern, urban, industrial, society. Late in the novel, the narrator reveals the message of the locomotive: "Trains said North" (148)—but it is not a message that John ever understands or acts upon. John also has a dream in which he and Lucy are directed down a white shell road by Alf Pearson—but this is ironic since the white road is not one that he can or will take (185). In contrast, the Zora of the autobiography leaves dust tracks on all manner of roads, emboldened by her insight that "the world is a whole family of Hurstons" (290).

Notes

1. See Robert Hemenway's discussions of Hurston's "dual consciousness" in his biography of the author (62, 100, 279).
2. Diana Miles provides a comprehensive summary of the autobiographical elements in *Jonah's Gourd Vine* in *Women, Violence, and Testimony in the Works of Zora Neale Hurston* (15).
3. See, for example, articles on *Dust Tracks* by Tanya Kam and Kathleen Hassall.
4. In a 1945 essay entitled "Crazy for This Democracy," Hurston characterized racism as a form of national "small-pox" (167).
5. See Bentley and Mace, eds. *Substitute Parents*.
6. See, for example, critical essays on *Dust Tracks* by Tanya Kam and Judith Robey.
7. This description is reminiscent of Steven Ozment's discussion of the ways in which, traditionally, parents have often "alternated small carrots with large sticks" in the instruction of daughters (93–100).
8. Just as recent histories of the family have redefined the family in broader and more complex terms, so does Hurston in her autobiography. See, for example, Ozment's *Ancestors* (2001).

9. Ozment observes that, "[if] parental advice to the young in past centuries might be marshaled into one sentence, it would be the priority of self-knowledge and self-mastery" (100), and this is the very advice that the godfather gives to Zora.
10. See Lynn Domina's brief analysis of this passage (207).
11. See, for example, John Kanthak's and Diana Miles's analyses of the novel.
12. The text never explicitly identifies Alf as John's father, but no critic has ever doubted his patrimony. See Miles for a useful catalog of implicit textual evidence for this point (30).

Works Cited

Bentley, Gillian, and Ruth Mace, eds. *Substitute Parents: Biological and Social Perspectives on Alloparenting in Human Societies.* Oxford: Berghahn, 2009.

Boi, Paola. "Zora Neale Hurston's Autobiographie Fictive: Dark Tracks on the Canon of a Female Writer." *The Black Columbiad: Defining Moments in African American Literature and Culture.* Eds. Werner Sollors and Maria Diedrich. Cambridge: Harvard UP, 1994. 191–200.

Domina, Lynn. "'Protection in my mouf': Self, Voice, and Community in Zora Neale Hurston's *Dust Tracks on a Road.*" *African American Review* 31.2 (1997): 197–209.

Genovese, Eugene. *Roll, Jordan, Roll: The World the Slaves Made.* 1974. New York: Vintage, 1976.

Hassall, Kathleen. "Text and Personality in Disguise and in the Open: Zora Neale Hurston's *Dust Tracks on a Road.*" *Zora in Florida.* Eds. Steve Glassman and Kathryn Lee Seidel. Orlando: U of Central Florida P, 1991. 159–73.

Hemenway, Robert. *Zora Neale Hurston: A Literary Biography.* Urbana: U of Illinois P, 1977.

Hurston, Zora Neale. "Crazy for This Democracy." 1945. *I Love Myself When I Am Laughing . . . and Then Again When I Am Looking Mean and Impressive: A Zora Neale Hurston Reader.* Ed. Alice Walker. New York: Feminist P, 1979. 165–68.

_____. *Dust Tracks on a Road.* 1942. New York: Arno, 1969.

_____. *Jonah's Gourd Vine.* 1934. New York: Harper, 2008.

Kam, Tanya Y. "Velvet Coats and Manicured Nails: The Body Speaks Resistance in *Dust Tracks on a Road.*" *Southern Literary Journal* 42.1 (2009): 73–87.

Kanthak, John F. "Legacy of Dysfunction: Family Systems in Zora Neale Hurston's *Jonah's Gourd Vine.*" *Journal of Modern Literature* 28.2 (2005): 113–29.

Miles, Diana. *Women, Violence, and Testimony in the Works of Zora Neale Hurston.* New York: Lang, 2003.

Ozment, Steven. *Ancestors: The Loving Family in Old Europe.* Cambridge: Harvard UP, 2001.

Robey, Judith. "Generic Strategies in Zora Neale Hurston's *Dust Tracks on a Road.*" *Black American Literature Forum* 24.4 (1990). Web. 18 May 2011.

The Bluest Family Eye: Emergence in Toni Morrison's Novel _____

Gillian Lachanski and John V. Knapp

Toni Morrison's *The Bluest Eye* has generated considerable critical response since it was first published in 1970. According to Margaret G. Lloyd, and as with critical approaches generally, many of these essays and book chapters have been somewhat mixed in their helpfulness for first-time readers of the novel; one quality they all seem to share is analyzing the various characters in Morrison's novel one-at-a-time rather than seeing most of the major figures as also part of a family configuration. As has been discussed elsewhere in this collection, families possess emergent properties where the whole can be greater than the sum of its parts and, as such, even minor characters play an important role in understanding the complex interactions among the several characters in family representations. For this chapter, we will focus on Cholly and Pauline, two seemingly minor characters, relatively speaking, whose marital roles are, in the light of the whole novel, far more important in understanding Morrison's overall achievement than has hitherto been mentioned in the criticism we have read, as noted by Jerome Bump and Cynthia Dubin Edelberg. While others—including Jennifer Gillan and Jane Kuenz—have noted how characters in *The Bluest Eye* are embedded in their cultural history and historical assumptions (including but not limited to race) and temporal (1940s) perspectives, our interest is in a marriage.

To help explain why analyzing minor characters can be profitable, we will begin with some ideas from two complementary critical models: family systems theory (FST) and Alan Palmer's *Social Minds in Fiction* (2010). Palmer's ideas concerning "aspectual points of view" and his idea of "situated identity" remind us that "the concept of aspectuality serves as a reminder that . . . the storyworld is also being

---

experienced differently, under other aspects, by all of the characters who are not currently being focalized in the text." He then notes an example of how aspectuality is "a way of bringing to centre stage previously marginalized characters whose voices may not often be heard" (22). Here, we elaborate on why earlier discussions of character in *The Bluest Eye* have been both negative and one-sided for and against two relatively marginalized characters in the Breedlove family, Cholly and Pauline.Examining the meanings of this critical bias generally, we will suggest some interesting ways of looking at Morrison's work from two recently developed and important critical directions.

Alan Palmer speaks of embodied consciousness in narratives to suggest that almost all mimetic (lifelike) characters (as well as real people) are assumed to be aware of physical sensations generally, and so perceive the physical storyworld through their senses. Embodied consciousness is particularly important for a character like Pauline and the deformed foot about which, we should assume, she is always mindful, shaping the choices she has made early in the novel and continues throughout.

Another important idea of Palmer's is aspectuality. Characters in Morrison's novel, or any other novel, can only experience their storyworld from one perspective at a time and the storyworld will therefore be unique to each unique character, in both perception and experience; each character's particular knowledge of the world will shape his or her worldview and inform their action in the plot (Palmer 12, 40). In Morrison's novel, Cholly's despicable act must be deplored by readers and other characters, but, at the same time, we ask ourselves: what was he thinking and feeling to do such a thing to his own child? From his perspective, what allows him even to consider such a thing? We reject his behavior, obviously, and given audience disgust, most readers and other characters dismiss him as animalistic (Morrison 18). However, the character Claudia avoids answering a crucial question at the very beginning of the novel: "There is really nothing more to say—except why. But since why is difficult to handle, one must take refuge in how"

(6). Readers are, on the other hand, much more interested in the why. The "why" leads to an important issue in *The Bluest Eye:* the problem of marital energy, even negative energy, that is irrespective of race.

II

The Bluest Eye tells the story of Pecola Breedlove, a young girl who is raped by her father. Interestingly, Toni Morrison reveals this important plot point in the first two sentences of the novel. The experienced reader quickly wonders, however, whether or if the rape of a child—so prominently displayed at the opening of the novel—may be secondary to speculation about both the how and why this rape occurred as we ask ourselves: how could a father could commit such a terrible transgression toward his own child?

In order to understand this terrible act, we must learn much more about Cholly. What kind of a man is Morrison representing? What kind of life had he led that might have allowed him to act the way he did? The narrative voice dismisses as having "catapulted himself beyond the reaches of human consideration." He had "joined the animals" and was an "old dog, a snake, a ratty nigger" (Morrison 18). In addition, we are told that the family's "innocence and face were no more productive than [Cholly's] lust or despair" (6). To be morally unproductive and yet able to produce a child suggest that characters, like real people, exhibit contradictory experiences.

To understand a character lower than a snake in Claudia's eyes, we must examine Cholly's family life: his wife, Pauline, and two children, their older son, Sammy, and daughter, Pecola. Their collective life is introduced through the physical images of their living space: "an abandoned store" that does not "recede into its background of leaden sky, nor harmonize with the gray frame houses and black telephone poles around it" (33). This is not a family in harmony, either with their surroundings or with one another. The narrator says that the house "is both irritating and melancholy" while visitors "wonder why it has not been torn down" and neighbors "simply look away when they pass it" (33).

Like the fictional characters, readers are also given permission to look away because the family is "nestled together" and "festering" (34). This disturbing image suggests a sick, suffering, rotting family. Note that Cholly is not festering in isolation, but with his family as one entity (34). Palmer's ideas of "social minds" and FST together lets readers see characters as individuals, as well as within their particular family system (Knapp, *Style* 3). These critical models detail a broken system where Cholly is only one facet; he has not only contributed to the family's demise, but has himself been affected by the other family members because "within the family system, each member helps determine the conditions for the development of all the other family members" (9). Therefore, the family festers jointly as determined by all their interactions, but specifically among the architects of the family, Cholly and Pauline. It is important to specify: those understanding families through a systems analysis would neither absolve Cholly from raping Pecola, nor blame Pecola for her father's violation. Rather, systems analysis helps the reader understand much of the how and the why: how the family dynamic and their living conditions contributed to Cholly's rape of Pecola.

Morrison's description of the storefront house and its relationship to the family dynamic suggests the Breedloves live in a dysfunctional and physically dirty environment, which speaks volumes about the family's psychological condition. Readers are told that in the front room, among various pieces of furniture, there is a "tiny artificial Christmas tree which had been there, decorated and dust-laden, for two years" (Morrison 35). The text goes on to emphasize the dispiriting nature of the room, which includes a broken down couch that was forced upon Cholly. The Christmas tree and the damaged couch both represent a lack of joy and a sense of powerlessness that exist in the family. Indeed, there seems to be "no memories to be cherished" in the Breedlove family (36). Cholly and Pauline's odd passiveness negatively affects the entire family.

As in all marriages, Cholly and Pauline's have a rhythm—a predictable cycle—where how they interact is determined in part by what each one brings into the marriage. One asks: who was Cholly before Pauline? Who was Pauline before Cholly? What individualized traits do they embody that help shape marital interactions. Understanding the family as a working system, where each member plays a part, helps readers understand how incestuous acts occurred. Indeed, "incest is but an additional symptom of a dysfunctional family" (Tinling 284). By reviewing the narrator's descriptions of Cholly and Pauline as individuals before marriage—as well as their families-of-origin—their behaviors will make more sense because they are continuing a pattern set by their predecessors.

Cholly Breedlove's mother, whom he never knew, "wrapped him in two blankets and one newspaper and placed him on a junk heap by the railroad" without naming him when he was four days old (Morrison 132). Aunt Jimmy, who "had saved him" on the ninth day and driven off her niece, raised Cholly. Jimmy tells him that "his mother wasn't right in the head" and his father "wasn't nowhere around when [he] was born" (132–33). Noticeable immediately is the narrator's and Jimmy's lack of empathy. Although Jimmy salvaged Cholly from the junk heap, she "took delight sometimes in telling him of how she had saved him" (132). One can't help but note her hint of self-glorification.

Cholly's informal adoption may explain his sense of loss and his subsequent vulnerability to psychological problems (Brodzinsky 10–11). A child who does not know his or her biological parents grieves their loss, leading to "many emotional and behavioral manifestations: shock, anger, depression, despair, helplessness, hopelessness" (11). Looking further into Cholly's life, we see these emotions manifest themselves in his relationship with Pauline and his children. Since family-of-origin experiences play a large role in adult personality development, we assume Cholly's loss of both parents leaves him feeling incomplete. Many psychologists think that situations like Cholly's, an abandoned child left to die, can only deepen his lack of self-worth and damage his self-esteem, as it "represents [. . .] judgments about whether aspects of our selves are good or bad, likable or dislikable, valuable or not" (13). Because Jimmy reinforces his negative self-image by reminding him that his mother threw him away, his behavior toward women becomes problematic: either he is unworthy, indebted, or both.

Morrison signals the reader to pay close attention to what seems initially like a protective and nurturing relationship. Interestingly, since Morrison has Aunt Jimmy name Cholly on the day he was saved—all on the ninth day—she intends for the reader to pay attention to this repetition because she is aware that nine, symbolically, is related to judgment (Mt. 27:46, 2 Kg. 17:6, 25:1, Mk. 15:25). The biblical connection complicates Cholly and Aunt Jimmy's relationship because it is possible to see Aunt Jimmy as a kind of Christ figure, a savior. Although Cholly is saved, his association with the number does not necessarily bode well.

First, note the description of Jimmy as Cholly experiences her physical presence. Cholly is "grateful for having been saved. Except sometimes." He watches Aunt Jimmy with disgust "eating collards with her fingers, sucking her four gold teeth, or . . . [wearing] the asafetida bag around her neck" (Morrison 132). Furthermore, "she made him sleep with her for warmth in the winter when he could see her old, wrinkled breast sagging in her nightgown" (132). It is at this point in the narrative that we become aware of Cholly's sadness when he wonders "whether it would have been just as well to have died . . . under the soft black Georgia sky" (132–33). These images and confusing boundaries between caretaker and child must conflict with the ideal of the family that adopted children often create (Brodzinsky 76).

When Cholly finds his aunt dead the image of bodily waste echoes again during the funeral: "There was grief over the waste of life, the stunned wonder at the ways of God, and the restoration of order and nature at the graveyard" (Morrison 143). During the funeral, Cholly seems curiously disconnected. After viewing Jimmy's body, "he had trudged back to his pew dry-eyed amid tearful shrieks and shouts of others, wondering if he should try to cry" (143). He is more caught up in the festivities being enmeshed in Jimmy's extended family: As "one of the bereaved, he was the object of a great deal of attention . . . they treated him like the child he was . . . [and] anticipated wishes he never had: meals appeared, hot water for the wooden tub, clothes laid out. At the wake he was allowed to fall asleep, and arms carried him to bed" (140). This is the only example where we see Cholly being nurtured by family. As readers, we feel that his lack of connectedness to the funeral, symptomatic of a child who has been abandoned by both parents, is an odd reaction to receiving caring attention from family.

However, this sense of belonging to an extended family is short lived, as he overhears a conversation between family members: "Well, what about the boy? What he gone do?" (142). For someone like Cholly, the normal "identity crisis" is even more complex and uncertain, especially as the family discusses whether he is biologically related to his cousins (143). Cholly's relationships to those he thought were his real family is now questionable, as is his sense of identity and belonging, which is confusing, unsettling, and once again threatening.

After the funeral, Cholly's cousin, Darlene, initiates flirting and sexual teasing when they find themselves alone in a "wild vineyard where the muscadine grew" (145). Cholly's feelings about Darlene "were mostly fear—fear that she would not like him, and fear that she would" (145). As Cholly and Darlene engage in intercourse, they are surprised by "two white men" who said, "Get on wid it. An' make it good, nigger, make it good" (148). Cholly's first intimate encounter with a woman unexpectedly becomes threatened by violence; helpless, Cholly is forced to finish a sexual act while being held at gunpoint. Unable to protect Darlene, he likewise fails to please her sexually, and his anger, not directed toward the two men, becomes aimed at Darlene: "Cholly moving faster, looked at Darlene. He hated her. He almost wished he could do it—long, hard, and painfully, he hated her so much" (148) because she was "the one who created the situation, the one who bore witness to his failure, his impotence" (151).

When Cholly runs for fear of impregnating Darlene, he unconsciously re-creates his father's actions and rationalizations. Even though Jimmy says that Samson Fuller, Cholly's father, "never come to no good end," Cholly fantasizes otherwise (133). Growing up without a father, his representations of fatherhood are not easily defined, and for him, there are "always a mythical 'other' set of parents out there who can hold qualities of goodness" (Brodzinsky 77).

Cholly eventually finds his father playing dice at the end of an alley and approaches him "dry-mouthed with excitement and apprehension"; he "always thought" about his idealized father whom he imagined "as a giant of a man" who would tell him where he belongs, who he looks like, and whom he might become (Morrison 154–55). When Cholly finally talks to his father, he sees for the first time "his eyes, his mouth, his whole head . . . his voice, his hands—all real" (155). Cholly discovers "that he was taller than his father. In fact, he was staring at a balding spot on his father's head, which he suddenly wanted to stroke" (155). Tentatively, Cholly speaks to him, but his father rejects him and says "get the fuck outta my face" (156). Cholly, frightened, runs away and soils himself (157). Again, he is humiliated, destroyed, and abandoned. Yet after being on his own after his father's rejection, Cholly comes to believe that he is free of his aunt, free of his father, and free of Darlene: "Dangerously free. Free to feel whatever he felt—fear, guilt, shame, love. . . . He was free to drink himself into a silly helplessness. . . . He was free to live his fantasies, and free even to die" (159). Cholly was not really free, however, but had to carry all of his fear, guilt, shame, love into a marriage.

Initially, Cholly's wife, Pauline, seems a less complicated character. Unlike Cholly, she is raised by both parents and is the ninth child of eleven. Again, we see the number nine that Morrison uses symbolically to connect her character to Cholly's, and at the same time, signals the reader of Pauline's impending doom, beginning in childhood with a foot injury resulting in a deformity. The narrator tells us "the easiest thing to do would be to build a case out of her foot. That is what she herself did" (110). But then we are told, however, that "to find out the truth about how dreams die, one should never take the word of the dreamer" (110). Interestingly, we come to know Pauline through her own words as well as the narrator's, yet we are warned in advance to question Pauline's aspectual experience of the storyworld. How are her perceptions of herself as a daughter, a wife, and a mother different from the narrative voices? We are told that her foot "saved . . . [her] from total anonymity," creating positive and negative interactions that complicate her role in the family (110).

First, Pauline is one of eleven children fighting for attention and a niche in a large family, yet one would think she would receive sympathetic attention. Instead, her foot not only gives her a "general feeling of separateness and unworthiness," but at the same time, justifies why she feels a loss of parental intimacy:

> This deformity explained for her many things that would have been otherwise incomprehensible: why she alone of all the children had no nickname; why there were no funny jokes and anecdotes about funny things she had done; why no one ever remarked on her food preferences—no saving of the wing or neck for her—no cooking of the peas in a separate pot without rice because she did not like rice; why nobody teased her; why she never felt at home anywhere, or that she belonged anyplace. (110–11)

Although we see her alienation, we notice a nagging inconsistency. When she "line[d] things up in rows" and arranged things: "jars on shelves, peach pits on the step, sticks, stones, leaves—the members of the family let these arrangements be" (111). One might surmise that the disorder Pauline feels because of the lack of parental affection—and her perceived inability to determine her own family identity—is the impetus for her need to order the world physically, granting her a sense of power and purpose. The narrator informs us of her family's reaction to this near-obsession: "When by some accident somebody scattered her rows, they always stopped to retrieve them for her, and she was never angry, for it gave her a chance to rearrange them again" (111). Initially, her family's considerate actions seem respectful and caring, but their response is inconsistent with the textual evidence that she is mostly ignored. Given these statements about Pauline, the narrator curiously points out that Pauline was neither angry nor aggressive in either situation, as if her emotional responses are unusual. Hence, a reader might speculate that Pauline may not be the unloved disabled child who goes unnoticed, nor is she incapable of determining her role in the family.

Alternatively, we will argue that Pauline controls much of how the family relates to her. Indeed, knowing that she is obsessed with ordering and lining up objects tells us a great deal about her personality. Persons (and characters representing them) with obsessive compulsive personalities tend to be perfectionists in their behavior and in their ethics and morals; their rigidity can affect their interpersonal and social relations (Pinto et al. 453–58). When family members feel the need to stop immediately to reorder her rows of objects, they are, in effect, being controlled by her obsessive behaviors and potential anger. Although the narrator mentions that "she was never angry," she also insists that "they *always* stopped to retrieve them for her" (Morrison 111; emphasis added). The family, as FST suggests, has tacitly agreed to adjust to Pauline's disability and her obsessive personality. The family allows Pauline "to build a case out of her foot," becoming enablers to avoid interpersonal conflicts. By unconsciously obeying the emerging hidden rules and rituals, the family imposes on Pauline her "feeling of separateness and unworthiness" as much as she does.

III

When Pauline first encounters Cholly, her romantic fantasy is realized. He becomes "a simple Presence, an all-embracing tenderness with strength and a promise of rest" (113). Cholly "bend[s] down tickling her broken foot and kissing her leg," fulfilling her dreams: "with gentle and penetrating eyes . . . before whose glance her foot straightened";

he is the "Presence [who] would know what to do" (113). In the same paragraph, Pauline combines biblical language with her romantic hopes: Cholly as redeemer delivered salvation and rebirth (113).

We wonder why Cholly chooses to caress Pauline's deformed foot. Was this kiss a seduction, or was he drawn to her foot because she was broken like himself? Family therapist Augustus Napier thinks "married people are exquisitely well matched in a number of ways—in their general maturity, in their capacity for intimacy, tolerance for anger . . . or a host of other psychological dimensions" (117). Both Cholly and Pauline struggle with feelings of unworthiness, rejection, and a sense of not belonging anyplace, as well as being nameless—Cholly nameless for nine days and Pauline without a childhood nickname. Cholly senses someone "very much like various members of his family of origin . . . [a] 'recognition of the familiar' . . . [allowing each] to feel safe" (Napier 222). Hence, they are "psychological twins" (117), as well as an "idealized figure. . . who will help [each] fill all the hunger and needs [brought to] the marriage" (116). Cholly enters the marriage in a "godlike state;" he is "free to feel what he felt—fear, guilt, shame, love, grief, pity" (Morrison 159). Therefore, his sense of omnipotence and her need of savior made them initially a perfect match.

But early in the marriage, real life intrudes. They move up north to find work, and Pauline is taken away from her family and all she knows. However, the transition is easier for Cholly because he makes friends easily and creates a social life that unwittingly excludes Pauline. Unemployed, Pauline is lonely and becomes increasingly dependent on Cholly "for reassurance, entertainment, for all things to fill the vacant places" (117), but the more dependent she becomes, the more he "began to resist her total dependence on him" (118).

Pauline tries to exert some independence by shopping for the right clothes in order to integrate herself with the other women. Cholly begins to argue about money she spends, forcing Pauline to find a job. Although he resents her dependency because it interferes with his social life, he panics when she asserts her independence by becoming employed. The initial informal marriage contract breaks down: he no longer her savior and she no longer passive. As she evolves, he resents her growing independence.

The pattern here is so familiar to marriage counselors that we need not go into detail about the fact that, often, the very trait or personality quality that draws one partner to another becomes a major source of conflict as each vies for a power balance within the dyad. An ideal marriage is one where "both partners are pretty secure, reasonably independent and strong, with a basic sense of self-confidence and self-reliance, [who] aren't likely to ask really *major* help from one another" (Napier 116). However, Pauline's need to be ratified by a Prince Charming cannot tolerate the days of loneliness while Cholly, who enjoys his freedom, still has dependency needs that he neither understands nor acknowledges (Morrison 160). Under such a burden many marriages either dissolve or degenerate into mutual name-calling or even violence. Hence, this discussion will end with an analysis of two scenes: the first is the battle between husband and wife over a seemingly trivial incident: who will get the coal? (39–44). This seemingly minor conflict stands as a reiterated metaphor of the countless battles of the Breedloves. The second analysis will connect this scene with the rape of Pecola and place this single incident (along with another that Pecola mentions to Claudia) inside the trajectory of the marriage. By doing so, we will offer some explanation about the "why" of Cholly's brutal attack on his own child.

The first incident elaborates on the habitual battles between husband and wife where both posit valid arguments about the other's misbehavior and where each amplifies the faults of the other in order to justify his or her own actions. The battle begins the night Cholly comes home and is too drunk to fight, therefore "the whole business would have to erupt [in the] morning" and it would, "calculated, uninspired, and deadly" (40). It begins with threatening noises as Pauline bangs around the kitchen and, in this case, the kitchen noises are nonverbal cues to Cholly, as well as the children, that the battle is about to escalate.

According to FST, these interactions are guided by unspoken transactional rules where an escalation of action and retaliation increases the intensity of conflicts (Napier 83). We see this pattern played out in the Breedloves' battle over the coal. Cholly, too drunk to fight until morning, and Pauline's loud kitchen noises cause even the children recognize the upcoming fight: "This awareness, supported by ample evidence from the past, made Pecola tighten her stomach muscles and ration her breath" (Morrison 40).

The battle, however, is not about the coal: "They all knew that Mrs. Breedlove could have, would have, and had, gotten the coal" (Morrison 41). Instead, these fights were "violent breaks in routine that were themselves routine" (41). As Napier says, "out of the forces acting on them and out of their decisions, they have shaped a model for living that is organized, predictable, and has unique and irreplaceable meaning for them" (80). Their violent interactions relieved them of "the tiresomeness of poverty, gave grandeur to the dead rooms" (Morrison 41). In the beginning of the marriage, each helped the other with minor problems, but more complicated problems led to each pulling away from the stress of the demands.

For the Breedloves, Pauline grows in strength as Cholly declines. Pauline becomes the breadwinner by finding an emotional niche in working for a white family. But at home, she must deal with the terrible ugliness of her life by "handling" it "as an actor does a prop: for the articulation of character, for the support of a role she frequently imagined was hers—martyrdom" (Morrison 39). Pauline finds meaning as an upright Christian and as the indispensable servant to her idealized white family, and Cholly continues to be problematic by providing "his habitual drunkenness and orneriness . . . the material they needed to make their lives tolerable" (42).

The children, Sammy and Pecola, also have roles in the family dance. Sammy "used his [ugliness] as a weapon to cause others pain," and regularly ran away and returned. Whereas Pecola "is behind hers . . . peeping out from behind the shroud very seldom, and then only to yearn for the return of her mask" (39). When Pauline and Cholly begin physically to beat each other, Sammy joins the fight and "suddenly began to hit his father about the head" (44). Interestingly, a parentified Sammy takes on the role as protector, standing with his mother against Cholly, who is now the outsider. Pauline accepts Sammy's help until he screams "Kill him! Kill him!" (44). Pauline is surprised; she and Cholly had no desire to actually kill one another because Cholly needed to "pour out on her the sum of his inarticulate fury and aborted desires" whereas she "needed Cholly's sins desperately" to make herself and her task "more splendid" (42). In the same passage, we learn that Cholly still remembers the humiliations, defeats, and emasculations which still "stir him into flights of depravity" (42).

In the context of their marriage, we better understand Cholly's psychological state when he rapes Pecola. Cholly is a drunk in part because "nothing, nothing interested him now" and that "only in drink was there some break, some floodlight, and when that closed, there was oblivion" (160). Cholly is a self-medicating depressive because, in his marriage, the "constantness, varietylessness, the sheer weight of sameness drove him to despair and froze his imagination" (160). Furthermore, he has lost standing in his family: Pauline is the breadwinner and parent to the children. He can neither provide for his family, nor parent his children: "Having no idea of how to raise children . . . he could not even comprehend what such a relationship should be" (160).

When Cholly sees Pecola hunched over the sink "his revulsion [is] a reaction to her young, helpless, hopeless presence" and he felt that "her misery was an accusation" (161). Cholly felt "revulsion, guilt, pity, then love" and "wanted to break her neck—but tenderly" (161). Amid his conflicting emotions—including his feelings toward Darlene and toward his wife—Cholly remembers his first encounter with Pauline as he watches Pecola's toe "scratching a velvet leg"; this reminds him intensely of Pauline's "small and simple gesture that . . . filled him then with wondering softness" (162). Cholly is once again stirred into depravity, and rapes Pecola. After the deed is done and he sees Pecola fainted on the floor, he feels "the hatred mixed with tenderness" and covers his child's body with a heavy quilt.

In brief, the marital battles of Cholly and Pauline contribute to the horrible deed done by a depressed and excluded Cholly, who is the direct agent of the crime. Through marriage, Cholly hoped to create the family-of-origin he never had. After being thrown away, emasculated by two white men, and rejected by his father, Cholly saw Pauline as his chance to regain his self-worth while, at the same time, he was also trying to solve some of the unresolved problems from his past. Once Pauline becomes the stronger spouse and parent because of her own need to control her environment and her husband, Cholly is once again emasculated. Cholly's fear of abandonment and Pauline's fear of engulfment determine their marital interactions. When Cholly encounters Pecola in the kitchen, she reminds him of Pauline back when Pauline thought he was her savior. He sees in her both his own sense of helplessness and his inability to help her. His rape, in a sense, is both a psychological bonding, a regaining of self, and a violent sex crime.

Works Cited

The Bible. Ed. Herbert May and Bruce Metzger. New York: Oxford UP, 1998. The New Oxford Annotated Bible with Apocrypha.

Brodzinsky, David M., Marshall D. Schecter, and Robin Marantz Henig. *Being Adopted: The Lifelong Search for Self*. New York: Anchor, 1993.

Bump, Jerome. "Family Systems Therapy and Narrative in Toni Morrison's *The Bluest Eye*." *Reading the Family Dance: Family Systems Therapy and Literary Studies*. Ed. John V. Knapp and Kenneth Womack. 2003: 151–70.

_____. "Racism and Appearance in *The Bluest Eye*: A Template for an Ethical-Emotive Criticism." *College Literature* 37.2 (2010): 147–70.

Cormier-Hamilton, Patrice. "Black Naturalism and Toni Morrison: The Journey Away from Self-Love in *The Bluest Eye*." *Melus* 19.4 (1994): 109.

Douglas, Christopher. "What *The Bluest Eye* Knows About Them: Culture, Race, Identity." *American Literature* 78.1 (2006): 141–68.

Edelberg, Cynthia Dubin. "Morrison's Voices: Formal Education, the Work Ethic, and the Bible." *American Literature* 58.2 (1986): 217–38.

Gillan, Jennifer. "Focusing on the Wrong Front: Historical Displacement, the Maginot Line, and *The Bluest Eye*." *African American Review* 36.2 (2002): 283–99.

Knapp, John V. "New Psychologies and Modern Assessments." *Style* 44.1–2 (2010): 1–59.

_____. *Striking at the Joints: Contemporary Psychology and Literary Criticism.* Lanham: UP of America, 1996.

Knapp, John V., and Kenneth Womack, eds. *Reading the Family Dance: Family Systems Therapy and Literary Studies.* Cranbury: U of Delaware P, 2003.

Kuenz, Jane. "*The Bluest Eye*: Notes on History, Community, and Black Female Subjectivity." *African American Review* 27.3 (1993): 421–32.

Lloyd, Margaret G. "A Thematic Approach to Teaching *The Bluest Eye.*" *Sage* 6.1 (1989) 59–62.

Morrison, Toni. *The Bluest Eye.* New York: Vintage, 2007.

Napier, Augustus, and Carl Whitaker. *The Family Crucible.* New York: Perennial Lib., 1988.

Palmer, Alan. *Social Minds in the Novel.* Columbus: Ohio State, UP: 2010.

Pinto, Anthony, Michael R. Liebowitz, Edna B. Foa, and H. Blair Simpson. "Obsessive Compulsive Personality Disorder as a Predictor of Exposure, and Ritual Prevention Outcome for Obsessive Compulsive Disorder." *Behavior Research and Therapy.* 49.8 (2011): 453–58.

Tinling, Lydia. "Perpetuation of Incest by Significant Others: Mothers Who Do Not Want to See." *Individual Psychology: Journal of Adlerian Theory, Research & Practice* 46.3 (1990): 280–97.

Whitaker, Carl A., and William M. Bumberry. *Dancing with the Family: A Symbolic-Experiential Approach.* New York: Brunner, 1988.

James Joyce's "The Dead": Gabriel's Epiphany and His Evolving Self_____

Sang-Wook Kim

The concept of an epiphany has long been a major reference point in reading the works of James Joyce, even though the Joycean epiphany had once been controversial in the matter of its significance as an overarching modernist technique weaving together all of his works. Some critics from the 1940s through the 1970s found the essence of Joycean epiphanies as "revelation": Irene Hendry identified the ways in which the "individual essence" of each Joycean character is "revealed" to the reader through objectifying the involved events and objects emblematic of the nature of each character. Florence L. Walzl took the Joycean epiphany as "a sudden revelation of spiritual or moral meaning, usually as to the essential being of a person or thing" because a story signifies through its narrative sequence (Scholes and Walzl 153). Others rejected the epiphany, considering it merely to be a Joycean literary leitmotif. Indeed, Robert Scholes dismisses the epiphany as "a literary device" (154) characteristic of Joyce's literary practices and considers it only as Stephen's aesthetic theory, not Joyce's (Scholes 66).

At the embryonic stage of conceiving *Dubliners* (1914), Joyce adumbrated his own idea of the epiphany as an artistic method, whose origin is religious—i.e., the Eucharist ritual. Applying the religious epiphany to his artistic creations, Joyce called them "manifestations or revelations" and considered them as "ironical observations of slips, and little errors and gestures [. . .] by which people betrayed the very things they were most careful to conceal" (Stanislaus Joyce 124). To put it another way, epiphanies are revelations of "the significance of trivial things" (Ellmann 163) in the insignificant procession of peoples' lives. In his posthumously published work *Stephen Hero*, Joyce had Stephen Dedalus explicate an epiphany as "a sudden spiritual

---

manifestation, whether in the vulgarity of speech or of gesture or in a memorable phase of the mind itself" (211). Stephen also expounded the epiphany in another way: "*Claritas* is *quidditas*. [. . .] This is the moment which I call epiphany [. . .] we recognize that it is *that* thing which it is. Its soul, its whatness, leaps to us from the vestment of its appearance" (213). Stanislaus Joyce testified that Joyce's sketches of epiphanies in his early career as a writer "served him in the formation of his style" (125). It clearly demonstrates that, for Joyce, epiphany is an artistic means to authenticate his insight into the Dublin life.

Dubliners is a collection of stories about the characters whose destiny is to fail to reinvent themselves even as they place their selves or their relationships with others into new perspectives; some of the stories, however, dramatize protagonists who move toward transforming the self by being awakened to a new reality. Joyce's task is to expose to the reader the self-deception of the characters who are stuck with their self-limiting view of personhood. Joyce's epiphanies in the collection are, "even if unstated, all the epiphanies of the characters themselves" (Bowen 106). In "Araby," for example, the young boy finds himself deluded by the romantic image of Mangan's sister found only in his own fantasy. In "A Painful Case," the adult loner ultimately distances and then excuses himself from any responsibility when he realizes that his lack of compassion for Mrs. Sinico's marital wretchedness helped lead to her suicide. In "A Mother," Mrs. Kearney's self-delusion as a loving mother is shattered by Kathleen's rebellion, one showing her deep resentment at her mother's excessiveness in her parental demands.

Dubliners represents the Irish city's social and family relationships, displaying the three stages of Dublin life: childhood, adolescence, and adulthood. This range of familial patterns suggests *Dubliners* to be a bildungsroman as is Joyce's *A Portrait of the Artist as a Young Man* (1916). In the latter work, Stephen grows into adolescence through an evolving process of commitment, moving through doubts about the authenticity of his received Catholic beliefs and insights, to emerging through some struggle into authenticating his new sense of self as an artist, a "priest of the eternal imagination" (221). Stanislaus Joyce's references to his brother's ideas of an epiphany as "vision new" in relation to a character's subjectivity could be seen in contemporary psychological terms as indicative of a kind of Piagetian cognitive developmentalism (125).

Piaget's most widely known observation is that intellectual development follows the biological principle of mutual interaction between organism and the environment. Just as a living organism adapts to changes in the environment, so too does a child change his or her mental or cognitive structure (schema) by adjusting to new stimuli, or new experience. The adult's schemata evolve from the child's schemata through the process of the constant interaction between internal mental structure (subject) and external stimuli (object)—i.e., "intellectual development is a constant process of construction and reconstruction" (Wadsworth 16). The epiphanies of the characters in *Dubliners* signify their cognitive growth grounded in modifications to their cognitive structures, especially those which no longer explain their new experiences. These epiphanies are, to put it another way, a more refined reasoning about the self and others from the evolving process of negotiations and renegotiations both of attachments to others (orientation toward object) and differentiation from others (orientation toward subject). In brief, Joyce's epiphanies exemplify Piaget's sense of the growth of the self as a constant balancing and rebalancing of the self in relation to both the world and to others.

The final story of *Dubliners*, "The Dead," is a coda to the Dublin stories in which Joyce addresses Dublin's "hospitality" as one of "the attractions of the City" (*Letters* 2 166) rather than its harsh reality featured in the rest of the stories. Following the thematic design intended by Joyce, who determined to show a congenial facet of Dublin life in his last story, "The Dead" deals with a family gathering, with its Irish exhibitions of greetings, drinking, eating, dancing, talking, and singing, all hosted by the Morkan spinsters, Kate and Julia, and their niece Mary Jane. This jovial appearance of congeniality, however, masks emotional patterns of inward conflict and tension for a married couple, Gabriel and Gretta Conroy. Joyce intended the title of "The Dead" to echo Henrik Ibsen's play *When We Dead Awaken* (1899). There are indeed several parallels between the short story and the play: the male protagonists Gabriel in Joyce's story and Rubek in Ibsen's *When We Dead Awaken* are both artists—one a writer, the other a sculptor. Both are more or less involved in marital conflict because of their masculine egoism in which they each attend primarily to their own self-interest while ignoring their wives' emotional demands.

In Ibsen's play, Rubek is portrayed as a person forcing himself into a rat race for the achievement of artistic mastery. He shows his visceral contempt for "a life of indolence and emptiness" (406) without artistic creation. Rubek sacrifices his wife, Maya, to art, "snap[ping] [her] up as an expedient" (405) for buffering his loneliness from his model Irene's abrupt disappearance when his statue—"The Day of the Resurrection," modeled on her—is completed. Rubek depreciates her solicitousness as a call for him to hearken to "her interests" (403), not to his own artistic needs. Her revolt against her husband's callousness takes her on an excursion to a mountain crest with Ulfhejam, a bear hunter, representing her journey toward freedom—"I have fled from my slavery" (421). Compared to Rubek, Gabriel in "The Dead" dismisses Gretta's aspiration to return to Galway, her former home not visited since her marriage, and ignores her emotional exhilaration in expectation of seeing it again. Gabriel is so obsessed with his own emotional disturbance since his mortification by Lily and Miss Ivors that he fails to see, much less care for, Gretta's inner feelings when she relates her memories of her deceased adolescent lover, Michael Furey, to explain her momentary emotional self-absorption.

What is perhaps the most striking analogy between Joyce's and Ibsen's male characters are the epiphanies of the two male protagonists and their ensuing enlightenments. When Irene derides his artistic vanity in pursuing merely abstract images without "earthly love" (430), Rubek realizes that he was "blind enough to place that dead image of clay above happiness—the happiness of life, of love" (430). In the end, Rubek becomes disillusioned with the emptiness of his artistic conceit and awakened to the fact that he has been a nominal person. At the end of Joyce's story, Gabriel feels "a strange friendly pity for" Gretta despite the revelation of her earlier heartbreak connected to Michael Furey's dying for her (222). Gabriel finally lifts the egocentric rigidity hindering the emotional intimacy between himself and his wife, wondering at "[the] riot of emotions" that has made him initially nervous about Gretta's confession, but has now suddenly collapsed (222). He finally reaches a state of emotional calm by rethinking of how poorly he performed in his marital relationship.

In 1900, Joyce wrote a critical essay titled "Ibsen's New Drama" concerned with *When We Dead Awaken.* Ibsen's drama addresses the marital conflicts between Rubek and Maya, one of which comes from an absence of an intellectual and emotional rapport between them: "You are not a sociable man, [Maya says,] you know that, Rubek. You like to be by yourself and occupy yourself with your own affairs" (403). It is remarkable, though, that, despite his own acknowledgment that most criticism takes the couple's marital trouble as the subject of Ibsen's play, Joyce belittles the significance of that topic and, instead, emphasizes Rubek's "epiphany" as the primary focus of the play.

Joyce's panegyric primarily discusses the revelatory power of the play in which Rubek is transformed into a man who redeems himself after reaching an epiphanic moment, a crucial juncture for him at which a new meaning of life from self-awareness comes about: "Thinking deeper and deeper on himself and on his former attitude towards this woman [Irene], it strikes him yet more forcibly that there are great gulfs set between his art and his life, and that even in his art his skill and genius are far from perfect" (*Critical Writings* 54). For Joyce, "The Resurrection Day" is "an all-embracing philosophy, a deep sympathy with the cross-purposes and contradictions of life, as they may be reconcilable with a hopeful awakening" (66). Hence, Joyce's philosophical exegesis of the statue by Rubek theorizes an evolving self, emphasizing

Rubek's transformation as a dynamic psychological process in which a new and larger experience demands an alteration of the old self. Emergence of the new self from out of the constraints of the old self is, for Joyce, like the regaining of a new life from a state of death on a symbolic level: "the facts that he is devoted to his art and that he has attained to a degree of mastery in it—mastery of hand linked with limitation of thought—tell us that there may be lying dormant in him a capacity for greater life, which may be exercised when he, a dead man, shall have risen from among the dead" (66).

As I will argue in detail ahead, "The Dead," as an Irish rendition of Ibsen's Norwegian drama, deals with Gabriel's epiphany as a self-transformative process, the self-transformative process impossible without the intellectual leap of becoming aware of two contending realities of the self: a narcissistically self-delusive self and an objectively self-evaluating self. Gabriel is destined to choose one of them as a corrective to his own previous self-deception that Gretta was merely an object in his willful emotional and intellectual egoism. I am also contending that his transformative process into greater maturity is pushed by the emotional pressure associated with his interactions with his wife in their family dynamic. In a broader sense, Gabriel's epiphany is a marker of his evolution as he reconstructs himself via adjustment to a family process he is newly awakened to.

II

Hence, Gabriel's epiphany is the outcome of family process, in particular, the dynamism of the interpersonal relationship between husband and wife. Two psychological theorists have discussed such dynamism from somewhat different approaches. Jean Piaget regards human personality as constructed along the sequence of social relationships, of which family processes are one of several interactional social relationships (71). Jerome Kagan also noticed the socially adaptive function of personality, allowing for both genetic factors and environmental factors in personality. Preferring the term *temperament* to *personality*,

Kagan distinguishes two opposite temperamental types by the degree to which the central nervous system is aroused—uninhibited and inhibited. Compared with uninhibited children, inhibited children tend to be more nervous among strangers or novel situations with a greater increase in arousal of the central nervous system—an increase in intensity of emotional reactions—relative to uninhibited children. The two temperaments are, Kagan says, not determined in actuality but are merely potentialities with their genetic profiles to be actualized in various ways as a consequence of interactions with the environment:

> Temperament is a potential. There is no guarantee of an indefinitely stable profile because environmental factors are always potent. [. . .] Thus, we borrow from biology the fruitful pair of concepts called *genotype*—the inherited genetic profile—and *phenotype*—the visible results of the interaction between that profile and the environment. (36)

Piaget's grand picture of cognitive development reflects his view of the adaptive process of the self's constant adjustment to the environment—i.e., the people surrounding the self, which aims at movement toward an equilibrium between the self and the other by reducing the gap—the state of disequilibrium—between them. In the Piagetian model of cognitive evolution, accordingly, personality is the *inter*personal reality constructed in the dialectic process between internal impulse and external pressure as the self reaches toward a point of interpersonal balance. One of the great findings by Piaget is that affectivity[1] provides the energy to vitalize an intellectual leap, and so cognitive development is activated by a new affective type appropriate to each developmental stage:

> Since structure does not exist without energetics and, reciprocally, since every new structure involves a new form of energetic regulation, a particular sort of cognitive structure will be found in concert with every new type of affective regulation (12).

Piaget posits, consequently, that "feeling, properly speaking, appears, disappears, and oscillates in intensity [. . .] because it is created, then dissipates, then is re-created. In other words, it is constructed or reconstructed on each occasion" (50–51).

An emotionally intense state, anxiety is a feeling emerging and perishing along the way in which interpersonal relationships are formed. Robert Kegan remarks that pressure for cognitive change is pushed by emotional intensity such as anxiety: "Central to the experiences of qualitative change or decentration (phenomenologically, the loss of my center) are the affects of loss—anxiety and depression" (82). Two family therapists, Michael Kerr and Murray Bowen, also note that anxiety is the energy to be mobilized in creating a new interpersonal relationship:

> An important consequence of anxiety is that it creates pressure on people *to adapt to one another* in ways that will reduce each other's anxiety. This pressure for adaptation can produce changes in each person's behavior that result in the anxiety being expressed, bound, or absorbed in certain aspects of the way people interact and function. (78)

In a family environment, for example, separation anxiety for the child is an intense emotion being displayed in accommodation of oneself to a new interpersonal relationship. It is not only the emotional distress about being separated from the mother but also about the child's growing differentiation from the old self and coming into a new state of self, i.e., "an evolutionary transformation" (Kegan 82). As the neo-Piagetian Henry Dupont states, "an emotion begins when some internal or external change puts the system into disequlibrium and a need is created. The emotion ends when the need is met" (5). Separation anxiety is also a sign of the child's excessive emotional dependence on mother. The emotional pattern underlying a child's adaptiveness to separation anxiety may be the archetype of all the family-emotional patterns beyond childhood psychology. Kerr and Bowen emphasize how family anxiety increases in proportion to the degree of emotional interdependency in family relationships:

> Since anxiety undermines a feeling of emotional well-being, people automatically act in ways designed to reduce anxiety. The greater the emotional interdependence of a relationship, therefore, the more easily people are threatened, the more anxiety they experience, and the more energy is invested in actions aimed at reducing that anxiety. (74)

Emotional maturity with little or no anxiety requires the logical reasoning part of one's mind to be more or less objectively conscious of the way others emotionally react to one's own emotional response to their feelings. In brief, maturity requires one always to put one's self into any response to that self by the other.

III

"The Dead" is, not surprisingly, a sequel to "The Sisters," as a sort of an adult version of the boy, the protagonist-narrator of the first story of *Dubliners*. As David G. Wright remarks, we find in "The Dead" "the links with the very first story" of *Dubliners* (289); the two sisters in "The Sisters" resonate with Gabriel's aunts, Julia and Kate. "The Sisters" begins with a boy taking seriously the issue of one's death, looking in from outside a dimly lit window of the priest's house that evokes the priest's imminent death, while "The Dead" ends with a man from inside a hotel room, looking out through a window on the snow-covered scenery gloomily lit by streetlamps, meditating on human mortality. As Wright notes, "'The Dead' operates as a kind of parody of the earlier stories in the collection" (288).

Apart from the analogy between the distinctive *mise en scène* of the earlier stories and that of "The Dead," Gabriel's hypersensitive personality is the most striking feature that enables the reader to connect his personality to the nervous dispositions of the boys in the childhood stories. The extremely nervous and bookish boys[2] in the stories of childhood and the loners in the stories of adolescence[3] are restated through Gabriel whose own marital issues show their likely fates in marriage. Insofar as each story of *Dubliners* is, retrospectively, one of the pieces of a puzzle whose collection makes the complete picture of Dublin life, the boys in the childhood stories are strongly correlated with Gabriel: they appear to indicate what his personality construction in the early life might look like and make us spot his tendencies toward emotional interdependency as the origin of his anxiety in adulthood, a tendency demanding a new logic to create a new interactive way of family process.

"The Dead" on the whole details the way in which Gabriel's temperament leads to his mood changes, as it dramatizes the nervousness he suffers from through his sensitive inward reactions in emotionally intensive situations. The first prominent sign of Gabriel's chronic anxiety is his sensitive rumination about Lily's unexpectedly painful rejoinder—"The men that is now is only all palaver and what they can get out of you"—to his affectionate greeting ("O, then, said Gabriel gaily, I suppose we'll be going to your wedding one of these fine days with your young man, eh?") and his intimidated feelings: "He was still discomposed by the girl's bitter and sudden retort. It had cast a gloom over him which he tried to dispel by arranging his cuffs and the bows of his tie" (*Dubliners* 178–79). His rumination brings about more anxiety, which generates more rumination, which, in turn, activates more anxiety. Upon barely dissipating his meditations on Lily's retort, he becomes instantly anxious about a forthcoming speech to be made by him after dinner:

He was undecided about the lines from Robert Browning for he feared they would be above the heads of his hearers. Some quotation that they could recognize from Shakespeare or from the Melodies would be better. The delicate clacking of the men's heels and the shuffling of their soles reminded him that their grade of culture differed from his. He would only make himself ridiculous by quoting poetry to them which they could not understand. They would think that he was airing his superior education. He would fail with them just as he had failed with the girl in the pantry. (179)

Gabriel's excessive nervousness prompts him anxiously to brood about anticipated responses to his speech from audiences. In particular, Miss Ivors's objection to his inclinations in his lifestyle and literary tastes to be pro-Continental rather than a Gaelic patriot plunges him into an emotional panic caused by his hypersensitive obsessions with what others think about him. The appellation for him, "a West Briton," which was given by Miss Ivors to taunt his susceptibility to foreign cultures, increases his anxiety: "A look of perplexity appeared on Gabriel's face" (188). Miss Ivors's repetitive interrogations about his ethnic identity drive him into emotional distress: "Gabriel glanced right and left nervously and tried to keep his good humor under the ordeal which was making a blush invade his forehead" (189). After an altercation with Miss Ivors, Gabriel ponders almost obsessively, as he usually did, what he should have told her, trying to dissipate the slanderous accusation by her: "Perhaps he ought not to have answered her like that. But she had no right to call him a West Briton before people, even in joke" (190). Miss Ivors's critical remarks on his apolitical view of literature haunt him for the rest of the night, as he becomes more nervous about her anticipated presence at the after-dinner speech: "It unnerved him to think that she would be at the supper-table, looking up at him while he spoke with her critical quizzing eyes" (192).

The high-level anxiety of Gabriel may be a sign of his unresolved emotional attachment to his family-of-origin. Gabriel's mother's oversolicitous care for her children resonates with the intrusively domineering motherhood by Mrs. Kearney in "A Mother," Queen Victoria in "Ivy Day in the Committee Room," Mrs. Mooney in "The Boarding House," and Eveline's dead mother in "Eveline." Like other *Dubliners* mothers, Gabriel's mother pushes her children into obeying her wishes. She tailors her sons' needs to her own narcissistic needs for admiration, as her self-centered intention in naming them suggests: "It was she who had chosen the names for her sons for she was very sensible of the dignity of family life" (186). Her overprotective mothering obviously contributes to her children's successes: "Thanks to her, Constantine was now senior curate in Balbriggan and, thanks to her, Gabriel himself had taken his degree in the Royal University" (186–87). The egocentric mother of Gabriel forces her sons to meet her demands inflicted on them behind the facade of maternal love. The symptomatically entangled relationship between mother and child appears to have impeded his development into a self-confident person, and has contributed to his increasingly timid individuality with an extremely sensitive but self-preoccupied mind.

For Gabriel, his mother's photograph, hung at the Morkans' house, brings up for him a painful memory of her refusal to accept Gretta as her daughter-in-law, which indicates his anguish at a demanding mother: "A shadow passed over his face as he remembered her sullen opposition to his marriage. Some slighting phrases she had used still rankled in his memory; she had once spoken of Gretta as being country cute and that was not true of Gretta at all" (187). Gabriel still harbors a deep "resentment" against his mother (187). His harsh memory of the dead mother and his anxiety about her even in her complete physical absence bring to light his unresolved emotional attachment to his mother, which could, in part, explain his emotional reliance on his wife. Their marital relationship indicates that Gabriel may have inherited the limited sense of his emotional autonomy—the degree to which he is emotionally dependent on others as witnessed by his excessive anxiety—from the way in which his family members seem to be emotionally duplicating those patterns from his family-of-origin. Gabriel could be seen to be repeating the relationships between himself and his mother in the interactional pattern with his wife. Kerr and Bowen spell out variations of individual anxiety in its relation to the level of differentiation of the self, or the degree of emotional separation of a child from parents:

The increased undifferentiation means that the functioning of family members is more relationship-dependent, *a dependence that spawns chronic anxiety*. The next level of observation for understanding the origin of this variation among individuals in anxiety levels is the emotional process in a nuclear family. An individual growing up in a given nuclear family is "imprinted" with a level of chronic anxiety characteristic of this branch. Anxiety "rubs off" on people; it is transmitted and absorbed without thinking. (115–16; emphasis added)

They further account for a multigenerational phenomenon of the interrelationship between the level of differentiation of the self and the level of anxiety:

When a person (second generation) who has less differentiation than his parents marries, he will, like his parents, select a mate who has the same level of differentiation. Whether the mate he selects has more or less differentiation than her parents depends on the patterns of emotional functioning in her original family. These two people become the "architects" of the emotional atmosphere in their new nuclear family and incorporate their children (third generation) into that atmosphere. (225–26)

Gabriel's own family, consisting of four members (Gabriel, Gretta, Tom, and Eva), is as dysfunctional a family as any other in *Dubliners*, displaying the same patterns of the emotional process as the other families do. Gabriel conflates his anxiety in living a public life with his wife in their family life, a reminder of Chandler in "A Little Cloud" or Farrington in "Counterparts." Gabriel's rejection of Gretta's suggestion to visit the Aran Isles stems from his anger at Miss Ivors, who made the outrageous slurs against his apolitical approaches to literature and his internationalism in contrast to her Irish patriotism:

—There were no words [in a talk with Miss Ivors], said Gabriel mood-
ily, only she wanted me to go for a trip to the west of Ireland and I said I
wouldn't.

His wife clasped her hands excitedly and gave a little jump.

—O, do go, Gabriel, she cried. I'd love to go see Galway again.

—You can go if you like, said Gabriel coldly. (191)

Gretta self-defensively reacts to Gabriel's embarrassingly bitter reaction to her gaiety: "She looked at him for a moment, then turned to
Mrs Malins and said: —There's a nice husband for you, Mrs Malins"
(191). Gabriel's repulsion causes her to feel alienated from her husband throughout the dance party and her emotional wounds along with
Bartell D'Arcy's singing prompt her to reminisce about her adolescent
worshipper, Michael Furey, as a self-defensive means for regaining her
self-esteem degraded by Gabriel. At the end of the party, the song sung
by Bartell D'Arcy—"The Lass of Aughrim"—touches Gretta's senti-
mentalism in which she is led to a memory of her old wooer as a way
to offset her snubbed feelings. Gabriel's demanding manner in treating
his wife is, too, detected in his children's mistreatment by him:

He's really an awful bother, what with green shades for Tom's eyes at
night and making him do the dumb-bells, and forcing Eva to eat the sti-
rabout. The poor child! And she simply hates the sight of it! . . . O, but
you'll never guess what he makes me wear now! (180)

The ending of "The Dead" illustrates Gabriel's meditation in which
he reaches a new perception of their relationship patterns—a different understanding of their marriage and of Gretta's own self-hood and
an awareness of the way to achieve more emotional balance in their
relationships. Gabriel has failed to see her emotional wound and her
intimidation caused by his harshness, her secret grief over her past
and dead lover, and her womanly wishes for romance exemplified in
her longing for Galway. Gretta has, too, failed to perceive her hus-

band's emotional vulnerability disguised in his facade of rigidity and his real affection for her in Gabriel's cavalier attitude in directing her. Gretta seems unaware of how bitterly her casual mention of Galway reminded her husband of the agony of his mortification by Miss Ivors. Gretta appears blind to Gabriel's unspoken care for her in his insistent demands for wearing "goloshes" to prevent her feet from being soaked by rain: "Goloshes! said Mrs Conroy. That's the latest. Whenever it's wet underfoot I must put on my goloshes. To-night even he wanted me to put them on, but I wouldn't" (180). Gabriel has felt nervous about the intolerable circumstances created by Lily's scornful retort against his benevolent joke; Gretta's sarcasms about his overbearing behavior that is in reality a sort of a defensive gesture against his timidity; and Miss Ivors's unrestrained criticism of his aestheticism, which is a validation of "literature [. . .] above politics" (188). As a self-defensive gesture against Miss Ivors's stigmatization of him, Gabriel makes a speech aimed at his absent enemy, Miss Ivors—the speech that puts emphasis on "hospitality" (203) and "humanity" in contrast to her, as Gabriel sees it, "propagandism" (192).

On the way back to a hotel, carnal desires overwhelm Gabriel's mood, leading him to misunderstand the eccentric immobility of Gretta "standing on the stairs in the shadow, listening to distant music" at the end of the party (210). He notes that "after the kindling again of so many memories, the first touch of her body, musical and strange and perfumed, sent through him a keen pang of lust" (215). Not until Gabriel and Gretta are later together alone in a hotel room does he realize that she is emotionally preoccupied. His timidity deprives him of courage to deal directly with the down mood, increasingly creating a nervous circumstance: "He was trembling now with annoyance. Why did she seem so abstracted? He did not know how he could begin. Was she annoyed, too, about something?" (217).

In the marital relationship between Gabriel and Gretta, he is the seemingly dominant person, who, from the very beginning of marriage, played the leading role in their marital relationship; however, in reality, he appears much more emotionally fragile than Gretta, as illustrated by how easily he was embarrassed by such unfamiliar experiences as Miss Ivors's slanderous remarks about his philosophy of internationalism, his wife's unusual stiffness, or Lily's unexpected rejoinder. His nervousness about unfamiliar experiences is, in part, the possible outcome of experience in his family-of-origin in which he would have adapted to his domineering mother by becoming hypervigilant, being required constantly to meet her emotional needs. Much of Gabriel's anxiety in the relationship with his spouse comes from his failure to accept her individuality, or his lack of effort to admit that she feels and thinks differently. He grows upset about an inattentiveness that is incomprehensible to him: "He longed to be master of her strange mood" (217). The rigidity in Gabriel's shyness obliged him to hope that Gretta would succumb to his emotional needs: "If she would only turn to him or come to him of her own accord!" (217). The impression of Gretta's unexpected rigidity in "her strange mood" exasperates Gabriel, and drives him into "a fever of rage." Gretta's final collapse, caused by her heartfelt memory of Michael Furey, misleads him to believe "the yielding mood had come upon her," as he feels relieved by her downfall; he thinks, "Now that she had fallen to him so easily he wondered why he had been so diffident" (218).

The abrupt confession by Gretta about her grief for her dead lover casts cold water on his romantic anticipation and disillusions. Gabriel, who had hitherto believed in his total dominance in the marital relationship with his wife, experiences a realization: "Gabriel felt humiliated by the failure of his irony and by the evocation of this figure from the dead, a boy in the gasworks. While he had been full of memories of their secret life together, full of tenderness and joy and desire, she had been comparing him in her mind with another" (219). Suddenly, Gabriel finds how emotionally dependent he has been on others: "He saw himself as a ludicrous figure, acting as a pennyboy for his aunts, a nervous well-meaning sentimentalist, orating to vulgarians and idealizing his own clownish lusts [. . .]" (220). Gabriel sees that he is emotionally overdependent on Gretta:

—I think he died for me, she answered. A vague terror seized Gabriel at this answer as if, at that hour when he had hoped to triumph, some impalpable and vindictive being was coming against him, gathering forces against him in its vague world. (220)

Gabriel's serious reflections on the relationship with his wife offer him a chance to reconfigure his role in this intense relationship, which has been dominated by a kind of forced togetherness and marked by intense and passionate closeness, and to objectify himself by rethinking the roles he played in the relationship system: "It hardly pained him now to think how poor a part he, her husband, had played in her life. He watched her while she slept as though he and she had never lived together as man and wife" (222). Gabriel finally releases his anxiety based upon his undue dependence on Gretta: "Generous tears filled Gabriel's eyes. He had never felt like that himself towards any woman but he knew that such a feeling must be love. [. . .] His own identity was fading out into a grey impalpable world" (223). Gabriel had accused his wife of no longer caring for him. But now, he no longer blames himself for being betrayed by his wife, whom he had believed to be subservient to his emotional demands. Now Gabriel accepts his own individuality as much as he admits Gretta's individuality.

Gabriel's epiphany comes up at the moment when he is conscious of an existential irony in which there is a gap between the self in subjective experience and the self in objective reality. Gabriel fully exposes himself to self-evaluation without self-defensive blaming of the other. Gabriel's equanimity is evidence of his distancing himself from an intensely embedded relationship, which comes from contemplation of the way in which he is involved in the relationship. His sense of betrayal is not a jealousy from the recognition of Michael Furey's occupation of Gretta's mind, which he earlier had considered the cause of her frigid inattentiveness to his emotional demands, but, rather, an interrogation of his selfhood. His sense of betrayal is, in essence, an ironic double on his part, as the double meaning of the word *betrayal* suggests: disbelief in his selfhood—disloyalty to his own self—he has believed to be legitimate and, as its ironic result, divulgement of the truth of self-delusion he is blind to. Joycean epiphany is obviously based upon revealing the ironic sense of the self. The epiphany is a dialectic process transpiring in the complementary relationship of affectivity and cognition from which to compel the self's movement for a further intellectual leap toward greater emotional maturity through the constant interaction between the self and the environment. In "The Dead," Gabriel resolves the crisis in "his own identity" by evolving into a more mature man and, in turn, accepting his wife Gretta's individuality. He appears to feel greater sensitivity to this relationship; Gabriel moves in this crisis from the emotional tensions created via a not-atypical family process—learning something new about their mutual past—and transforms his selfhood to fit into his new comprehension of his wife and his life with her by dialectically rethinking their interactional patterns in their total life span.

Notes

1. *Affectivity* is a broader term than *emotion* or *feelings*. Affectivity includes drives and the will as well as emotion and feelings (Piaget 2).
2. In "The Sisters," the boy displays his hypersensitivity in obsession with Father Flynn's death, which entails a hallucination; the boy of "An Encounter" is "studious" and "lacking in robustness" and he fears to be less bookish in the eyes of the old man and to look serious in the eyes of his classmates (20); the boy of "Araby" is the person of nervous disposition uncontrollably fixated with Mangan's sister in his fantasy.
3. Doran in "The Boarding House" is a grown-up version of the boys who were the first-person narrators in the stories of childhood. He enjoys celibacy in strict adherence to "his religious duties" but his religious scrupulosity causes his nerves to be frayed (66). Lenehan's solitary life in "Two Gallants" dramatizes his reserved demeanor as contrasted with his overbearing friend, Corley.

Works Cited

Bowen, Jack. "Joyce and the Epiphany Concept: A New Approach." *Journal of Modern Literature* 9 (1981): 103–14.

Dupont, Henry. *Emotional Development, Theory and Applications: A Neo-Piagetian Perspective*. London: Praeger, 1994.

Ellmann, Richard. *James Joyce*. Rev. ed. Oxford: Oxford UP, 1982.

Hendry, Irene. "Joyce's Epiphanies." *The Sewanee Review* 54 (1946): 449–67.

Ibsen, Henrik. *Last Plays of Henrik Ibsen*. Trans. Arvid Paulson. New York: Bantam, 1962.

Joyce, James. *The Critical Writings of James Joyce*. Ed. Ellsworth Mason and Richard Ellmann. New York: Viking, 1959.

_____. *Dubliners*. Ed. Robert Scholes and A. Walton Litz. New York: Viking, 1967.

_____. *Letters of James Joyce*. Ed. Stuart Gilbert and Richard Ellmann. 3 vols. New York: Viking, 1966.

_____. *A Portrait of the Artist as a Young Man*. Ed. Chester G. Anderson. New York: Viking, 1964.

_____. *Stephen Hero*. Ed. Theodore Spencer. New York: New Directions. 1963.

Joyce, Stanislaus. *My Brother's Keeper: James Joyce's Early Years*. Ed. Richard Ellmann. New York: Viking, 1958.

Kagan, Jerome. *Galen's Prophecy: Temperament in Human Nature*. New York: Basic, 1994.

Kegan, Robert. *The Evolving Self: Problem and Process in Human Development*. Cambridge: Harvard UP, 1982.

Kerr, Michael E., and Murray Bowen. *Family Evaluation: An Approach Based on Bowen Theory*. New York: Norton, 1988.

Piaget, Jean. *Intelligence and Affectivity: Their Relationship During Child Development*. Trans. and ed. T. A. Brown and C. E. Kaegi. Palo Alto: Annual Rev., 1981.

Scholes, Robert. "Joyce and the Epiphany: The Key to the Labyrinth?" *The Sewanee Review* 72 (1964): 65–77.

Scholes, Robert, and Florence L. Walzl. "The Epiphanies of Joyce." *PMLA* 82 (1967): 152–54.

Wadsworth, Barry J. *Piaget's Theory of Cognitive and Affective Development: Foundations of Constructivism*. 5th ed. New York: Longman, 1996.

Wright, David G. "Interactive Stories in Dubliners." *Studies in Short Fiction* 32 (1995): 285–93.

RESOURCES

Additional Works on Family

Drama

The Oresteia by Aeschylus, 458 BCE
Richard III by William Shakespeare, 1592
Hamlet by William Shakespeare, 1600
The Cherry Orchard by Anton Chekhov, 1904
The Little Foxes by Lillian Hellman, 1939
The Glass Menagerie by Tennessee Williams, 1944
Death of a Salesman by Arthur Miller, 1949
Long Day's Journey into Night by Eugene O'Neill, 1956
The Homecoming by Harold Pinter, 1965
Fences by August Wilson, 1985

Long Fiction

Wuthering Heights by Emily Brönte, 1847
The Mill on the Floss by George Eliot, 1860
Great Expectations by Charles Dickens, 1860–1861
The Death of Ivan Ilyich by Leo Tolstoy, 1886
Buddenbrooks by Thomas Mann, 1901
The Good Soldier by Ford Madox Ford, 1915
To the Lighthouse by Virginia Woolf, 1927
As I Lay Dying by William Faulkner, 1930
Brideshead Revisited by Evelyn Waugh, 1945
Rabbit Run by John Updike, 1960
Song of Solomon by Toni Morrison, 1977
The Joy Luck Club by Amy Tan, 1989
Therapy by David Lodge, 1995
Prisoner's Dilemma by Richard Powers, 1996
A Thousand Acres by Jane Smiley, 1996
We Were the Mulvaneys by Joyce Carol Oates, 1997
The Corrections by Jonathan Franzen, 2001
Spies by Michael Frayn, 2003

Nonfiction

Memories of a Catholic Girlhood, by Mary McCarthy, 1957
I Know Why the Caged Bird Sings by Maya Angelou, 1969
The Woman Warrior by Maxine Hong Kingston, 1976

Nonfiction (continued)

An American Childhood by Annie Dillard, 1987
Brother, I'm Dying by Edwidge Danticat, 2007

Poetry

The Odyssey by Homer, c. 725 BCE
Kaddish by Allen Ginsberg, 1961
Ariel by Sylvia Plath, 1965
Selected Poems by Denise Levertov, 1986
Opened Ground by Seamus Heaney, 1998
Blessings the Boats: New and Selected Poems, 1988–2000 by Lucille Clifton, 2000
The Essential Gwendolyn Brooks by Gwendolyn Brooks, 2005
Selected Poems, 1946–1985 by James Merrill, 2008

Short Fiction

"Barn Burning" by William Faulkner, 1939

Bibliography

Ariel, Shlomo. *Culturally Competent Family Therapy*. Westport: Praeger, 1999.

Boyd, Brian. *On the Origin of Stories: Evolution, Cognition, and Fiction*. Cambridge: Harvard UP, 2009.

Carroll, Joseph. *Literary Darwinism: Evolution, Human Nature, and Literature*. New York: Routledge, 2004.

Coles, Robert. *Handling One Another: Literature and Social Reflection*. New York: Random, 2010.

Culpeper, Jonathan. *Language and Characterization: People in Plays and Other Texts*. Essex: Pearson, 2001.

Di Nicola, Vincenzo. *A Stranger in the Family: Culture, Families, and Therapy*. New York: Norton, 1997.

Gerrig, Richard J., and David W. Allbritton. "The Construction of Literary Character: A View from Cognitive Psychology." *Style* 24.3 (1990): 380–91.

Gottschall, Jonathan. *Literature, Science, and the New Humanities*. New York: Palgrave, 2008.

Gottschall, Jonathan, and David Sloan Wilson. *The Literary Animal: Evolution and the Nature of Narrative*. Evanston: Northwestern UP, 2005.

Graff, Gerald. *Professing Literature: An Institutional History*. Chicago: U of Chicago P, 1987.

Grunbaum, Adolph. *The Foundations of Psychoanalysis: A Philosophic Critique*. Berkeley: U of California P, 1984.

Houlbrooke, Ralph. *The English Family, 1450–1700*. London: Longman, 1984.

Kagan, Jerome. *Three Cultures: Natural Sciences, Social Sciences, and the Humanities in the 21st Century*. New York: Cambridge UP, 2009.

Knapp, John V. "Family Games and Imbroglio in *Hamlet*." *Reading the Family Dance*. Ed. John V. Knapp and Kenneth Womack. Newark: U of Delaware P, 2003: 194–218.

_____. "Family Systems Psychotherapy and Psychoanalytic Literary Criticism: A Comparative Critique." *Mosaic* 37.1 (March 2004): 149–66.

Ozment, Steven. *Ancestors: The Loving Family in Old Europe*. Cambridge: Harvard UP, 2001.

_____. *When Fathers Ruled: Family Life in Reformation Europe*. Cambridge: Harvard UP, 1983.

Palmer, Alan. *Fictional Minds*. Lincoln: U of Nebraska P, 2004.

_____, ed. "Social Minds in Fiction and Criticism." *Style*, 45.2 (2011).

Phelan, James. *Reading People, Reading Plots: Character, Progression, and the Interpretation of Narrative*. Chicago: U of Chicago P, 1989.

Reiss, David, Jenae M. Neiderhiser, E. Mavis Hetherington, and Robert Plomin. *The Relationship Code: Deciphering Genetic and Social Influences on Adolescent Development.* Cambridge: Harvard UP, 2000.

Rogoff, Barbara. *The Cultural Nature of Human Development.* New York: Oxford UP, 2003.

Salmon, Catherine A., and Todd K. Shackelford. *Family Relationships: An Evolutionary Perspective.* New York: Oxford UP, 2008.

Vermeule, Blakey. *Why Do We Care About Literary Characters?* Baltimore: Johns Hopkins UP, 2010.

Whitaker, Carl A., and William M. Bumberry. *Dancing with the Family: A Symbolic-Experiential Approach.* New York: Brunner, 1988.

Zunshine, Lisa. *Why We Read Fiction: Theory of Mind and the Novel.* Columbus: Ohio State UP, 2006.

CRITICAL INSIGHTS

About the Editor _____

John V. Knapp is the editor of this volume and professor of English at Northern Illinois University where he has regularly taught courses in modern literatures, literary criticism and theory, and teacher education since 1971. Knapp holds doctorates in modern literatures (University of Illinois at Urbana–Champaign, 1971) and in educational psychology (University of Wisconsin–Madison, 2000). He has published four books, including *Learning from Scant Beginnings: English Professor Expertise* (2008), *Reading the Family Dance: Family Systems Therapy and Literary Study* (2003), *Striking at the Joints: Contemporary Psychology and Literary Criticism* (1996), and *Literary Character* (1993), plus over fifty articles and reviews. Knapp has been editor of the literary journal *Style* since 2007.

Contributors

John V. Knapp is professor of English at Northern Illinois University and the author of *Learning from Scant Beginnings: English Professor Expertise* (2008) and *Striking at the Joints: Contemporary Psychology and Literary Criticism* (1996), as well as the editor of *Literary Character* (1993). He co-edited (with Ken Womack) *Reading the Family Dance: Family Systems Therapy and Literary Study* (2003), and two issues of *Style* (in 1997 and 2010) devoted to the new psychologies in literary study, as well as over fifty essays and reviews. Knapp has also been the editor of the literary journal *Style* since 2007.

Steven Mintz is the director of the Graduate School of Arts and Sciences Teaching Center and professor of history at Columbia University. He is the author and editor of thirteen books, including *Domestic Revolutions: A Social History of American Family Life* (1988) and *Huck's Raft: A History of American Childhood* (2004). He is also the creator of the Digital History website. A former fellow at the Center for Advanced Study in the Behavioral Sciences at Stanford University, he is past president of the Society for the History of Children and Youth and past chair of the Council on Contemporary Families.

Catherine M. Leen is a lecturer in Spanish at the National University of Ireland, Maynooth. Her research interests include Chicana and Chicano literature and cinema, particularly the works of Sandra Cisneros, Denise Chávez, filmmaker Lourdes Portillo, and filmmaker and performance artist Guillermo Gómez-Peña. She has also published book chapters and articles on Chicano writers Sandra Cisneros and Luis Valdez, and on Latin American cinema. Leen is working on a monograph on Latina and Latino filmmakers and Mexico. She is also co-authoring a volume on international perspectives on Chicana and Chicano studies with Niamh Thornton of the University of Ulster.

Joseph Carroll is Curators' Professor of English at the University of Missouri–St. Louis. His first two books were monographs on Matthew Arnold and Wallace Stevens. Since the mid-1990s, he has focused on integrating literary theory with evolutionary theory. He is author of *Evolution and Literary Theory* (1995), *Literary Darwinism: Evolution, Human Nature, and Literature* (2004), and *Reading Human Nature: Literary Darwinism in Theory and Practice* (2011). He produced an edition of Charles Darwin's *Origin of Species* (2003), co-edited the first two annual volumes of *The Evolutionary Review: Art, Science, Culture* (2010 and 2011), and co-edited *Evolution, Literature, and Film: A Reader* (2010).

Thomas M. McCann is associate professor of English at Northern Illinois University. His primary research interests focus on the concerns of beginning teachers, the teaching of writing, and classroom discourse. He is the co-author of *Supporting Beginning English Teachers* (2005), *Talking in Class* (2006), and *The Dynamics of English Instruction* (2010).

Susan Callahan teaches courses in English education and serves as the college coordinator for Teacher Preparation and Development at Northern Illinois University. Previously, she taught at Kentucky State University, a historically African American institution, where her students brought a wide range of experiences and opinions into class discussions. Most of her research has been in the area of portfolio assessment and has appeared in *Research in the Teaching of English, Educational Assessment, and Assessing Writing*. Her interest in university–high school collaboration led to an article in *English Education* detailing some of the communication problems that often interfere with such work. She is researching a co-teaching model for student teaching that is being implemented in an area professional development school.

Beth McFarland-Wilson is lead consultant with the University Writing Center at Northern Illinois University and a supervisor with the English Teacher Certification Program. She holds a BA in English and psychology from North Central College, an MS from Eastern Illinois University, and an MA in English from Northern Illinois University. Her article applying a family systems interpretation of Richard Powers's *Prisoner's Dilemma* appeared in *Style* in 2010 and she presented a paper on the family system in D. H. Lawrence's "The Horse Dealer's Daughter" at the 2009 Modern Language Association (MLA) Convention.

James Postema is professor of English at Concordia College where he specializes in twentieth-century American literature and Native American literatures. He wrote his doctoral dissertation on temporal structures in Robert Frost's poetry, using narrative theory to study the lyric form. He has written on lyric structures in Edgar Allen Poe's work, colonialist constructions in the Groenlendinga Saga, or Greenlanders' Saga, and Eurocentrism in Garrison Keillor's Lake Wobegon Days—and he is transcribing the diary of the Reverend Oscar Elmer, who founded the original Prairie Home Cemetery.

Nicla Riverso is a lecturer in the division of French and Italian studies at the University of Washington. She completed a PhD in comparative literature at the University of Washington, with a dissertation titled "Paolo Sarpi: A Scholar in an Age of Transformation." She has previously published a book titled *Alfabetizzazione e Umanesimo nell' Italia dei secoli XIV e XV* (1997), which focuses on the process of education in Italian towns that began during the late Middle Ages. Her interests include late medieval and Renaissance literary culture in Italy, and early modern natural philosophy and textual culture in Europe, emphasizing the ways in which other natural philosophers (Sagredo, Sarpi, Santorio, Marius, Scheiner, Capra, and de Dominis) directly or indirectly helped Galileo reach his achievements in physics and astronomy.

Brian Edwards is working on his dissertation assessing Graham Greene's fiction with several of the newer psychologies, including evolutionary psychology. In addition to his chapter on modern British poetry and the family in England, Edwards published the article "The Inhibited Temperament in *Sons and Lovers*" in *Style*. His publications also include a review essay "Perennially Greene" in a 2010 issue of *Style*.

Brett Cooke is Professor of Russian at Texas A&M University. He is the author of *Human Nature in Utopia: Zamyatin's We* (2002) and *Pushkin and the Creative Process* (1998). He co-edited *Sociobiology and the Arts* (1998) with Jan Baptist Bedaux, *Biopoetics: Evolutionary Explorations in the Arts* (1999) with Frederick Turner, and *The Fantastic Other* (1998) with George E. Slusser and Jaume Marti-Olivella. His articles cover evolutionary criticism, Tolstoy, Dostoevsky, Pushkin, science fiction, and opera. He is writing a book on Tolstoy's use of family members as prototypes for the principal characters of *War and Peace*.

Massimiliano Morini is an associate professor of language and translation at the University of Udine. His main research interests are the theory, practice, and history of translation (*Tudor Translation in Theory and Practice*, 2006) and literary stylistics (*Jane Austen's Narrative Techniques: A Stylistic and Pragmatic Analysis*, 2009). He has contributed articles for, among others, *Target*, *Style*, and *Language and Literature*. He is also a literary translator.

Tim Ryan is an assistant professor at Northern Illinois University, where he teaches courses on twentieth-century American, Southern, and African American literature and culture. He has also taught in the American Studies program at King's College London. He took his BA at the University of Reading, England, and completed his MA and PhD at the University of Nevada, Reno. His first book, *Calls and Responses: The American Novel of Slavery since* Gone with the Wind (2008), won the Jules and Frances Landry Award. He has also published articles in such venues as *Mississippi Quarterly* and *Journal of American Culture*. He is working on a second book, a comparative thematic analysis of William Faulkner's fiction and the classic songs of the Delta Blues.

Gillian Lachanski works in the Glenbard, Illinois, school district as a specialist in helping basic learners improve their reading and writing skills. A graduate of Northern Illinois University in English, she lives in Wheaton. Her scholarly interests include the Bible as literature, and the writings of G. K. Chesterton.

Sang-wook Kim is an assistant professor at the School of Global Communication at Kyung Hee University and has published numerous journal articles about Irish culture and literature, East-West literary liaison, and literary sociobiology. His essay

"Shelley's *Frankenstein* and Rousseau's *Essay on the Origin of Languages*" won the 2008 ELLAK (The English Language and Literature Association of Korea) Award for the best journal article in English language and literature studies. He has also written the article "Irish Bloom and Korean Goobo: Modernism and Global Commodity Culture," a study of the intertextuality in global capitalism between *Ulysses* and its Korean rendition, *A Day of Mr. Goobo, the Novelist*. He is working on the Korean reception of Irish literature in the 1920s and 1930s.

Index

father-daughter relationship, 71, 143, 145–46, 187–88, 252–54, 256
father-son relationship, 40, 69, 115, 188–90, 207–09, 260–62, 272
female characters in Chicano literature, 74–75
Freud, Sigmund
    Freudian theory, 15–17
    Oedipus complex, 15
    sexual abuse, views on, 24
Frost, Robert
    childhood, 160–61, 163
    Elinor White and, 162
    poetry and poetic voice, 163–64

gender roles. See women's roles
godparents. See alloparents
Great Depression, effect on families, 59
grief and loss, 166–67, 168

Hansberry, Lorraine, 122
Heaney, Seamus, 206
Helmer, Nora (A Doll's House), 140–41, 144–49, 150–51
"Home Burial" (Frost), 166–70
homeostasis, 155
housing, 52
"How Cruel Is the Story of Eve" (Smith), 202–03
human nature, 88–89
Hurston, Zora Neale
    family and childhood, 250–54
    family in works, 247–48
    racial identity, 248, 255

illigitimate children. See paternity
immigrants and immigrant families, 67

Jonah's Gourd Vine (Hurston), 258–63
Joyce, James, 281–82

King Lear (Shakespeare), 83–100

Larkin, Philip, 198–99
Lear (King Lear), 94–95

"Maiden Name" (Larkin), 209–12
maiden names. See names and naming
marriage. See also divorce
    ancient practices, 50, 51
    early years, 35, 275
    marital relations, 140, 143–44, 151, 169–71, 276, 297
    portrayal in literature, 58, 216
    proposals, 239–40
    remarriage, 183
matchmaking, 223
Mexican Americans
    families, 72
    history of, 66–68
"Miss Eire" (Boland), 203–05
Morel, Paul (Sons and Lovers), 44–45
Morel, William (Sons and Lovers), 39–43
morphogenesis, 21
mother-son relationship, 29

names and naming
    first names, 219
    middle names, 209–12, 219
    surnames, 217–18
narratives. See stories and myths in the family
New Historicism, 87
normative universals, 91

Oedipus complex, 15

pair-bonds. See dyads
Palmer, Alan, 10, 265
parentification, 143

parents of deceased children, 166, 176. *See also* death in the family
paternity, 222–23
patriarchy, 55, 106–07, 217–19
patronyms. *See* names and naming
Pearson, John (*Jonah's Gourd Vine*), 258–63
Piaget, Jean, 287
poetry
    Frost, Robert, 160–77
    modern, 197–213
    women authors, 197, 198
poor families, 72
poststructuralism, 90
Pride and Prejudice (Austen), 232–45
Prospero (*The Tempest*), 108–12, 116–18
Protagonist (*. . . And the Earth Did Not Devour Him*), 69–70
pseudoparents. *See* alloparents

race and racism in literature, 249–50, 254–55
Raisin in the Sun, A (Hansberry), 121–38
Reyes, Lala (*Caramelo*), 70, 71
Rivera, Tomás, 68

secrets and secretiveness, 20, 146–47
separation anxiety, 288
Smith, Stevie (Florence Margaret Smith), 199
social classes
    mobility, 235

rural gentry, 236
working class, 126
social marginalization, 72
Sons and Lovers (Lawrence), 29–45
stories and myths in the family
    creation and propagation of, 78
    influence on behavior, 22–23
    narratives, 122, 124, 127
substitute parents. *See* alloparents

T-bond, 19
Tempest, The (Shakespeare), 104–19

universals. *See* normative universals

When We Dead Awaken (Ibsen), 285
women poets. *See* poetry
women's roles
    identity in marriage, 209–12
    in Chicano culture, 73
    in Roman culture, 192–94
    unequal status, 221–22
working-class families, 126
World War II, effect on families, 59–60

Younger, Beneatha (*A Raisin in the Sun*), 131–32
Younger, Mama Lena (*A Raisin in the Sun*), 129–30
Younger, Ruth (*A Raisin in the Sun*), 132–34
Younger, Walter (*A Raisin in the Sun*), 125–29, 135–37